MW00948056

The Complete
Air Fryer
Cookbook for Beginners

2000+ Days of Quick and Flavorful Recipes for Effortless Cooking and Wholesome Meals, Unleash the Potential of Your Air Fryer

Alden Deville

Copyright© 2023 By Alden Deville

All rights reserved worldwide.

No part of this book may be reproduced or transmitted in any form or by any means, electronic or mechanical, including photo- copying, recording or by any information storage and retrieval system, without written permission from the publisher, except for the inclusion of brief quotations in a review.

Warning-Disclaimer

The purpose of this book is to educate and entertain. The author or publisher does not guarantee that anyone following the techniques, suggestions, tips, ideas, or strategies will become successful. The author and publisher shall have neither liability or responsibility to anyone with respect to any loss or damage caused, or alleged to be caused, directly or indirectly by the information contained in this book.

Table of Contents

Chapter 4 Beef, Pork, and Lamb — 24

Chapter 5 Poultry — 35

Chapter 6 Fish and Seafood 47

Chapter 7 Vegetables and Sides 58

Chapter 8 Vegetarian Mains

Chapter 9 Snacks and Appetizers

Chapter 10 Desserts

Appendix Air Fryer Cooking Chart

INTRODUCTION

Welcome to the world of culinary exploration with air frying! If you're looking for a healthier way to enjoy your favorite fried foods without all the grease and fat, then an air fryer is the perfect solution for you. This innovative kitchen appliance uses hot air to cook your food, giving it that crispy texture you love without all the excess oil.

Air fryers have been gaining popularity as a healthier and more convenient alternative to deep-frying, which meansyou can indulge in all your favorite dishes without the added oil and calories. If you're looking to invest in an air fryer or you already have one, you're in luck. Our cookbook offers a wide range of recipes with helpful tips and tricks for using an air fryer.

What sets this air fryer cookbook apart from others is its focus on using fresh and wholesome ingredients. You won't find any processed or pre-packaged foods here. Instead, you'll learn how to transform fresh produce and lean proteins into delicious, crispy meals. Plus, with the air fryer's ability to use minimal oil, you'll be able to indulge in your favorite comfort foods without the guilt.

What to Expect?

In this cookbook, you'll find a wide variety of delicious and healthy recipes that are perfect for your air fryer. From appetizers and snacks to main dishes and desserts, there's something for everyone in this collection. Whether you're a seasoned cook or just starting out, you'll love how easy these recipes are to follow and how quickly you can whip up a delicious meal.

One of the great things about air frying is that it's incredibly versatile. You can use it to cook all your favorite foods, from chicken wings and french fries to fish and vegetables. And because air frying is so much healthier than traditional frying, you can feel good about indulging in your favorite treats without worrying about your waistline.

In this cookbook, you'll learn how to make all kinds of delicious dishes using your air fryer, including crispy fried chicken, savory roasted vegetables, and even sweet treats like donuts and churros. You'll also find tips and tricks for getting the most out of your air fryer, including how to clean and maintain it for optimal performance.

Let's Get Cooking

Whether you're a health-conscious foodie looking to try something new or a busy professional looking for quick and easy meal ideas, this air fryer cookbook has everything you need to get started. With its delicious recipes and helpful tips, you'll be whipping up healthy and delicious meals in no time. In today's fast-paced world, it's important to have kitchen appliances that save time and energy. An air fryer cookbook is the perfect solution for anyone who wants to eat healthier without sacrificing flavor. With this cookbook, you'll have all the guidance you need to create delicious, crispy meals that your whole family will love. So why wait? Invest in an air fryer and start exploring the endless possibilities today!

Chapter 1 Breakfasts

Chocolate Doughnut Holes

Prep time: 10 minutes | Cook time: 8 to 12 minutes per batch | Makes 24 doughnut holes

◁ 1 (8-count) can refrigerated biscuits
◁ Cooking oil spray
◁ 48 semisweet chocolate
◁ chips
◁ 3 tablespoons melted unsalted butter
◁ ¼ cup confectioners' sugar

1. Separate the biscuits and cut each biscuit into thirds, for 24 pieces. 2. Flatten each biscuit piece slightly and put 2 chocolate chips in the center. Wrap the dough around the chocolate and seal the edges well. 3. Insert the crisper plate into the basket and the basket into the unit. Preheat the unit by selecting AIR FRY, setting the temperature to 330ºF (166ºC), and setting the time to 3 minutes. Select START/STOP to begin. 4. Once the unit is preheated, spray the crisper plate with cooking oil. Brush each doughnut hole with a bit of the butter and place it into the basket. Select AIR FRY, set the temperature to 330ºF (166ºC), and set the time between 8 and 12 minutes. Select START/STOP to begin. 5. The doughnuts are done when they are golden brown. When the cooking is complete, place the doughnut holes on a plate and dust with the confectioners' sugar. Serve warm.

Sausage and Egg Breakfast Burrito

Prep time: 5 minutes | Cook time: 30 minutes | Serves 6

◁ 6 eggs
◁ Salt and pepper, to taste
◁ Cooking oil
◁ ½ cup chopped red bell pepper
◁ ½ cup chopped green bell pepper
◁ 8 ounces (227 g) ground chicken sausage
◁ ½ cup salsa
◁ 6 medium (8-inch) flour tortillas
◁ ½ cup shredded Cheddar cheese

1. In a medium bowl, whisk the eggs. Add salt and pepper to taste. 2. Place a skillet on medium-high heat. Spray with cooking oil. Add the eggs. Scramble for 2 to 3 minutes, until the eggs are fluffy. Remove the eggs from the skillet and set aside. 3. If needed, spray the skillet with more oil. Add the chopped red and green bell peppers. Cook for 2 to 3 minutes, until the peppers are soft. 4. Add the ground sausage to the skillet. Break the sausage into smaller pieces using a spatula or spoon. Cook for 3 to 4 minutes, until the sausage is brown. 5. Add the salsa and scrambled eggs. Stir to combine. Remove the skillet from heat. 6. Spoon the mixture evenly onto the tortillas. 7. To form the burritos, fold the sides of each tortilla in toward the middle and then roll up from the bottom. You can secure each burrito with a toothpick. Or you can moisten the outside edge of the tortilla with a small amount of water. I prefer to use a cooking brush, but you can also dab with your fingers. 8. Spray the burritos with cooking oil and place them in the air fryer. Do not stack. Cook the burritos in batches if they do not all fit in the basket. Air fry at 400ºF (204ºC) for 8 minutes. 9. Open the air fryer and flip the burritos. Cook for an additional 2 minutes or until crisp. 10. If necessary, repeat steps 8 and 9 for the remaining burritos. 11. Sprinkle the Cheddar cheese over the burritos. Cool before serving.

Cheddar Soufflés

Prep time: 15 minutes | Cook time: 12 minutes | Serves 4

◁ 3 large eggs, whites and yolks separated
◁ ¼ teaspoon cream of tartar
◁ ½ cup shredded sharp
◁ Cheddar cheese
◁ 3 ounces (85 g) cream cheese, softened

1. In a large bowl, beat egg whites together with cream of tartar until soft peaks form, about 2 minutes. 2. In a separate medium bowl, beat egg yolks, Cheddar, and cream cheese together until frothy, about 1 minute. Add egg yolk mixture to whites, gently folding until combined. 3. Pour mixture evenly into four ramekins greased with cooking spray. Place ramekins into air fryer basket. Adjust the temperature to 350ºF (177ºC) and bake for 12 minutes. Eggs will be browned on the top and firm in the center when done. Serve warm.

Vanilla Granola

Prep time: 5 minutes | Cook time: 40 minutes | Serves 4

◁ 1 cup rolled oats
◁ 3 tablespoons maple syrup
◁ 1 tablespoon sunflower oil
◁ 1 tablespoon coconut sugar
◁ ¼ teaspoon vanilla
◁ ¼ teaspoon cinnamon
◁ ¼ teaspoon sea salt

1. Preheat the air fryer to 248ºF (120ºC). 2. Mix together the oats, maple syrup, sunflower oil, coconut sugar, vanilla, cinnamon, and sea salt in a medium bowl and stir to combine. Transfer the mixture to a baking pan. 3. Place the pan in the air fryer basket and bake for 40 minutes, or until the granola is mostly dry and lightly browned. Stir the granola four times during cooking. 4. Let the granola stand for 5 to 10 minutes before serving.

Bacon Hot Dogs

Prep time: 5 minutes | Cook time: 15 minutes | Serves 4

- 3 brazilian sausages, cut into 3 equal pieces
- 9 slices bacon
- 1 tablespoon Italian herbs
- Salt and ground black pepper, to taste

1. Preheat the air fryer to 355°F (179°C). 2. Take each slice of bacon and wrap around each piece of sausage. Sprinkle with Italian herbs, salt and pepper. 3. Air fry the sausages in the preheated air fryer for 15 minutes. 4. Serve warm.

Southwestern Ham Egg Cups

Prep time: 5 minutes | Cook time: 12 minutes | Serves 2

- 4 (1 ounce / 28 g) slices deli ham
- 4 large eggs
- 2 tablespoons full-fat sour cream
- ¼ cup diced green bell pepper
- 2 tablespoons diced red bell pepper
- 2 tablespoons diced white onion
- ½ cup shredded medium Cheddar cheese

1. Place one slice of ham on the bottom of four baking cups. 2. In a large bowl, whisk eggs with sour cream. Stir in green pepper, red pepper, and onion. 3. Pour the egg mixture into ham-lined baking cups. Top with Cheddar. Place cups into the air fryer basket. 4. Adjust the temperature to 320°F (160°C) and bake for 12 minutes or until the tops are browned. 5. Serve warm.

Meritage Eggs

Prep time: 5 minutes | Cook time: 8 minutes | Serves 2

- 2 teaspoons unsalted butter (or coconut oil for dairy-free), for greasing the ramekins
- 4 large eggs
- 2 teaspoons chopped fresh thyme
- ½ teaspoon fine sea salt
- ¼ teaspoon ground black pepper
- 2 tablespoons heavy cream (or unsweetened, unflavored almond milk for dairy-free)
- 3 tablespoons finely grated Parmesan cheese (or Kite Hill brand chive cream cheese style spread, softened, for dairy-free)
- Fresh thyme leaves, for garnish (optional)

1. Preheat the air fryer to 400°F (204°C). Grease two (4 ounces / 113 g) ramekins with the butter. 2. Crack 2 eggs into each ramekin and divide the thyme, salt, and pepper between the ramekins. Pour 1 tablespoon of the heavy cream into each ramekin. Sprinkle each ramekin with 1½ tablespoons of the Parmesan cheese. 3. Place the ramekins in the air fryer and bake for 8 minutes for soft-cooked yolks (longer if you desire a harder yolk). 4. Garnish with a sprinkle of ground black pepper and thyme leaves, if desired. Best served fresh.

Pita and Pepperoni Pizza

Prep time: 10 minutes | Cook time: 6 minutes | Serves 1

- 1 teaspoon olive oil
- 1 tablespoon pizza sauce
- 1 pita bread
- 6 pepperoni slices
- ¼ cup grated Mozzarella cheese
- ¼ teaspoon garlic powder
- ¼ teaspoon dried oregano

1. Preheat the air fryer to 350°F (177°C). Grease the air fryer basket with olive oil. 2. Spread the pizza sauce on top of the pita bread. Put the pepperoni slices over the sauce, followed by the Mozzarella cheese. 3. Season with garlic powder and oregano. 4. Put the pita pizza inside the air fryer and place a trivet on top. 5. Bake in the preheated air fryer for 6 minutes and serve.

Breakfast Cobbler

Prep time: 20 minutes | Cook time: 30 minutes | Serves 4

Filling:
- 10 ounces (283 g) bulk pork sausage, crumbled
- ¼ cup minced onions
- 2 cloves garlic, minced
- ½ teaspoon fine sea salt
- ½ teaspoon ground black pepper
- 1 (8 ounces / 227 g) package cream cheese (or Kite Hill brand cream cheese style spread for dairy-free), softened
- ¾ cup beef or chicken broth

Biscuits:
- 3 large egg whites
- ¾ cup blanched almond flour
- 1 teaspoon baking powder
- ¼ teaspoon fine sea salt
- 2½ tablespoons very cold unsalted butter, cut into ¼-inch pieces
- Fresh thyme leaves, for garnish

1. Preheat the air fryer to 400°F (204°C). 2. Place the sausage, onions, and garlic in a pie pan. Using your hands, break up the sausage into small pieces and spread it evenly throughout the pie pan. Season with the salt and pepper. Place the pan in the air fryer and bake for 5 minutes. 3. While the sausage cooks, place the cream cheese and broth in a food processor or blender and purée until smooth. 4. Remove the pork from the air fryer and use a fork or metal spatula to crumble it more. Pour the cream cheese mixture into the sausage and stir to combine. Set aside. 5. Make the biscuits: Place the egg whites in a medium-sized mixing bowl or the bowl of a stand mixer and whip with a hand mixer or stand mixer until stiff peaks form. 6. In a separate medium-sized bowl, whisk together the almond flour, baking powder, and salt, then cut in the butter. When you are done, the mixture should still have chunks of butter. Gently fold the flour mixture into the egg whites with a rubber spatula. 7. Use a large spoon or ice cream scoop to scoop the dough into 4 equal-sized biscuits, making sure the butter is evenly distributed. Place the biscuits on top of the sausage and cook in the air fryer for 5 minutes, then turn the heat down to 325°F (163°C) and bake for another 17 to 20 minutes, until the biscuits are golden brown. Serve garnished with fresh thyme leaves. 8. Store leftovers in an airtight container in the refrigerator for up to 3 days. Reheat in a preheated 350°F (177°C) air fryer for 5 minutes, or until warmed through.

Bacon, Cheese, and Avocado Melt

Prep time: 5 minutes | Cook time: 3 to 5 minutes | Serves 2

◄ 1 avocado
◄ 4 slices cooked bacon, chopped
◄ 2 tablespoons salsa
◄ 1 tablespoon heavy cream
◄ ¼ cup shredded Cheddar cheese

1. Preheat the air fryer to 400ºF (204ºC). 2. Slice the avocado in half lengthwise and remove the stone. To ensure the avocado halves do not roll in the basket, slice a thin piece of skin off the base. 3. In a small bowl, combine the bacon, salsa, and cream. Divide the mixture between the avocado halves and top with the cheese. 4. Place the avocado halves in the air fryer basket and air fry for 3 to 5 minutes until the cheese has melted and begins to brown. Serve warm.

Oat and Chia Porridge

Prep time: 10 minutes | Cook time: 5 minutes | Serves 4

◄ 2 tablespoons peanut butter
◄ 4 tablespoons honey
◄ 1 tablespoon butter, melted
◄ 4 cups milk
◄ 2 cups oats
◄ 1 cup chia seeds

1. Preheat the air fryer to 390ºF (199ºC). 2. Put the peanut butter, honey, butter, and milk in a bowl and stir to mix. Add the oats and chia seeds and stir. 3. Transfer the mixture to a bowl and bake in the air fryer for 5 minutes. Give another stir before serving.

Mississippi Spice Muffins

Prep time: 15 minutes | Cook time: 13 minutes | Makes 12 muffins

◄ 4 cups all-purpose flour
◄ 1 tablespoon ground cinnamon
◄ 2 teaspoons baking soda
◄ 2 teaspoons allspice
◄ 1 teaspoon ground cloves
◄ 1 teaspoon salt
◄ 1 cup (2 sticks) butter, room

temperature
◄ 2 cups sugar
◄ 2 large eggs, lightly beaten
◄ 2 cups unsweetened applesauce
◄ ¼ cup chopped pecans
◄ 1 to 2 tablespoons oil

1. In a large bowl, whisk the flour, cinnamon, baking soda, allspice, cloves, and salt until blended. 2. In another large bowl, combine the butter and sugar. Using an electric mixer, beat the mixture for 2 to 3 minutes until light and fluffy. Add the beaten eggs and stir until blended. 3. Add the flour mixture and applesauce, alternating between the two and blending after each addition. Stir in the pecans. 4. Preheat the air fryer to 325ºF (163ºC). Spritz 12 silicone muffin cups with oil. 5. Pour the batter into the prepared muffin cups, filling each halfway. Place the muffins in the air fryer basket. 6. Air fry for 6 minutes. Shake the basket and air fry for 7 minutes

more. The muffins are done when a toothpick inserted into the middle comes out clean.

Bacon and Cheese Quiche

Prep time: 5 minutes | Cook time: 12 minutes | Serves 2

◄ 3 large eggs
◄ 2 tablespoons heavy whipping cream
◄ ¼ teaspoon salt
◄ 4 slices cooked sugar-free bacon, crumbled
◄ ½ cup shredded mild Cheddar cheese

1. In a large bowl, whisk eggs, cream, and salt together until combined. Mix in bacon and Cheddar. 2. Pour mixture evenly into two ungreased ramekins. Place into air fryer basket. Adjust the temperature to 320ºF (160ºC) and bake for 12 minutes. Quiche will be fluffy and set in the middle when done. 3. Let quiche cool in ramekins 5 minutes. Serve warm.

Gold Avocado

Prep time: 5 minutes | Cook time: 6 minutes | Serves 4

◄ 2 large avocados, sliced
◄ ¼ teaspoon paprika
◄ Salt and ground black pepper, to taste
◄ ½ cup flour
◄ 2 eggs, beaten
◄ 1 cup bread crumbs

1. Preheat the air fryer to 400ºF (204ºC). 2. Sprinkle paprika, salt and pepper on the slices of avocado. 3. Lightly coat the avocados with flour. Dredge them in the eggs, before covering with bread crumbs. 4. Transfer to the air fryer and air fry for 6 minutes. 5. Serve warm.

Fried Cheese Grits

Prep time: 10 minutes | Cook time: 10 to 12 minutes | Serves 4

◄ ⅔ cup instant grits
◄ 1 teaspoon salt
◄ 1 teaspoon freshly ground black pepper
◄ ¾ cup whole or 2% milk
◄ 3 ounces (85 g) cream
cheese, at room temperature
◄ 1 large egg, beaten
◄ 1 tablespoon butter, melted
◄ 1 cup shredded mild Cheddar cheese
◄ Cooking spray

1. Mix the grits, salt, and black pepper in a large bowl. Add the milk, cream cheese, beaten egg, and melted butter and whisk to combine. Fold in the Cheddar cheese and stir well. 2. Preheat the air fryer to 400ºF (204ºC). Spray a baking pan with cooking spray. 3. Spread the grits mixture into the baking pan and place in the air fryer basket. 4. Air fry for 1o to 12 minutes, or until the grits are cooked and a knife inserted in the center comes out clean. Stir the mixture once halfway through the cooking time. 5. Rest for 5 minutes and serve warm.

Double-Dipped Mini Cinnamon Biscuits

Prep time: 15 minutes | Cook time: 13 minutes | Makes 8 biscuits

- 2 cups blanched almond flour
- ½ cup Swerve confectioners'-style sweetener or equivalent amount of liquid or powdered sweetener
- 1 teaspoon baking powder
- ½ teaspoon fine sea salt
- ¼ cup plus 2 tablespoons (¾ stick) very cold unsalted butter
- ¼ cup unsweetened, unflavored almond milk
- 1 large egg
- 1 teaspoon vanilla extract
- 3 teaspoons ground cinnamon
- Glaze:
- ½ cup Swerve confectioners'-style sweetener or equivalent amount of powdered sweetener
- ¼ cup heavy cream or unsweetened, unflavored almond milk

1. Preheat the air fryer to 350ºF (177ºC). Line a pie pan that fits into your air fryer with parchment paper. 2. In a medium-sized bowl, mix together the almond flour, sweetener (if powdered; do not add liquid sweetener), baking powder, and salt. Cut the butter into ½-inch squares, then use a hand mixer to work the butter into the dry ingredients. When you are done, the mixture should still have chunks of butter. 3. In a small bowl, whisk together the almond milk, egg, and vanilla extract (if using liquid sweetener, add it as well) until blended. Using a fork, stir the wet ingredients into the dry ingredients until large clumps form. Add the cinnamon and use your hands to swirl it into the dough. 4. Form the dough into sixteen 1-inch balls and place them on the prepared pan, spacing them about ½ inch apart. (If you're using a smaller air fryer, work in batches if necessary.) Bake in the air fryer until golden, 10 to 13 minutes. Remove from the air fryer and let cool on the pan for at least 5 minutes. 5. While the biscuits bake, make the glaze: Place the powdered sweetener in a small bowl and slowly stir in the heavy cream with a fork. 6. When the biscuits have cooled somewhat, dip the tops into the glaze, allow it to dry a bit, and then dip again for a thick glaze. 7. Serve warm or at room temperature. Store unglazed biscuits in an airtight container in the refrigerator for up to 3 days or in the freezer for up to a month. Reheat in a preheated 350ºF (177ºC) air fryer for 5 minutes, or until warmed through, and dip in the glaze as instructed above.

Mexican Breakfast Pepper Rings

Prep time: 5 minutes | Cook time: 10 minutes | Serves 4

- Olive oil
- 1 large red, yellow, or orange bell pepper, cut into four ¾-inch rings
- 4 eggs
- Salt and freshly ground black pepper, to taste
- 2 teaspoons salsa

1. Preheat the air fryer to 350ºF (177ºC). Lightly spray a baking pan with olive oil. 2. Place 2 bell pepper rings on the pan. Crack one egg into each bell pepper ring. Season with salt and black pepper.

3. Spoon ½ teaspoon of salsa on top of each egg. 4. Place the pan in the air fryer basket. Air fry until the yolk is slightly runny, 5 to 6 minutes or until the yolk is fully cooked, 8 to 10 minutes. 5. Repeat with the remaining 2 pepper rings. Serve hot.

Two-Cheese Grits

Prep time: 10 minutes | Cook time: 10 to 12 minutes | Serves 4

- ⅔ cup instant grits
- 1 teaspoon salt
- 1 teaspoon freshly ground black pepper
- ¾ cup milk, whole or 2%
- 1 large egg, beaten
- 3 ounces (85 g) cream cheese, at room temperature
- 1 tablespoon butter, melted
- 1 cup shredded mild Cheddar cheese
- 1 to 2 tablespoons oil

1. In a large bowl, combine the grits, salt, and pepper. Stir in the milk, egg, cream cheese, and butter until blended. Stir in the Cheddar cheese. 2. Preheat the air fryer to 400ºF (204ºC). Spritz a baking pan with oil. 3. Pour the grits mixture into the prepared pan and place it in the air fryer basket. 4. Cook for 5 minutes. Stir the mixture and cook for 5 minutes more for soupy grits or 7 minutes more for firmer grits.

Apple Rolls

Prep time: 20 minutes | Cook time: 20 to 24 minutes | Makes 12 rolls

Apple Rolls:
- 2 cups all-purpose flour, plus more for dusting
- 2 tablespoons granulated sugar
- 1 teaspoon salt
- 3 tablespoons butter, at room temperature

Icing:
- ½ cup confectioners' sugar
- ½ teaspoon vanilla extract
- ¾ cup milk, whole or 2%
- ½ cup packed light brown sugar
- 1 teaspoon ground cinnamon
- 1 large Granny Smith apple, peeled and diced
- 1 to 2 tablespoons oil
- 2 to 3 tablespoons milk, whole or 2%

Make the Apple Rolls 1. In a large bowl, whisk the flour, granulated sugar, and salt until blended. Stir in the butter and milk briefly until a sticky dough forms. 2. In a small bowl, stir together the brown sugar, cinnamon, and apple. 3. Place a piece of parchment paper on a work surface and dust it with flour. Roll the dough on the prepared surface to ¼ inch thickness. 4. Spread the apple mixture over the dough. Roll up the dough jelly roll-style, pinching the ends to seal. Cut the dough into 12 rolls. 5. Preheat the air fryer to 320ºF (160ºC). 6. Line the air fryer basket with parchment paper and spritz it with oil. Place 6 rolls on the prepared parchment. 7. Bake for 5 minutes. Flip the rolls and bake for 5 to 7 minutes more until lightly browned. Repeat with the remaining rolls. Make the Icing 8. In a medium bowl, whisk the confectioners' sugar, vanilla, and milk until blended. 9. Drizzle over the warm rolls.

Breakfast Sammies

Prep time: 15 minutes | Cook time: 20 minutes | Serves 5

Biscuits:
- 6 large egg whites
- 2 cups blanched almond flour, plus more if needed
- 1½ teaspoons baking powder
- ½ teaspoon fine sea salt
- ¼ cup (½ stick) very cold unsalted butter (or lard for dairy-free), cut into ¼-inch pieces

Eggs:
- 5 large eggs
- ½ teaspoon fine sea salt
- ¼ teaspoon ground black pepper
- 5 (1 ounce / 28 g) slices Cheddar cheese (omit for dairy-free)
- 10 thin slices ham

1. Spray the air fryer basket with avocado oil. Preheat the air fryer to 350°F (177°C). Grease two pie pans or two baking pans that will fit inside your air fryer. 2. Make the biscuits: In a medium-sized bowl, whip the egg whites with a hand mixer until very stiff. Set aside. 3. In a separate medium-sized bowl, stir together the almond flour, baking powder, and salt until well combined. Cut in the butter. Gently fold the flour mixture into the egg whites with a rubber spatula. If the dough is too wet to form into mounds, add a few tablespoons of almond flour until the dough holds together well. 4. Using a large spoon, divide the dough into 5 equal portions and drop them about 1 inch apart on one of the greased pie pans. (If you're using a smaller air fryer, work in batches if necessary.) Place the pan in the air fryer and bake for 11 to 14 minutes, until the biscuits are golden brown. Remove from the air fryer and set aside to cool. 5. Make the eggs: Set the air fryer to 375°F (191°C). Crack the eggs into the remaining greased pie pan and sprinkle with the salt and pepper. Place the eggs in the air fryer to bake for 5 minutes, or until they are cooked to your liking. 6. Open the air fryer and top each egg yolk with a slice of cheese (if using). Bake for another minute, or until the cheese is melted. 7. Once the biscuits are cool, slice them in half lengthwise. Place 1 cooked egg topped with cheese and 2 slices of ham in each biscuit. 8. Store leftover biscuits, eggs, and ham in separate airtight containers in the fridge for up to 3 days. Reheat the biscuits and eggs on a baking sheet in a preheated 350°F (177°C) air fryer for 5 minutes, or until warmed through.

Gluten-Free Granola Cereal

Prep time: 7 minutes | Cook time: 30 minutes | Makes 3½ cups

- Oil, for spraying
- 1½ cups gluten-free rolled oats
- ½ cup chopped walnuts
- ½ cup chopped almonds
- ½ cup pumpkin seeds
- ¼ cup maple syrup or honey
- 1 tablespoon toasted sesame oil or vegetable oil
- 1 teaspoon ground cinnamon
- ½ teaspoon salt
- ½ cup dried cranberries

1. Preheat the air fryer to 250°F (121°C). Line the air fryer basket with parchment and spray lightly with oil. (Do not skip the step of lining the basket; the parchment will keep the granola from falling through the holes.) 2. In a large bowl, mix together the oats, walnuts, almonds, pumpkin seeds, maple syrup, sesame oil, cinnamon, and salt. 3. Spread the mixture in an even layer in the prepared basket. 4. Cook for 30 minutes, stirring every 10 minutes. 5. Transfer the granola to a bowl, add the dried cranberries, and toss to combine. 6. Let cool to room temperature before storing in an airtight container.

Kale and Potato Nuggets

Prep time: 10 minutes | Cook time: 18 minutes | Serves 4

- 1 teaspoon extra virgin olive oil
- 1 clove garlic, minced
- 4 cups kale, rinsed and chopped
- 2 cups potatoes, boiled and mashed
- ⅛ cup milk
- Salt and ground black pepper, to taste
- Cooking spray

1. Preheat the air fryer to 390°F (199°C). 2. In a skillet over medium heat, sauté the garlic in the olive oil, until it turns golden brown. Sauté with the kale for an additional 3 minutes and remove from the heat. 3. Mix the mashed potatoes, kale and garlic in a bowl. Pour in the milk and sprinkle with salt and pepper. 4. Shape the mixture into nuggets and spritz with cooking spray. 5. Put in the air fryer basket and air fry for 15 minutes, flip the nuggets halfway through cooking to make sure the nuggets fry evenly. 6. Serve immediately.

Hearty Blueberry Oatmeal

Prep time: 10 minutes | Cook time: 25 minutes | Serves 6

- 1½ cups quick oats
- 1¼ teaspoons ground cinnamon, divided
- ½ teaspoon baking powder
- Pinch salt
- 1 cup unsweetened vanilla almond milk
- ¼ cup honey
- 1 teaspoon vanilla extract
- 1 egg, beaten
- 2 cups blueberries
- Olive oil
- 1½ teaspoons sugar, divided
- 6 tablespoons low-fat whipped topping (optional)

1. In a large bowl, mix together the oats, 1 teaspoon of cinnamon, baking powder, and salt. 2. In a medium bowl, whisk together the almond milk, honey, vanilla and egg. 3. Pour the liquid ingredients into the oats mixture and stir to combine. Fold in the blueberries. 4. Lightly spray a baking pan with oil. 5. Add half the blueberry mixture to the pan. 6. Sprinkle ⅛ teaspoon of cinnamon and ½ teaspoon sugar over the top. 7. Cover the pan with aluminum foil and place gently in the air fryer basket. 8. Air fry at 360°F (182°C) for 20 minutes. Remove the foil and air fry for an additional 5 minutes. Transfer the mixture to a shallow bowl. 9. Repeat with the remaining blueberry mixture, ½ teaspoon of sugar, and ⅛ teaspoon of cinnamon. 10. To serve, spoon into bowls and top with whipped topping.

Not-So-English Muffins

Prep time: 5 minutes | Cook time: 10 minutes | Serves 4

- ◀ 2 strips turkey bacon, cut in half crosswise
- ◀ 2 whole grain English muffins, split
- ◀ 1 cup fresh baby spinach, long stems removed
- ◀ ¼ ripe pear, peeled and thinly sliced
- ◀ 4 slices Provolone cheese

1. Place bacon strips in air fryer basket and air fry at 390ºF (199ºC) for 2 minutes. Check and separate strips if necessary so they cook evenly. Cook for 3 to 4 more minutes, until crispy. Remove and drain on paper towels. 2. Place split muffin halves in air fryer basket and cook for 2 minutes, just until lightly browned. 3. Open air fryer and top each muffin with a quarter of the baby spinach, several pear slices, a strip of bacon, and a slice of cheese. 4. Air fry at 360ºF (182ºC) for 1 to 2 minutes, until cheese completely melts.

Fried Chicken Wings with Waffles

Prep time: 10 minutes | Cook time: 30 minutes | Serves 4

- ◀ 8 whole chicken wings
- ◀ 1 teaspoon garlic powder
- ◀ Chicken seasoning, for preparing the chicken
- ◀ Freshly ground black pepper, to taste
- ◀ ½ cup all-purpose flour
- ◀ Cooking oil spray
- ◀ 8 frozen waffles
- ◀ Pure maple syrup, for serving (optional)

1. In a medium bowl, combine the chicken and garlic powder and season with chicken seasoning and pepper. Toss to coat. 2. Transfer the chicken to a resealable plastic bag and add the flour. Seal the bag and shake it to coat the chicken thoroughly. 3. Insert the crisper plate into the basket and the basket into the unit. Preheat the unit by selecting AIR FRY, setting the temperature to 400ºF (204ºC), and setting the time to 3 minutes. Select START/STOP to begin. 4. Once the unit is preheated, spray the crisper plate with cooking oil. Using tongs, transfer the chicken from the bag to the basket. It is okay to stack the chicken wings on top of each other. Spray them with cooking oil. 5. Select AIR FRY, set the temperature to 400ºF (204ºC), and set the time to 20 minutes. Select START/STOP to begin. 6. After 5 minutes, remove the basket and shake the wings. Reinsert the basket to resume cooking. Remove and shake the basket every 5 minutes until the chicken is fully cooked. 7. When the cooking is complete, remove the cooked chicken from the basket; cover to keep warm. 8. Rinse the basket and crisper plate with warm water. Insert them back into the unit. 9. Select AIR FRY, set the temperature to 360ºF (182ºC), and set the time to 3 minutes. Select START/STOP to begin. 10. Once the unit is preheated, spray the crisper plate with cooking spray. Working in batches, place the frozen waffles into the basket. Do not stack them. Spray the waffles with cooking oil. 11. Select AIR FRY, set the temperature to 360ºF (182ºC), and set the time to 6 minutes. Select START/STOP to begin. 12. When the cooking is complete, repeat steps 10 and 11 with the remaining waffles. 13. Serve the waffles with the chicken and a touch of maple syrup, if desired.

Ham and Cheese Crescents

Prep time: 5 minutes | Cook time: 7 minutes | Makes 8 rolls

- ◀ Oil, for spraying
- ◀ 1 (8 ounces / 227 g) can refrigerated crescent rolls
- ◀ 4 slices deli ham
- ◀ 8 slices American cheese
- ◀ 2 tablespoons unsalted butter, melted

1. Line the air fryer basket with parchment and spray lightly with oil. 2. Separate the dough into 8 pieces. 3. Tear the ham slices in half and place 1 piece on each piece of dough. Top each with 1 slice of cheese. 4. Roll up each piece of dough, starting on the wider side. 5. Place the rolls in the prepared basket. Brush with the melted butter. 6. Air fry at 320ºF (160ºC) for 6 to 7 minutes, or until puffed and golden brown and the cheese is melted.

Hearty Cheddar Biscuits

Prep time: 10 minutes | Cook time: 22 minutes | Makes 8 biscuits

- ◀ 2⅓ cups self-rising flour
- ◀ 2 tablespoons sugar
- ◀ ½ cup butter (1 stick), frozen for 15 minutes
- ◀ ½ cup grated Cheddar cheese, plus more to melt on top
- ◀ 1⅓ cups buttermilk
- ◀ 1 cup all-purpose flour, for shaping
- ◀ 1 tablespoon butter, melted

1. Line a buttered 7-inch metal cake pan with parchment paper or a silicone liner. 2. Combine the flour and sugar in a large mixing bowl. Grate the butter into the flour. Add the grated cheese and stir to coat the cheese and butter with flour. Then add the buttermilk and stir just until you can no longer see streaks of flour. The dough should be quite wet. 3. Spread the all-purpose (not self-rising) flour out on a small cookie sheet. With a spoon, scoop 8 evenly sized balls of dough into the flour, making sure they don't touch each other. With floured hands, coat each dough ball with flour and toss them gently from hand to hand to shake off any excess flour. Put each floured dough ball into the prepared pan, right up next to the other. This will help the biscuits rise, rather than spreading out. 4. Preheat the air fryer to 380ºF (193ºC). 5. Transfer the cake pan to the basket of the air fryer. Let the ends of the aluminum foil sling hang across the cake pan before returning the basket to the air fryer. 6. Air fry for 20 minutes. Check the biscuits twice to make sure they are not getting too brown on top. If they are, re-arrange the aluminum foil strips to cover any brown parts. After 20 minutes, check the biscuits by inserting a toothpick into the center of the biscuits. It should come out clean. If it needs a little more time, continue to air fry for two extra minutes. Brush the tops of the biscuits with some melted butter and sprinkle a little more grated cheese on top if desired. Pop the basket back into the air fryer for another 2 minutes. 7. Remove the cake pan from the air fryer. Let the biscuits cool for just a minute or two and then turn them out onto a plate and pull apart. Serve immediately.

Classic British Breakfast

Prep time: 5 minutes | Cook time: 25 minutes | Serves 2

◄ 1 cup potatoes, sliced and diced
◄ 2 cups beans in tomato sauce
◄ 2 eggs
◄ 1 tablespoon olive oil
◄ 1 sausage
◄ Salt, to taste

1. Preheat the air fryer to 390ºF (199ºC) and allow to warm. 2. Break the eggs onto a baking dish and sprinkle with salt. 3. Lay the beans on the dish, next to the eggs. 4. In a bowl, coat the potatoes with the olive oil. Sprinkle with salt. 5. Transfer the bowl of potato slices to the air fryer and bake for 10 minutes. 6. Swap out the bowl of potatoes for the dish containing the eggs and beans. Bake for another 10 minutes. Cover the potatoes with parchment paper. 7. Slice up the sausage and throw the slices on top of the beans and eggs. Bake for another 5 minutes. 8. Serve with the potatoes.

Cinnamon Rolls

Prep time: 10 minutes | Cook time: 20 minutes | Makes 12 rolls

◄ 2½ cups shredded Mozzarella cheese
◄ 2 ounces (57 g) cream cheese, softened
◄ 1 cup blanched finely ground almond flour
◄ ½ teaspoon vanilla extract
◄ ½ cup confectioners' erythritol
◄ 1 tablespoon ground cinnamon

1. In a large microwave-safe bowl, combine Mozzarella cheese, cream cheese, and flour. Microwave the mixture on high 90 seconds until cheese is melted. 2. Add vanilla extract and erythritol, and mix 2 minutes until a dough forms. 3. Once the dough is cool enough to work with your hands, about 2 minutes, spread it out into a 12 × 4-inch rectangle on ungreased parchment paper. Evenly sprinkle dough with cinnamon. 4. Starting at the long side of the dough, roll lengthwise to form a log. Slice the log into twelve even pieces. 5. Divide rolls between two ungreased round nonstick baking dishes. Place one dish into air fryer basket. Adjust the temperature to 375ºF (191ºC) and bake for 10 minutes. 6. Cinnamon rolls will be done when golden around the edges and mostly firm. Repeat with second dish. Allow rolls to cool in dishes 10 minutes before serving.

Cauliflower Avocado Toast

Prep time: 15 minutes | Cook time: 8 minutes | Serves 2

◄ 1 (12 ounces / 340 g) steamer bag cauliflower
◄ 1 large egg
◄ ½ cup shredded Mozzarella cheese
◄ 1 ripe medium avocado
◄ ½ teaspoon garlic powder
◄ ¼ teaspoon ground black pepper

1. Cook cauliflower according to package instructions. Remove from bag and place into cheesecloth or clean towel to remove excess moisture. 2. Place cauliflower into a large bowl and mix in egg and Mozzarella. Cut a piece of parchment to fit your air fryer basket. Separate the cauliflower mixture into two, and place it on the parchment in two mounds. Press out the cauliflower mounds into a ¼-inch-thick rectangle. Place the parchment into the air fryer basket. 3. Adjust the temperature to 400ºF (204ºC) and set the timer for 8 minutes. 4. Flip the cauliflower halfway through the cooking time. 5. When the timer beeps, remove the parchment and allow the cauliflower to cool 5 minutes. 6. Cut open the avocado and remove the pit. Scoop out the inside, place it in a medium bowl, and mash it with garlic powder and pepper. Spread onto the cauliflower. Serve immediately.

Cinnamon-Raisin Bagels

Prep time: 30 minutes | Cook time: 10 minutes | Makes 4 bagels

◄ Oil, for spraying
◄ ¼ cup raisins
◄ 1 cup self-rising flour, plus more for dusting
◄ 1 cup plain Greek yogurt
◄ 1 teaspoon ground cinnamon
◄ 1 large egg

1. Line the air fryer basket with parchment and spray lightly with oil. 2. Place the raisins in a bowl of hot water and let sit for 10 to 15 minutes, until they have plumped. This will make them extra juicy. 3. In a large bowl, mix together the flour, yogurt, and cinnamon with your hands or a large silicone spatula until a ball is formed. It will be quite sticky for a while. 4. Drain the raisins and gently work them into the ball of dough. 5. Place the dough on a lightly floured work surface and divide into 4 equal pieces. Roll each piece into an 8- or 9-inch-long rope and shape it into a circle, pinching the ends together to seal. 6. In a small bowl, whisk the egg. Brush the egg onto the tops of the dough. 7. Place the dough in the prepared basket. 8. Air fry at 350ºF (177ºC) for 10 minutes. Serve immediately.

White Bean–Oat Waffles

Prep time: 10 minutes | Cook time: 20 minutes | Serves 2

◄ 1 large egg white
◄ 2 tablespoons finely ground flaxseed
◄ ½ cup water
◄ ¼ teaspoon salt
◄ 1 teaspoon vanilla extract
◄ ½ cup cannellini beans,
drained and rinsed
◄ 1 teaspoon coconut oil
◄ 1 teaspoon liquid stevia
◄ ½ cup old-fashioned rolled oats
◄ Extra-virgin olive oil cooking spray

1. In a blender, combine the egg white, flaxseed, water, salt, vanilla, cannellini beans, coconut oil, and stevia. Blend on high for 90 seconds. 2. Add the oats. Blend for 1 minute more. 3. Preheat the waffle iron. The batter will thicken to the correct consistency while the waffle iron preheats. 4. Spray the heated waffle iron with cooking spray. 5. Add ¾ cup of batter. Close the waffle iron. Cook for 6 to 8 minutes, or until done. Repeated with the remaining batter. 6. Serve hot, with your favorite sugar-free topping.

Turkey Breakfast Sausage Patties

Prep time: 5 minutes | Cook time: 10 minutes | Serves 4

- 1 tablespoon chopped fresh thyme
- 1 tablespoon chopped fresh sage
- 1¼ teaspoons kosher salt
- 1 teaspoon chopped fennel seeds
- ¾ teaspoon smoked paprika
- ½ teaspoon onion powder
- ½ teaspoon garlic powder
- ⅛ teaspoon crushed red pepper flakes
- ⅛ teaspoon freshly ground black pepper
- 1 pound (454 g) 93% lean ground turkey
- ½ cup finely minced sweet apple (peeled)

1. Thoroughly combine the thyme, sage, salt, fennel seeds, paprika, onion powder, garlic powder, red pepper flakes, and black pepper in a medium bowl. 2. Add the ground turkey and apple and stir until well incorporated. Divide the mixture into 8 equal portions and shape into patties with your hands, each about ¼ inch thick and 3 inches in diameter. 3. Preheat the air fryer to 400ºF (204ºC). 4. Place the patties in the air fryer basket in a single layer. You may need to work in batches to avoid overcrowding. 5. Air fry for 5 minutes. Flip the patties and air fry for 5 minutes, or until the patties are nicely browned and cooked through. 6. Remove from the basket to a plate and repeat with the remaining patties. 7. Serve warm.

Apple Cider Doughnut Holes

Prep time: 10 minutes | Cook time: 6 minutes | Makes 10 mini doughnuts

Doughnut Holes:
- 1½ cups all-purpose flour
- 2 tablespoons granulated sugar
- 2 teaspoons baking powder
- 1 teaspoon baking soda
- ½ teaspoon kosher salt
- Pinch of freshly grated nutmeg
- ¼ cup plus 2 tablespoons buttermilk, chilled
- 2 tablespoons apple cider (hard or nonalcoholic), chilled
- 1 large egg, lightly beaten
- Vegetable oil, for brushing

Glaze:
- ½ cup powdered sugar
- 2 tablespoons unsweetened applesauce
- ¼ teaspoon vanilla extract
- Pinch of kosher salt

1. Make the doughnut holes: In a bowl, whisk together the flour, granulated sugar, baking powder, baking soda, salt, and nutmeg until smooth. Add the buttermilk, cider, and egg and stir with a small rubber spatula or spoon until the dough just comes together. 2. Using a 1 ounce (28 g) ice cream scoop or 2 tablespoons, scoop and drop 10 balls of dough into the air fryer basket, spaced evenly apart, and brush the tops lightly with oil. Air fry at 350ºF (177ºC) until the doughnut holes are golden brown and fluffy, about 6 minutes. Transfer the doughnut holes to a wire rack to cool completely. 3. Make the glaze: In a small bowl, stir together the powdered sugar, applesauce, vanilla, and salt until smooth. 4. Dip the tops of the doughnuts holes in the glaze, then let stand until the glaze sets before serving. If you're impatient and want warm doughnuts, have the glaze ready to go while the doughnuts cook, then use the glaze as a dipping sauce for the warm doughnuts, fresh out of the air fryer.

Mozzarella Bacon Calzones

Prep time: 15 minutes | Cook time: 12 minutes | Serves 4

- 2 large eggs
- 1 cup blanched finely ground almond flour
- 2 cups shredded Mozzarella cheese
- 2 ounces (57 g) cream cheese, softened and broken into small pieces
- 4 slices cooked sugar-free bacon, crumbled

1. Beat eggs in a small bowl. Pour into a medium nonstick skillet over medium heat and scramble. Set aside. 2. In a large microwave-safe bowl, mix flour and Mozzarella. Add cream cheese to the bowl. 3. Place bowl in microwave and cook 45 seconds on high to melt cheese, then stir with a fork until a soft dough ball forms. 4. Cut a piece of parchment to fit air fryer basket. Separate dough into two sections and press each out into an 8-inch round. 5. On half of each dough round, place half of the scrambled eggs and crumbled bacon. Fold the other side of the dough over and press to seal the edges. 6. Place calzones on ungreased parchment and into air fryer basket. Adjust the temperature to 350ºF (177ºC) and set the timer for 12 minutes, turning calzones halfway through cooking. Crust will be golden and firm when done. 7. Let calzones cool on a cooking rack 5 minutes before serving.

Breakfast Calzone

Prep time: 15 minutes | Cook time: 15 minutes | Serves 4

- 1½ cups shredded Mozzarella cheese
- ½ cup blanched finely ground almond flour
- 1 ounce (28 g) full-fat cream cheese
- 1 large whole egg
- 4 large eggs, scrambled
- ½ pound (227 g) cooked breakfast sausage, crumbled
- 8 tablespoons shredded mild Cheddar cheese

1. In a large microwave-safe bowl, add Mozzarella, almond flour, and cream cheese. Microwave for 1 minute. Stir until the mixture is smooth and forms a ball. Add the egg and stir until dough forms. 2. Place dough between two sheets of parchment and roll out to ¼-inch thickness. Cut the dough into four rectangles. 3. Mix scrambled eggs and cooked sausage together in a large bowl. Divide the mixture evenly among each piece of dough, placing it on the lower half of the rectangle. Sprinkle each with 2 tablespoons Cheddar. 4. Fold over the rectangle to cover the egg and meat mixture. Pinch, roll, or use a wet fork to close the edges completely. 5. Cut a piece of parchment to fit your air fryer basket and place the calzones onto the parchment. Place parchment into the air fryer basket. 6. Adjust the temperature to 380ºF (193ºC) and air fry for 15 minutes. 7. Flip the calzones halfway through the cooking time. When done, calzones should be golden in color. Serve immediately.

Egg in a Hole

◄ 1 slice bread
◄ 1 teaspoon butter, softened
◄ 1 egg
◄ Salt and pepper, to taste
◄ 1 tablespoon shredded Cheddar cheese
◄ 2 teaspoons diced ham

1. Preheat the air fryer to 330ºF (166ºC). Place a baking dish in the air fryer basket. 2. On a flat work surface, cut a hole in the center of the bread slice with a 2½-inch-diameter biscuit cutter. 3. Spread the butter evenly on each side of the bread slice and transfer to the baking dish. 4. Crack the egg into the hole and season as desired with salt and pepper. Scatter the shredded cheese and diced ham on top. 5. Bake in the preheated air fryer for 5 minutes until the bread is lightly browned and the egg is cooked to your preference. 6. Remove from the basket and serve hot.

Onion Omelet

◄ 3 eggs
◄ Salt and ground black pepper, to taste
◄ ½ teaspoons soy sauce
◄ 1 large onion, chopped
◄ 2 tablespoons grated Cheddar cheese
◄ Cooking spray

1. Preheat the air fryer to 355ºF (179ºC). 2. In a bowl, whisk together the eggs, salt, pepper, and soy sauce. 3. Spritz a small pan with cooking spray. Spread the chopped onion across the bottom of the pan, then transfer the pan to the air fryer. 4. Bake in the preheated air fryer for 6 minutes or until the onion is translucent. 5. Add the egg mixture on top of the onions to coat well. Add the cheese on top, then continue baking for another 6 minutes. 6. Allow to cool before serving.

Pork Sausage Eggs with Mustard Sauce

◄ 1 pound (454 g) pork sausage
◄ 8 soft-boiled or hard-boiled eggs, peeled
◄ 1 large egg
◄ 2 tablespoons milk
◄ 1 cup crushed pork rinds
◄ Smoky Mustard Sauce:
◄ ¼ cup mayonnaise
◄ 2 tablespoons sour cream
◄ 1 tablespoon Dijon mustard
◄ 1 teaspoon chipotle hot sauce

1. Preheat the air fryer to 390ºF (199ºC). 2. Divide the sausage into 8 portions. Take each portion of sausage, pat it down into a patty, and place 1 egg in the middle, gently wrapping the sausage around the egg until the egg is completely covered. (Wet your hands slightly if you find the sausage to be too sticky.) Repeat with the remaining eggs and sausage. 3. In a small shallow bowl, whisk the egg and milk until frothy. In another shallow bowl, place the crushed pork rinds. Working one at a time, dip a sausage-wrapped egg into the beaten egg and then into the pork rinds, gently rolling to coat evenly. Repeat with the remaining sausage-wrapped eggs. 4. Arrange the eggs in a single layer in the air fryer basket, and lightly spray with olive oil. Air fry for 10 to 12 minutes, pausing halfway through the baking time to turn the eggs, until the eggs are hot and the sausage is cooked through. 5. To make the sauce: In a small bowl, combine the mayonnaise, sour cream, Dijon, and hot sauce. Whisk until thoroughly combined. Serve with the Scotch eggs.

Baked Potato Breakfast Boats

◄ 2 large russet potatoes, scrubbed
◄ Olive oil
◄ Salt and freshly ground black pepper, to taste
◄ 4 eggs
◄ 2 tablespoons chopped, cooked bacon
◄ 1 cup shredded Cheddar cheese

1. Poke holes in the potatoes with a fork and microwave on full power for 5 minutes. 2. Turn potatoes over and cook an additional 3 to 5 minutes, or until the potatoes are fork-tender. 3. Cut the potatoes in half lengthwise and use a spoon to scoop out the inside of the potato. Be careful to leave a layer of potato so that it makes a sturdy "boat." 4. Preheat the air fryer to 350ºF (177ºC). 5. Lightly spray the air fryer basket with olive oil. Spray the skin side of the potatoes with oil and sprinkle with salt and pepper to taste. 6. Place the potato skins in the air fryer basket, skin-side down. Crack one egg into each potato skin. 7. Sprinkle ½ tablespoon of bacon pieces and ¼ cup of shredded cheese on top of each egg. Sprinkle with salt and pepper to taste. 8. Air fry until the yolk is slightly runny, 5 to 6 minutes, or until the yolk is fully cooked, 7 to 10 minutes.

Lemon-Blueberry Muffins

◄ 1¼ cups almond flour
◄ 3 tablespoons Swerve
◄ 1 teaspoon baking powder
◄ 2 large eggs
◄ 3 tablespoons melted butter
◄ 1 tablespoon almond milk
◄ 1 tablespoon fresh lemon juice
◄ ½ cup fresh blueberries

1. Preheat the air fryer to 350ºF (177ºC). Lightly coat 6 silicone muffin cups with vegetable oil. Set aside. 2. In a large mixing bowl, combine the almond flour, Swerve, and baking soda. Set aside. 3. In a separate small bowl, whisk together the eggs, butter, milk, and lemon juice. Add the egg mixture to the flour mixture and stir until just combined. Fold in the blueberries and let the batter sit for 5 minutes. 4. Spoon the muffin batter into the muffin cups, about two-thirds full. Air fry for 20 to 25 minutes, or until a toothpick inserted into the center of a muffin comes out clean. 5. Remove the basket from the air fryer and let the muffins cool for about 5 minutes before transferring them to a wire rack to cool completely.

Cheesy Scrambled Eggs

Prep time: 2 minutes | Cook time: 9 minutes | Serves 2

◄ 1 teaspoon unsalted butter
◄ 2 large eggs
◄ 2 tablespoons milk
◄ 2 tablespoons shredded

Cheddar cheese
◄ Salt and freshly ground
   black pepper, to taste

1. Preheat the air fryer to 300ºF (149ºC). Place the butter in a baking pan and cook for 1 to 2 minutes, until melted. 2. In a small bowl, whisk together the eggs, milk, and cheese. Season with salt and black pepper. Transfer the mixture to the pan. 3. Cook for 3 minutes. Stir the eggs and push them toward the center of the pan. 4. Cook for another 2 minutes, then stir again. Cook for another 2 minutes, until the eggs are just cooked. Serve warm.

Asparagus and Bell Pepper Strata

Prep time: 10 minutes | Cook time: 14 to 20 minutes | Serves 4

◄ 8 large asparagus spears,
   trimmed and cut into 2-inch
   pieces
◄ ⅓ cup shredded carrot
◄ ½ cup chopped red bell
   pepper
◄ 2 slices low-sodium whole-

wheat bread, cut into ½-inch
cubes
◄ 3 egg whites
◄ 1 egg
◄ 3 tablespoons 1% milk
◄ ½ teaspoon dried thyme

1. In a baking pan, combine the asparagus, carrot, red bell pepper, and 1 tablespoon of water. Bake in the air fryer at 330ºF (166ºC) for 3 to 5 minutes, or until crisp-tender. Drain well. 2. Add the bread cubes to the vegetables and gently toss. 3. In a medium bowl, whisk the egg whites, egg, milk, and thyme until frothy. 4. Pour the egg mixture into the pan. Bake for 11 to 15 minutes, or until the strata is slightly puffy and set and the top starts to brown. Serve.

Pancake for Two

Prep time: 5 minutes | Cook time: 30 minutes | Serves 2

◄ 1 cup blanched finely ground
   almond flour
◄ 2 tablespoons granular
   erythritol
◄ 1 tablespoon salted butter,

melted
◄ 1 large egg
◄ ⅓ cup unsweetened almond
   milk
◄ ½ teaspoon vanilla extract

1. In a large bowl, mix all ingredients together, then pour half the batter into an ungreased round nonstick baking dish. 2. Place dish into air fryer basket. Adjust the temperature to 320ºF (160ºC) and bake for 15 minutes. The pancake will be golden brown on top and firm, and a toothpick inserted in the center will come out clean when done. Repeat with remaining batter. 3. Slice in half in dish and serve warm.

Cheddar Eggs

Prep time: 5 minutes | Cook time: 15 minutes | Serves 2

◄ 4 large eggs
◄ 2 tablespoons unsalted
   butter, melted

◄ ½ cup shredded sharp
   Cheddar cheese

1. Crack eggs into a round baking dish and whisk. Place dish into the air fryer basket. 2. Adjust the temperature to 400ºF (204ºC) and set the timer for 10 minutes. 3. After 5 minutes, stir the eggs and add the butter and cheese. Let cook 3 more minutes and stir again. 4. Allow eggs to finish cooking an additional 2 minutes or remove if they are to your desired liking. 5. Use a fork to fluff. Serve warm.

Spaghetti Squash Fritters

Prep time: 15 minutes | Cook time: 8 minutes | Serves 4

◄ 2 cups cooked spaghetti
   squash
◄ 2 tablespoons unsalted
   butter, softened
◄ 1 large egg

◄ ¼ cup blanched finely
   ground almond flour
◄ 2 stalks green onion, sliced
◄ ½ teaspoon garlic powder
◄ 1 teaspoon dried parsley

1. Remove excess moisture from the squash using a cheesecloth or kitchen towel. 2. Mix all ingredients in a large bowl. Form into four patties. 3. Cut a piece of parchment to fit your air fryer basket. Place each patty on the parchment and place into the air fryer basket. 4. Adjust the temperature to 400ºF (204ºC) and set the timer for 8 minutes. 5. Flip the patties halfway through the cooking time. Serve warm.

Egg Muffins

Prep time: 10 minutes | Cook time: 11 to 13 minutes | Serves 4

◄ 4 eggs
◄ Salt and pepper, to taste
◄ Olive oil
◄ 4 English muffins, split

◄ 1 cup shredded Colby Jack
   cheese
◄ 4 slices ham or Canadian
   bacon

1. Preheat the air fryer to 390ºF (199ºC). 2. Beat together eggs and add salt and pepper to taste. Spray a baking pan lightly with oil and add eggs. Bake for 2 minutes, stir, and continue cooking for 3 or 4 minutes, stirring every minute, until eggs are scrambled to your preference. Remove pan from air fryer. 3. Place bottom halves of English muffins in air fryer basket. Take half of the shredded cheese and divide it among the muffins. Top each with a slice of ham and one-quarter of the eggs. Sprinkle remaining cheese on top of the eggs. Use a fork to press the cheese into the egg a little so it doesn't slip off before it melts. 4. Air fry at 360ºF (182ºC) for 1 minute. Add English muffin tops and cook for 2 to 4 minutes to heat through and toast the muffins.

Nutty Granola

Prep time: 5 minutes | Cook time: 1 hour | Serves 4

- ½ cup pecans, coarsely chopped
- ½ cup walnuts or almonds, coarsely chopped
- ¼ cup unsweetened flaked coconut
- ¼ cup almond flour
- ¼ cup ground flaxseed or chia seeds
- 2 tablespoons sunflower seeds
- 2 tablespoons melted butter
- ¼ cup Swerve
- ½ teaspoon ground cinnamon
- ½ teaspoon vanilla extract
- ¼ teaspoon ground nutmeg
- ¼ teaspoon salt
- 2 tablespoons water

1. Preheat the air fryer to 250ºF (121ºC). Cut a piece of parchment paper to fit inside the air fryer basket. 2. In a large bowl, toss the nuts, coconut, almond flour, ground flaxseed or chia seeds, sunflower seeds, butter, Swerve, cinnamon, vanilla, nutmeg, salt, and water until thoroughly combined. 3. Spread the granola on the parchment paper and flatten to an even thickness. 4. Air fry for about an hour, or until golden throughout. Remove from the air fryer and allow to fully cool. Break the granola into bite-size pieces and store in a covered container for up to a week.

Cheddar-Ham-Corn Muffins

Prep time: 10 minutes | Cook time: 6 to 8 minutes per batch | Makes 8 muffins

- ¾ cup yellow cornmeal
- ¼ cup flour
- 1½ teaspoons baking powder
- ¼ teaspoon salt
- 1 egg, beaten
- 2 tablespoons canola oil
- ½ cup milk
- ½ cup shredded sharp Cheddar cheese
- ½ cup diced ham
- 8 foil muffin cups, liners removed and sprayed with cooking spray

1. Preheat the air fryer to 390ºF (199ºC). 2. In a medium bowl, stir together the cornmeal, flour, baking powder, and salt. 3. Add egg, oil, and milk to dry ingredients and mix well. 4. Stir in shredded cheese and diced ham. 5. Divide batter among the muffin cups. 6. Place 4 filled muffin cups in air fryer basket and bake for 5 minutes. 7. Reduce temperature to 330ºF (166ºC) and bake for 1 to 2 minutes or until toothpick inserted in center of muffin comes out clean. 8. Repeat steps 6 and 7 to cook remaining muffins.

Potatoes Lyonnaise

Prep time: 10 minutes | Cook time: 31 minutes | Serves 4

- 1 Vidalia onion, sliced
- 1 teaspoon butter, melted
- 1 teaspoon brown sugar
- 2 large russet potatoes (about 1 pound / 454 g in total), sliced
- ½-inch thick
- 1 tablespoon vegetable oil
- Salt and freshly ground black pepper, to taste

1. Preheat the air fryer to 370ºF (188ºC). 2. Toss the sliced onions, melted butter and brown sugar together in the air fryer basket. Air fry for 8 minutes, shaking the basket occasionally to help the onions cook evenly. 3. While the onions are cooking, bring a saucepan of salted water to a boil on the stovetop. Par-cook the potatoes in boiling water for 3 minutes. Drain the potatoes and pat them dry with a clean kitchen towel. 4. Add the potatoes to the onions in the air fryer basket and drizzle with vegetable oil. Toss to coat the potatoes with the oil and season with salt and freshly ground black pepper. 5. Increase the air fryer temperature to 400ºF (204ºC) and air fry for 20 minutes, tossing the vegetables a few times during the cooking time to help the potatoes brown evenly. 6. Season with salt and freshly ground black pepper and serve warm.

Chapter 2 Family Favorites

Elephant Ears

Prep time: 5 minutes | Cook time: 5 minutes | Serves 8

- Oil, for spraying
- 1 (8 ounces / 227 g) can buttermilk biscuits
- 3 tablespoons sugar
- 1 tablespoon ground
- cinnamon
- 3 tablespoons unsalted butter, melted
- 8 scoops vanilla ice cream (optional)

1. Line the air fryer basket with parchment and spray lightly with oil. 2. Separate the dough. Using a rolling pin, roll out the biscuits into 6- to 8-inch circles. 3. Place the dough circles in the prepared basket and spray liberally with oil. You may need to work in batches, depending on the size of your air fryer. 4. Air fry at 350°F (177°C) for 5 minutes, or until lightly browned. 5. In a small bowl, mix together the sugar and cinnamon. 6. Brush the elephant ears with the melted butter and sprinkle with the cinnamon-sugar mixture. 7. Top each serving with a scoop of ice cream (if using).

Pecan Rolls

Prep time: 20 minutes | Cook time: 20 to 24 minutes | Makes 12 rolls

- 2 cups all-purpose flour, plus more for dusting
- 2 tablespoons granulated sugar, plus ¼ cup, divided
- 1 teaspoon salt
- 3 tablespoons butter, at room temperature
- ¾ cup milk, whole or 2%
- ¼ cup packed light brown sugar
- ½ cup chopped pecans, toasted
- 1 to 2 tablespoons oil
- ¼ cup confectioners' sugar (optional)

1. In a large bowl, whisk the flour, 2 tablespoons granulated sugar, and salt until blended. Stir in the butter and milk briefly until a sticky dough forms. 2. In a small bowl, stir together the brown sugar and remaining ¼ cup of granulated sugar. 3. Place a piece of parchment paper on a work surface and dust it with flour. Roll the dough on the prepared surface to ¼ inch thickness. 4. Spread the sugar mixture over the dough. Sprinkle the pecans on top. Roll up the dough jelly roll-style, pinching the ends to seal. Cut the dough into 12 rolls. 5. Preheat the air fryer to 320°F (160°C). 6. Line the air fryer basket with parchment paper and spritz the parchment with oil. Place 6 rolls on the prepared parchment. 7. Bake for 5 minutes. Flip the rolls and bake for 5 to 7 minutes more until lightly browned. Repeat with the remaining rolls. 8. Sprinkle with confectioners' sugar (if using).

Cajun Shrimp

Prep time: 15 minutes | Cook time: 9 minutes | Serves 4

- Oil, for spraying
- 1 pound (454 g) jumbo raw shrimp, peeled and deveined
- 1 tablespoon Cajun seasoning
- 6 ounces (170 g) cooked kielbasa, cut into thick slices
- ½ medium zucchini, cut into ¼-inch-thick slices
- ½ medium yellow squash, cut into ¼-inch-thick slices
- 1 green bell pepper, seeded and cut into 1-inch pieces
- 2 tablespoons olive oil
- ½ teaspoon salt

1. Preheat the air fryer to 400°F (204°C). Line the air fryer basket with parchment and spray lightly with oil. 2. In a large bowl, toss together the shrimp and Cajun seasoning. Add the kielbasa, zucchini, squash, bell pepper, olive oil, and salt and mix well. 3. Transfer the mixture to the prepared basket, taking care not to overcrowd. You may need to work in batches, depending on the size of your air fryer. 4. Cook for 9 minutes, shaking and stirring every 3 minutes. Serve immediately.

Phyllo Vegetable Triangles

Prep time: 15 minutes | Cook time: 6 to 11 minutes | Serves 6

- 3 tablespoons minced onion
- 2 garlic cloves, minced
- 2 tablespoons grated carrot
- 1 teaspoon olive oil
- 3 tablespoons frozen baby peas, thawed
- 2 tablespoons nonfat cream cheese, at room temperature
- 6 sheets frozen phyllo dough, thawed
- Olive oil spray, for coating the dough

1. In a baking pan, combine the onion, garlic, carrot, and olive oil. Air fry at 390°F (199°C) for 2 to 4 minutes, or until the vegetables are crisp-tender. Transfer to a bowl. 2. Stir in the peas and cream cheese to the vegetable mixture. Let cool while you prepare the dough. 3. Lay one sheet of phyllo on a work surface and lightly spray with olive oil spray. Top with another sheet of phyllo. Repeat with the remaining 4 phyllo sheets; you'll have 3 stacks with 2 layers each. Cut each stack lengthwise into 4 strips (12 strips total). 4. Place a scant 2 teaspoons of the filling near the bottom of each strip. Bring one corner up over the filling to make a triangle; continue folding the triangles over, as you would fold a flag. Seal the edge with a bit of water. Repeat with the remaining strips and filling. 5. Air fry the triangles, in 2 batches, for 4 to 7 minutes, or until golden brown. Serve.

Bacon-Wrapped Hot Dogs

Prep time: 5 minutes | Cook time: 10 minutes | Serves 4

◄ Oil, for spraying
◄ 4 bacon slices
◄ 4 all-beef hot dogs
◄ 4 hot dog buns
◄ Toppings of choice

1. Line the air fryer basket with parchment and spray lightly with oil. 2. Wrap a strip of bacon tightly around each hot dog, taking care to cover the tips so they don't get too crispy. Secure with a toothpick at each end to keep the bacon from shrinking. 3. Place the hot dogs in the prepared basket. 4. Air fry at 380ºF (193ºC) for 8 to 9 minutes, depending on how crispy you like the bacon. For extra-crispy, cook the hot dogs at 400ºF (204ºC) for 6 to 8 minutes. 5. Place the hot dogs in the buns, return them to the air fryer, and cook for another 1 to 2 minutes, or until the buns are warm. Add your desired toppings and serve.

Mixed Berry Crumble

Prep time: 10 minutes | Cook time: 11 to 16 minutes | Serves 4

◄ ½ cup chopped fresh strawberries
◄ ½ cup fresh blueberries
◄ ⅓ cup frozen raspberries
◄ 1 tablespoon freshly squeezed lemon juice
◄ 1 tablespoon honey
◄ ⅔ cup whole-wheat pastry flour
◄ 3 tablespoons packed brown sugar
◄ 2 tablespoons unsalted butter, melted

1. In a baking pan, combine the strawberries, blueberries, and raspberries. Drizzle with the lemon juice and honey. 2. In a small bowl, mix the pastry flour and brown sugar. 3. Stir in the butter and mix until crumbly. Sprinkle this mixture over the fruit. 4. Bake at 380ºF (193ºC) for 11 to 16 minutes, or until the fruit is tender and bubbly and the topping is golden brown. Serve warm.

Puffed Egg Tarts

Prep time: 10 minutes | Cook time: 42 minutes | Makes 4 tarts

◄ Oil, for spraying
◄ All-purpose flour, for dusting
◄ 1 (12 ounces / 340 g) sheet frozen puff pastry, thawed
◄ ¾ cup shredded Cheddar
cheese, divided
◄ 4 large eggs
◄ 2 teaspoons chopped fresh parsley
◄ Salt and freshly ground black pepper, to taste

1. Preheat the air fryer to 390ºF (199ºC). Line the air fryer basket with parchment and spray lightly with oil. 2. Lightly dust your work surface with flour. Unfold the puff pastry and cut it into 4 equal squares. Place 2 squares in the prepared basket. 3. Cook for 10 minutes. 4. Remove the basket. Press the center of each tart shell with a spoon to make an indentation. 5. Sprinkle 3 tablespoons of cheese into each indentation and crack 1 egg into the center of each tart shell. 6. Cook for another 7 to 11 minutes, or until the eggs are cooked to your desired doneness. 7. Repeat with the remaining puff pastry squares, cheese, and eggs. 8. Sprinkle evenly with the parsley, and season with salt and black pepper. Serve immediately.

Meatball Subs

Prep time: 15 minutes | Cook time: 19 minutes | Serves 6

◄ Oil, for spraying
◄ 1 pound (454 g) 85% lean ground beef
◄ ½ cup Italian bread crumbs
◄ 1 tablespoon dried minced onion
◄ 1 tablespoon minced garlic
◄ 1 large egg
◄ 1 teaspoon salt
◄ 1 teaspoon freshly ground black pepper
◄ 6 hoagie rolls
◄ 1 (18 ounces / 510 g) jar marinara sauce
◄ 1½ cups shredded Mozzarella cheese

1. Line the air fryer basket with parchment and spray lightly with oil. 2. In a large bowl, mix together the ground beef, bread crumbs, onion, garlic, egg, salt, and black pepper. Roll the mixture into 18 meatballs. 3. Place the meatballs in the prepared basket. 4. Air fry at 390ºF (199ºC) for 15 minutes. 5. Place 3 meatballs in each hoagie roll. Top with marinara and Mozzarella cheese. 6. Place the loaded rolls in the air fryer and cook for 3 to 4 minutes, or until the cheese is melted. You may need to work in batches, depending on the size of your air fryer. Serve immediately.

Apple Pie Egg Rolls

Prep time: 10 minutes | Cook time: 8 minutes | Makes 6 rolls

◄ Oil, for spraying
◄ 1 (21 ounces / 595 g) can apple pie filling
◄ 1 tablespoon all-purpose flour
◄ ½ teaspoon lemon juice
◄ ¼ teaspoon ground nutmeg
◄ ¼ teaspoon ground cinnamon
◄ 6 egg roll wrappers

1. Preheat the air fryer to 400ºF (204ºC). Line the air fryer basket with parchment and spray lightly with oil. 2. In a medium bowl, mix together the pie filling, flour, lemon juice, nutmeg, and cinnamon. 3. Lay out the egg roll wrappers on a work surface and spoon a dollop of pie filling in the center of each. 4. Fill a small bowl with water. Dip your finger in the water and, working one at a time, moisten the edges of the wrappers. Fold the wrapper like an envelope: First fold one corner into the center. Fold each side corner in, and then fold over the remaining corner, making sure each corner overlaps a bit and the moistened edges stay closed. Use additional water and your fingers to seal any open edges. 5. Place the rolls in the prepared basket and spray liberally with oil. You may need to work in batches, depending on the size of your air fryer. 6. Cook for 4 minutes, flip, spray with oil, and cook for another 4 minutes, or until crispy and golden brown. Serve immediately.

Coconut Chicken Tenders

Prep time: 10 minutes | Cook time: 12 minutes | Serves 4

◄ Oil, for spraying
◄ 2 large eggs
◄ ¼ cup milk
◄ 1 tablespoon hot sauce
◄ 1½ cups sweetened flaked coconut
◄ ¾ cup panko bread crumbs
◄ 1 teaspoon salt
◄ ½ teaspoon freshly ground black pepper
◄ 1 pound (454 g) chicken tenders

1. Line the air fryer basket with parchment and spray lightly with oil. 2. In a small bowl, whisk together the eggs, milk, and hot sauce. 3. In a shallow dish, mix together the coconut, bread crumbs, salt, and black pepper. 4. Coat the chicken in the egg mix, then dredge in the coconut mixture until evenly coated. 5. Place the chicken in the prepared basket and spray liberally with oil. 6. Air fry at 400°F (204°C) for 6 minutes, flip, spray with more oil, and cook for another 6 minutes, or until the internal temperature reaches 165°F (74°C).

Veggie Tuna Melts

Prep time: 15 minutes | Cook time: 7 to 11 minutes | Serves 4

◄ 2 low-sodium whole-wheat English muffins, split
◄ 1 (6 ounces / 170 g) can chunk light low-sodium tuna, drained
◄ 1 cup shredded carrot
◄ ⅓ cup chopped mushrooms
◄ 2 scallions, white and green parts, sliced
◄ ⅓ cup nonfat Greek yogurt
◄ 2 tablespoons low-sodium stone ground mustard
◄ 2 slices low-sodium low-fat Swiss cheese, halved

1. Place the English muffin halves in the air fryer basket. Air fry at 340°F (171°C) for 3 to 4 minutes, or until crisp. Remove from the basket and set aside. 2. In a medium bowl, thoroughly mix the tuna, carrot, mushrooms, scallions, yogurt, and mustard. Top each half of the muffins with one-fourth of the tuna mixture and a half slice of Swiss cheese. 3. Air fry for 4 to 7 minutes, or until the tuna mixture is hot and the cheese melts and starts to brown. Serve immediately.

Scallops with Green Vegetables

Prep time: 15 minutes | Cook time: 8 to 11 minutes | Serves 4

◄ 1 cup green beans
◄ 1 cup frozen peas
◄ 1 cup frozen chopped broccoli
◄ 2 teaspoons olive oil
◄ ½ teaspoon dried basil
◄ ½ teaspoon dried oregano
◄ 12 ounces (340 g) sea scallops

1. In a large bowl, toss the green beans, peas, and broccoli with the olive oil. Place in the air fryer basket. Air fry at 400°F (204°C) for 4 to 6 minutes, or until the vegetables are crisp-tender. 2. Remove the vegetables from the air fryer basket and sprinkle with the herbs. Set aside. 3. In the air fryer basket, put the scallops and air fry for 4 to 5 minutes, or until the scallops are firm and reach an internal temperature of just 145°F (63°C) on a meat thermometer. 4. Toss scallops with the vegetables and serve immediately.

Beignets

Prep time: 30 minutes | Cook time: 6 minutes | Makes 9 beignets

◄ Oil, for greasing and spraying
◄ 3 cups all-purpose flour, plus more for dusting
◄ 1½ teaspoons salt
◄ 1 (2¼-teaspoon) envelope active dry yeast
◄ 1 cup milk
◄ 2 tablespoons packed light brown sugar
◄ 1 tablespoon unsalted butter
◄ 1 large egg
◄ 1 cup confectioners' sugar

1. Oil a large bowl. 2. In a small bowl, mix together the flour, salt, and yeast. Set aside. 3. Pour the milk into a glass measuring cup and microwave in 1-minute intervals until it boils. 4. In a large bowl, mix together the brown sugar and butter. Pour in the hot milk and whisk until the sugar has dissolved. Let cool to room temperature. 5. Whisk the egg into the cooled milk mixture and fold in the flour mixture until a dough forms. 6. On a lightly floured work surface, knead the dough for 3 to 5 minutes. 7. Place the dough in the oiled bowl and cover with a clean kitchen towel. Let rise in a warm place for about 1 hour, or until doubled in size. 8. Roll the dough out on a lightly floured work surface until it's about ¼ inch thick. Cut the dough into 3-inch squares and place them on a lightly floured baking sheet. Cover loosely with a kitchen towel and let rise again until doubled in size, about 30 minutes. 9. Line the air fryer basket with parchment and spray lightly with oil. 10. Place the dough squares in the prepared basket and spray lightly with oil. You may need to work in batches, depending on the size of your air fryer. 11. Air fry at 390°F (199°C) for 3 minutes, flip, spray with oil, and cook for another 3 minutes, until crispy. 12. Dust with the confectioners' sugar before serving.

Cheesy Roasted Sweet Potatoes

Prep time: 7 minutes | Cook time: 18 to 23 minutes | Serves 4

◄ 2 large sweet potatoes, peeled and sliced
◄ 1 teaspoon olive oil
◄ 1 tablespoon white balsamic
    vinegar
◄ 1 teaspoon dried thyme
◄ ¼ cup grated Parmesan cheese

1. In a large bowl, drizzle the sweet potato slices with the olive oil and toss. 2. Sprinkle with the balsamic vinegar and thyme and toss again. 3. Sprinkle the potatoes with the Parmesan cheese and toss to coat. 4. Roast the slices, in batches, in the air fryer basket at 400°F (204°C) for 18 to 23 minutes, tossing the sweet potato slices in the basket once during cooking, until tender. 5. Repeat with the remaining sweet potato slices. Serve immediately.

Chinese-Inspired Spareribs

Prep time: 30 minutes | Cook time: 8 minutes | Serves 4

- ◄ Oil, for spraying
- ◄ 12 ounces (340 g) boneless pork spareribs, cut into 3-inch-long pieces
- ◄ 1 cup soy sauce
- ◄ ¾ cup sugar
- ◄ ½ cup beef or chicken stock
- ◄ ¼ cup honey
- ◄ 2 tablespoons minced garlic
- ◄ 1 teaspoon ground ginger
- ◄ 2 drops red food coloring (optional)

1. Line the air fryer basket with parchment and spray lightly with oil. 2. Combine the ribs, soy sauce, sugar, beef stock, honey, garlic, ginger, and food coloring (if using) in a large zip-top plastic bag, seal, and shake well until completely coated. Refrigerate for at least 30 minutes. 3. Place the ribs in the prepared basket. 4. Air fry at 375ºF (191ºC) for 8 minutes, or until the internal temperature reaches 165ºF (74ºC).

Beef Jerky

Prep time: 30 minutes | Cook time: 2 hours | Serves 8

- ◄ Oil, for spraying
- ◄ 1 pound (454 g) round steak, cut into thin, short slices
- ◄ ¼ cup soy sauce
- ◄ 3 tablespoons packed light
- brown sugar
- ◄ 1 tablespoon minced garlic
- ◄ 1 teaspoon ground ginger
- ◄ 1 tablespoon water

1. Line the air fryer basket with parchment and spray lightly with oil. 2. Place the steak, soy sauce, brown sugar, garlic, ginger, and water in a zip-top plastic bag, seal, and shake well until evenly coated. Refrigerate for 30 minutes. 3. Place the steak in the prepared basket in a single layer. You may need to work in batches, depending on the size of your air fryer. 4. Air fry at 180ºF (82ºC) for at least 2 hours. Add more time if you like your jerky a bit tougher.

Fish and Vegetable Tacos

Prep time: 15 minutes | Cook time: 9 to 12 minutes | Serves 4

- ◄ 1 pound (454 g) white fish fillets, such as sole or cod
- ◄ 2 teaspoons olive oil
- ◄ 3 tablespoons freshly squeezed lemon juice, divided
- ◄ 1½ cups chopped red
- cabbage
- ◄ 1 large carrot, grated
- ◄ ½ cup low-sodium salsa
- ◄ ⅓ cup low-fat Greek yogurt
- ◄ 4 soft low-sodium whole-wheat tortillas

1. Brush the fish with the olive oil and sprinkle with 1 tablespoon of lemon juice. Air fry in the air fryer basket at 390ºF (199ºC) for 9 to 12 minutes, or until the fish just flakes when tested with a fork. 2. Meanwhile, in a medium bowl, stir together the remaining 2 tablespoons of lemon juice, the red cabbage, carrot, salsa, and yogurt. 3. When the fish is cooked, remove it from the air fryer basket and break it up into large pieces. 4. Offer the fish, tortillas, and the cabbage mixture, and let each person assemble a taco.

Old Bay Tilapia

Prep time: 15 minutes | Cook time: 6 minutes | Serves 4

- ◄ Oil, for spraying
- ◄ 1 cup panko bread crumbs
- ◄ 2 tablespoons Old Bay seasoning
- ◄ 2 teaspoons granulated garlic
- ◄ 1 teaspoon onion powder
- ◄ ½ teaspoon salt
- ◄ ¼ teaspoon freshly ground black pepper
- ◄ 1 large egg
- ◄ 4 tilapia fillets

1. Preheat the air fryer to 400ºF (204ºC). Line the air fryer basket with parchment and spray lightly with oil. 2. In a shallow bowl, mix together the bread crumbs, Old Bay, garlic, onion powder, salt, and black pepper. 3. In a small bowl, whisk the egg. 4. Coat the tilapia in the egg, then dredge in the bread crumb mixture until completely coated. 5. Place the tilapia in the prepared basket. You may need to work in batches, depending on the size of your air fryer. Spray lightly with oil. 6. Cook for 4 to 6 minutes, depending on the thickness of the fillets, until the internal temperature reaches 145ºF (63ºC). Serve immediately.

Fried Green Tomatoes

Prep time: 15 minutes | Cook time: 6 to 8 minutes | Serves 4

- ◄ 4 medium green tomatoes
- ◄ ⅓ cup all-purpose flour
- ◄ 2 egg whites
- ◄ ¼ cup almond milk
- ◄ 1 cup ground almonds
- ◄ ½ cup panko bread crumbs
- ◄ 2 teaspoons olive oil
- ◄ 1 teaspoon paprika
- ◄ 1 clove garlic, minced

1. Rinse the tomatoes and pat dry. Cut the tomatoes into ½-inch slices, discarding the thinner ends. 2. Put the flour on a plate. In a shallow bowl, beat the egg whites with the almond milk until frothy. And on another plate, combine the almonds, bread crumbs, olive oil, paprika, and garlic and mix well. 3. Dip the tomato slices into the flour, then into the egg white mixture, then into the almond mixture to coat. 4. Place four of the coated tomato slices in the air fryer basket. Air fry at 400ºF (204ºC) for 6 to 8 minutes or until the tomato coating is crisp and golden brown. Repeat with remaining tomato slices and serve immediately.

Buffalo Cauliflower

Prep time: 15 minutes | Cook time: 5 minutes | Serves 6

◄ 1 large head cauliflower, separated into small florets
◄ 1 tablespoon olive oil
◄ ½ teaspoon garlic powder
◄ ⅓ cup low-sodium hot wing sauce

◄ ⅔ cup nonfat Greek yogurt
◄ ½ teaspoons Tabasco sauce
◄ 1 celery stalk, chopped
◄ 1 tablespoon crumbled blue cheese

1. In a large bowl, toss the cauliflower florets with the olive oil. Sprinkle with the garlic powder and toss again to coat. Put half of the cauliflower in the air fryer basket. Air fry at 380ºF (193ºC) for 5 to 7 minutes, until the cauliflower is browned, shaking the basket once during cooking. 2. Transfer to a serving bowl and toss with half of the wing sauce. Repeat with the remaining cauliflower and wing sauce. 3. In a small bowl, stir together the yogurt, Tabasco sauce, celery, and blue cheese. Serve with the cauliflower for dipping.

Chapter 3 Fast and Easy Everyday Favorites

Baked Halloumi with Greek Salsa

Prep time: 15 minutes | Cook time: 6 minutes | Serves 4

Salsa:
- 1 small shallot, finely diced
- 3 garlic cloves, minced
- 2 tablespoons fresh lemon juice
- 2 tablespoons extra-virgin olive oil
- 1 teaspoon freshly cracked black pepper
- Pinch of kosher salt

Cheese:
- 8 ounces (227 g) Halloumi cheese, sliced into ½-inch-thick pieces
- ½ cup finely diced English cucumber
- 1 plum tomato, deseeded and finely diced
- 2 teaspoons chopped fresh parsley
- 1 teaspoon snipped fresh dill
- 1 teaspoon snipped fresh oregano
- 1 tablespoon extra-virgin olive oil

1. Preheat the air fryer to 375ºF (191ºC). 2. For the salsa: Combine the shallot, garlic, lemon juice, olive oil, pepper, and salt in a medium bowl. Add the cucumber, tomato, parsley, dill, and oregano. Toss gently to combine; set aside. 3. For the cheese: Place the cheese slices in a medium bowl. Drizzle with the olive oil. Toss gently to coat. Arrange the cheese in a single layer in the air fryer basket. Bake for 6 minutes. 4. Divide the cheese among four serving plates. Top with the salsa and serve immediately.

South Carolina Shrimp and Corn Bake

Prep time: 10 minutes | Cook time: 18 minutes | Serves 2

- 1 ear corn, husk and silk removed, cut into 2-inch rounds
- 8 ounces (227 g) red potatoes, unpeeled, cut into 1-inch pieces
- 2 teaspoons Old Bay Seasoning, divided
- 2 teaspoons vegetable oil, divided
- ¼ teaspoon ground black pepper
- 8 ounces (227 g) large shrimps (about 12 shrimps), deveined
- 6 ounces (170 g) andouille or chorizo sausage, cut into 1-inch pieces
- 2 garlic cloves, minced
- 1 tablespoon chopped fresh parsley

1. Preheat the air fryer to 400ºF (204ºC). 2. Put the corn rounds and potatoes in a large bowl. Sprinkle with 1 teaspoon of Old Bay seasoning and drizzle with vegetable oil. Toss to coat well.

3. Transfer the corn rounds and potatoes on a baking sheet, then put in the preheated air fryer. 4. Bake for 12 minutes or until soft and browned. Shake the basket halfway through the cooking time. 5. Meanwhile, cut slits into the shrimps but be careful not to cut them through. Combine the shrimps, sausage, remaining Old Bay seasoning, and remaining vegetable oil in the large bowl. Toss to coat well. 6. When the baking of the potatoes and corn rounds is complete, add the shrimps and sausage and bake for 6 more minutes or until the shrimps are opaque. Shake the basket halfway through the cooking time. 7. When the baking is finished, serve them on a plate and spread with parsley before serving.

Garlicky Knots with Parsley

Prep time: 10 minutes | Cook time: 10 minutes | Makes 8 knots

- 1 teaspoon dried parsley
- ¼ cup melted butter
- 2 teaspoons garlic powder
- 1 (11 ounces / 312 g) tube refrigerated French bread dough, cut into 8 slices

1. Preheat the air fryer to 350ºF (177ºC). 2. Combine the parsley, butter, and garlic powder in a bowl. Stir to mix well. 3. Place the French bread dough slices on a clean work surface, then roll each slice into a 6-inch long rope. Tie the ropes into knots and arrange them on a plate. Brush the knots with butter mixture. 4. Transfer the knots into the air fryer. You need to work in batches to avoid overcrowding. 5. Air fry for 5 minutes or until the knots are golden brown. Flip the knots halfway through the cooking time. 6. Serve immediately.

Easy Roasted Asparagus

Prep time: 5 minutes | Cook time: 6 minutes | Serves 4

- 1 pound (454 g) asparagus, trimmed and halved crosswise
- 1 teaspoon extra-virgin olive
- oil
- Salt and pepper, to taste
- Lemon wedges, for serving

1. Preheat the air fryer to 400ºF (204ºC). 2. Toss the asparagus with the oil, ⅛ teaspoon salt, and ⅛ teaspoon pepper in bowl. Transfer to air fryer basket. 3. Place the basket in air fryer and roast for 6 to 8 minutes, or until tender and bright green, tossing halfway through cooking. 4. Season with salt and pepper and serve with lemon wedges.

Cheesy Chile Toast

Prep time: 5 minutes | Cook time: 5 minutes | Serves 1

◄ 2 tablespoons grated
  Parmesan cheese
◄ 2 tablespoons grated
  Mozzarella cheese
◄ 2 teaspoons salted butter, at

  room temperature
◄ 10 to 15 thin slices serrano
  chile or jalapeño
◄ 2 slices sourdough bread
◄ ½ teaspoon black pepper

1. Preheat the air fryer to 325ºF (163ºC). 2. In a small bowl, stir together the Parmesan, Mozzarella, butter, and chiles. 3. Spread half the mixture onto one side of each slice of bread. Sprinkle with the pepper. Place the slices, cheese-side up, in the air fryer basket. Bake for 5 minutes, or until the cheese has melted and started to brown slightly. 4. Serve immediately.

Baked Chorizo Scotch Eggs

Prep time: 5 minutes | Cook time: 15 to 20 minutes | Makes 4 eggs

◄ 1 pound (454 g) Mexican
  chorizo or other seasoned
  sausage meat
◄ 4 soft-boiled eggs plus 1 raw
  egg

◄ 1 tablespoon water
◄ ½ cup all-purpose flour
◄ 1 cup panko bread crumbs
◄ Cooking spray

1. Divide the chorizo into 4 equal portions. Flatten each portion into a disc. Place a soft-boiled egg in the center of each disc. Wrap the chorizo around the egg, encasing it completely. Place the encased eggs on a plate and chill for at least 30 minutes. 2. Preheat the air fryer to 360ºF (182ºC). 3. Beat the raw egg with 1 tablespoon of water. Place the flour on a small plate and the panko on a second plate. Working with 1 egg at a time, roll the encased egg in the flour, then dip it in the egg mixture. Dredge the egg in the panko and place on a plate. Repeat with the remaining eggs. 4. Spray the eggs with oil and place in the air fryer basket. Bake for 10 minutes. Turn and bake for an additional 5 to 10 minutes, or until browned and crisp on all sides. 5. Serve immediately.

Beery and Crunchy Onion Rings

Prep time: 10 minutes | Cook time: 16 minutes | Serves 2 to 4

◄ ⅔ cup all-purpose flour
◄ 1 teaspoon paprika
◄ ½ teaspoon baking soda
◄ 1 teaspoon salt
◄ ½ teaspoon freshly ground
  black pepper
◄ 1 egg, beaten

◄ ¾ cup beer
◄ 1½ cups breadcrumbs
◄ 1 tablespoons olive oil
◄ 1 large Vidalia onion, peeled
  and sliced into ½-inch rings
◄ Cooking spray

1. Preheat the air fryer to 360ºF (182ºC). Spritz the air fryer basket with cooking spray. 2. Combine the flour, paprika, baking soda, salt, and ground black pepper in a bowl. Stir to mix well. 3. Combine the egg and beer in a separate bowl. Stir to mix well. 4. Make a well in the center of the flour mixture, then pour the egg mixture in the well. Stir to mix everything well. 5. Pour the breadcrumbs and olive oil in a shallow plate. Stir to mix well. 6. Dredge the onion rings gently into the flour and egg mixture, then shake the excess off and put into the plate of breadcrumbs. Flip to coat the both sides well. 7. Arrange the onion rings in the preheated air fryer. Air fry in batches for 16 minutes or until golden brown and crunchy. Flip the rings and put the bottom rings to the top halfway through. 8. Serve immediately.

Crispy Potato Chips with Lemony Cream Dip

Prep time: 20 minutes | Cook time: 15 minutes | Serves 2 to 4

◄ 2 large russet potatoes,
  sliced into ⅛-inch slices,
  rinsed
◄ Sea salt and freshly ground
  black pepper, to taste
◄ Cooking spray
◄ Lemony Cream Dip:
◄ ½ cup sour cream

◄ ¼ teaspoon lemon juice
◄ 2 scallions, white part only,
  minced
◄ 1 tablespoon olive oil
◄ ¼ teaspoon salt
◄ Freshly ground black pepper,
  to taste

1. Soak the potato slices in water for 10 minutes, then pat dry with paper towels. 2. Preheat the air fryer to 300ºF (149ºC). 3. Transfer the potato slices in the preheated air fryer. Spritz the slices with cooking spray. You may need to work in batches to avoid overcrowding. 4. Air fry for 15 minutes or until crispy and golden brown. Shake the basket periodically. Sprinkle with salt and ground black pepper in the last minute. 5. Meanwhile, combine the ingredients for the dip in a small bowl. Stir to mix well. 6. Serve the potato chips immediately with the dip.

Air Fried Zucchini Sticks

Prep time: 5 minutes | Cook time: 20 minutes | Serves 4

◄ 1 medium zucchini, cut into
  48 sticks
◄ ¼ cup seasoned breadcrumbs

◄ 1 tablespoon melted buttery
  spread
◄ Cooking spray

1. Preheat the air fryer to 360ºF (182ºC). Spritz the air fryer basket with cooking spray and set aside. 2. In 2 different shallow bowls, add the seasoned breadcrumbs and the buttery spread. 3. One by one, dredge the zucchini sticks into the buttery spread, then roll in the breadcrumbs to coat evenly. Arrange the crusted sticks on a plate. 4. Place the zucchini sticks in the prepared air fryer basket. Work in two batches to avoid overcrowding. 5. Air fry for 10 minutes, or until golden brown and crispy. Shake the basket halfway through to cook evenly. 6. When the cooking time is over, transfer the fries to a wire rack. Rest for 5 minutes and serve warm.

Simple Pea Delight

Prep time: 5 minutes | Cook time: 15 minutes | Serves 2 to 4

- 1 cup flour
- 1 teaspoon baking powder
- 3 eggs
- 1 cup coconut milk
- 1 cup cream cheese
- 3 tablespoons pea protein
- ½ cup chicken or turkey strips
- Pinch of sea salt
- 1 cup Mozzarella cheese

1. Preheat the air fryer to 390ºF (199ºC). 2. In a large bowl, mix all ingredients together using a large wooden spoon. 3. Spoon equal amounts of the mixture into muffin cups and bake for 15 minutes. 4. Serve immediately.

Cheesy Jalapeño Cornbread

Prep time: 10 minutes | Cook time: 20 minutes | Serves 8

- ⅔ cup cornmeal
- ⅓ cup all-purpose flour
- ¾ teaspoon baking powder
- 2 tablespoons buttery spread, melted
- ½ teaspoon kosher salt
- 1 tablespoon granulated sugar
- ¾ cup whole milk
- 1 large egg, beaten
- 1 jalapeño pepper, thinly sliced
- ⅓ cup shredded sharp Cheddar cheese
- Cooking spray

1. Preheat the air fryer to 300ºF (149ºC). Spritz the air fryer basket with cooking spray. 2. Combine all the ingredients in a large bowl. Stir to mix well. Pour the mixture in a baking pan. 3. Arrange the pan in the preheated air fryer. Bake for 20 minutes or until a toothpick inserted in the center of the bread comes out clean. 4. When the cooking is complete, remove the baking pan from the air fryer and allow the bread to cool for a few minutes before slicing to serve.

Purple Potato Chips with Rosemary

Prep time: 10 minutes | Cook time: 9 to 14 minutes | Serves 6

- 1 cup Greek yogurt
- 2 chipotle chiles, minced
- 2 tablespoons adobo sauce
- 1 teaspoon paprika
- 1 tablespoon lemon juice
- 10 purple fingerling potatoes
- 1 teaspoon olive oil
- 2 teaspoons minced fresh rosemary leaves
- ⅛ teaspoon cayenne pepper
- ¼ teaspoon coarse sea salt

1. Preheat the air fryer to 400ºF (204ºC). 2. In a medium bowl, combine the yogurt, minced chiles, adobo sauce, paprika, and lemon juice. Mix well and refrigerate. 3. Wash the potatoes and dry them with paper towels. Slice the potatoes lengthwise, as thinly

as possible. You can use a mandoline, a vegetable peeler, or a very sharp knife. 4. Combine the potato slices in a medium bowl and drizzle with the olive oil; toss to coat. 5. Air fry the chips, in batches, in the air fryer basket, for 9 to 14 minutes. Use tongs to gently rearrange the chips halfway during cooking time. 6. Sprinkle the chips with the rosemary, cayenne pepper, and sea salt. Serve with the chipotle sauce for dipping.

Sweet Corn and Carrot Fritters

Prep time: 10 minutes | Cook time: 8 to 11 minutes | Serves 4

- 1 medium-sized carrot, grated
- 1 yellow onion, finely chopped
- 4 ounces (113 g) canned sweet corn kernels, drained
- 1 teaspoon sea salt flakes
- 1 tablespoon chopped fresh cilantro
- 1 medium-sized egg, whisked
- 2 tablespoons plain milk
- 1 cup grated Parmesan cheese
- ¼ cup flour
- ⅓ teaspoon baking powder
- ⅓ teaspoon sugar
- Cooking spray

1. Preheat the air fryer to 350ºF (177ºC). 2. Place the grated carrot in a colander and press down to squeeze out any excess moisture. Dry it with a paper towel. 3. Combine the carrots with the remaining ingredients. 4. Mold 1 tablespoon of the mixture into a ball and press it down with your hand or a spoon to flatten it. Repeat until the rest of the mixture is used up. 5. Spritz the balls with cooking spray. 6. Arrange in the air fryer basket, taking care not to overlap any balls. Bake for 8 to 11 minutes, or until they're firm. 7. Serve warm.

Parsnip Fries with Garlic-Yogurt Dip

Prep time: 10 minutes | Cook time: 10 minutes | Serves 4

- 3 medium parsnips, peeled, cut into sticks
- ¼ teaspoon kosher salt
Dip:
- ¼ cup plain Greek yogurt
- ⅛ teaspoon garlic powder
- 1 tablespoon sour cream
- 1 teaspoon olive oil
- 1 garlic clove, unpeeled
- Cooking spray
- ¼ teaspoon kosher salt
- Freshly ground black pepper, to taste

1. Preheat the air fryer to 360ºF (182ºC). Spritz the air fryer basket with cooking spray. 2. Put the parsnip sticks in a large bowl, then sprinkle with salt and drizzle with olive oil. 3. Transfer the parsnip into the preheated air fryer and add the garlic. 4. Air fry for 5 minutes, then remove the garlic from the air fryer and shake the basket. Air fry for 5 more minutes or until the parsnip sticks are crisp. 5. Meanwhile, peel the garlic and crush it. Combine the crushed garlic with the ingredients for the dip. Stir to mix well. 6. When the frying is complete, remove the parsnip fries from the air fryer and serve with the dipping sauce.

Spinach and Carrot Balls

Prep time: 10 minutes | Cook time: 10 minutes | Serves 4

- ◄ 2 slices toasted bread
- ◄ 1 carrot, peeled and grated
- ◄ 1 package fresh spinach, blanched and chopped
- ◄ ½ onion, chopped
- ◄ 1 egg, beaten
- ◄ ½ teaspoon garlic powder
- ◄ 1 teaspoon minced garlic
- ◄ 1 teaspoon salt
- ◄ ½ teaspoon black pepper
- ◄ 1 tablespoon nutritional yeast
- ◄ 1 tablespoon flour

1. Preheat the air fryer to 390ºF (199ºC). 2. In a food processor, pulse the toasted bread to form bread crumbs. Transfer into a shallow dish or bowl. 3. In a bowl, mix together all the other ingredients. 4. Use your hands to shape the mixture into small-sized balls. Roll the balls in the bread crumbs, ensuring to cover them well. 5. Put in the air fryer basket and air fry for 10 minutes. 6. Serve immediately.

Simple Air Fried Crispy Brussels Sprouts

Prep time: 5 minutes | Cook time: 20 minutes | Serves 4

- ◄ ¼ teaspoon salt
- ◄ ⅛ teaspoon ground black pepper
- ◄ 1 tablespoon extra-virgin
- olive oil
- ◄ 1 pound (454 g) Brussels sprouts, trimmed and halved
- ◄ Lemon wedges, for garnish

1. Preheat the air fryer to 350ºF (177ºC). 2. Combine the salt, black pepper, and olive oil in a large bowl. Stir to mix well. 3. Add the Brussels sprouts to the bowl of mixture and toss to coat well. 4. Arrange the Brussels sprouts in the preheated air fryer. Air fry for 20 minutes or until lightly browned and wilted. Shake the basket two times during the air frying. 5. Transfer the cooked Brussels sprouts to a large plate and squeeze the lemon wedges on top to serve.

Beet Salad with Lemon Vinaigrette

Prep time: 10 minutes | Cook time: 12 to 15 minutes | Serves 4

- ◄ 6 medium red and golden beets, peeled and sliced
- ◄ 1 teaspoon olive oil
- ◄ ¼ teaspoon kosher salt
- ◄ ½ cup crumbled feta cheese
- ◄ 8 cups mixed greens
- ◄ Cooking spray
- ◄ Vinaigrette:
- ◄ 2 teaspoons olive oil
- ◄ 2 tablespoons chopped fresh chives
- ◄ Juice of 1 lemon

1. Preheat the air fryer to 360ºF (182ºC). 2. In a large bowl, toss the beets, olive oil, and kosher salt. 3. Spray the air fryer basket with cooking spray, then place the beets in the basket and air fry for 12 to 15 minutes or until tender. 4. While the beets cook, make the vinaigrette in a large bowl by whisking together the olive oil, lemon juice, and chives. 5. Remove the beets from the air fryer, toss in the vinaigrette, and allow to cool for 5 minutes. Add the feta and serve on top of the mixed greens.

Bacon Pinwheels

Prep time: 10 minutes | Cook time: 10 minutes | Makes 8 pinwheels

- ◄ 1 sheet puff pastry
- ◄ 2 tablespoons maple syrup
- ◄ ¼ cup brown sugar
- ◄ 8 slices bacon
- ◄ Ground black pepper, to taste
- ◄ Cooking spray

1. Preheat the air fryer to 360ºF (182ºC). Spritz the air fryer basket with cooking spray. 2. Roll the puff pastry into a 10-inch square with a rolling pin on a clean work surface, then cut the pastry into 8 strips. 3. Brush the strips with maple syrup and sprinkle with sugar, leaving a 1-inch far end uncovered. 4. Arrange each slice of bacon on each strip, leaving a ⅛-inch length of bacon hang over the end close to you. Sprinkle with black pepper. 5. From the end close to you, roll the strips into pinwheels, then dab the uncovered end with water and seal the rolls. 6. Arrange the pinwheels in the preheated air fryer and spritz with cooking spray. 7. Air fry for 10 minutes or until golden brown. Flip the pinwheels halfway through. 8. Serve immediately.

Air Fried Butternut Squash with Chopped Hazelnuts

Prep time: 10 minutes | Cook time: 20 minutes | Makes 3 cups

- ◄ 2 tablespoons whole hazelnuts
- ◄ 3 cups butternut squash, peeled, deseeded, and cubed
- ◄ ¼ teaspoon kosher salt
- ◄ ¼ teaspoon freshly ground black pepper
- ◄ 2 teaspoons olive oil
- ◄ Cooking spray

1. Preheat the air fryer to 300ºF (149ºC). Spritz the air fryer basket with cooking spray. 2. Arrange the hazelnuts in the preheated air fryer. Air fry for 3 minutes or until soft. 3. Chopped the hazelnuts roughly and transfer to a small bowl. Set aside. 4. Set the air fryer temperature to 360ºF (182ºC). Spritz with cooking spray. 5. Put the butternut squash in a large bowl, then sprinkle with salt and pepper and drizzle with olive oil. Toss to coat well. 6. Transfer the squash in the air fryer. Air fry for 20 minutes or until the squash is soft. Shake the basket halfway through the frying time. 7. When the frying is complete, transfer the squash onto a plate and sprinkle with chopped hazelnuts before serving.

Easy Cinnamon Toast

Prep time: 5 minutes | Cook time: 20 minutes | Serves 6

◄ 1½ teaspoons cinnamon
◄ 1½ teaspoons vanilla extract
◄ ½ cup sugar
◄ 2 teaspoons ground black

pepper
◄ 2 tablespoons melted coconut oil
◄ 12 slices whole wheat bread

1. Preheat the air fryer to 400ºF (204ºC). 2. Combine all the ingredients, except for the bread, in a large bowl. Stir to mix well. 3. Dunk the bread in the bowl of mixture gently to coat and infuse well. Shake the excess off. 4. Arrange the bread slices in the preheated air fryer. Air fry for 5 minutes or until golden brown. Flip the bread halfway through. You may need to cook in batches to avoid overcrowding. 5. Remove the bread slices from the air fryer and slice to serve.

Herb-Roasted Veggies

Prep time: 10 minutes | Cook time: 14 to 18 minutes | Serves 4

◄ 1 red bell pepper, sliced
◄ 1 (8 ounces / 227 g) package sliced mushrooms
◄ 1 cup green beans, cut into 2-inch pieces

◄ ⅓ cup diced red onion
◄ 3 garlic cloves, sliced
◄ 1 teaspoon olive oil
◄ ½ teaspoon dried basil
◄ ½ teaspoon dried tarragon

1. Preheat the air fryer to 350ºF (177ºC). 2. In a medium bowl, mix the red bell pepper, mushrooms, green beans, red onion, and garlic. Drizzle with the olive oil. Toss to coat. 3. Add the herbs and toss again. 4. Place the vegetables in the air fryer basket. Roast for 14 to 18 minutes, or until tender. Serve immediately.

Garlicky Zoodles

Prep time: 10 minutes | Cook time: 10 minutes | Serves 4

◄ 2 large zucchini, peeled and spiralized
◄ 2 large yellow summer squash, peeled and spiralized
◄ 1 tablespoon olive oil,

divided
◄ ½ teaspoon kosher salt
◄ 1 garlic clove, whole
◄ 2 tablespoons fresh basil, chopped
◄ Cooking spray

1. Preheat the air fryer to 360ºF (182ºC). Spritz the air fryer basket with cooking spray. 2. Combine the zucchini and summer squash with 1 teaspoon olive oil and salt in a large bowl. Toss to coat well. 3. Transfer the zucchini and summer squash in the preheated air fryer and add the garlic. 4. Air fry for 10 minutes or until tender and fragrant. Toss the spiralized zucchini and summer squash halfway through the cooking time. 5. Transfer the cooked zucchini and summer squash onto a plate and set aside. 6. Remove the garlic from the air fryer and allow to cool for a few minutes. Mince the garlic and combine with remaining olive oil in a small bowl. Stir to mix well. 7. Drizzle the spiralized zucchini and summer squash with garlic oil and sprinkle with basil. Toss to serve.

Classic Poutine

Prep time: 15 minutes | Cook time: 25 minutes | Serves 2

◄ 2 russet potatoes, scrubbed and cut into ½-inch sticks
◄ 2 teaspoons vegetable oil
◄ 2 tablespoons butter
◄ ¼ onion, minced
◄ ¼ teaspoon dried thyme
◄ 1 clove garlic, smashed
◄ 3 tablespoons all-purpose

flour
◄ 1 teaspoon tomato paste
◄ 1½ cups beef stock
◄ 2 teaspoons Worcestershire sauce
◄ Salt and freshly ground black pepper, to taste
◄ ⅔ cup chopped string cheese

1. Bring a pot of water to a boil, then put in the potato sticks and blanch for 4 minutes. 2. Preheat the air fryer to 400ºF (204ºC). 3. Drain the potato sticks and rinse under running cold water, then pat dry with paper towels. 4. Transfer the sticks in a large bowl and drizzle with vegetable oil. Toss to coat well. 5. Place the potato sticks in the preheated air fryer. Air fry for 25 minutes or until the sticks are golden brown. Shake the basket at least three times during the frying. 6. Meanwhile, make the gravy: Heat the butter in a saucepan over medium heat until melted. 7. Add the onion, thyme, and garlic and sauté for 5 minutes or until the onion is translucent. 8. Add the flour and sauté for an additional 2 minutes. Pour in the tomato paste and beef stock and cook for 1 more minute or until lightly thickened. 9. Drizzle the gravy with Worcestershire sauce and sprinkle with salt and ground black pepper. Reduce the heat to low to keep the gravy warm until ready to serve. 10. Transfer the fried potato sticks onto a plate, then sprinkle with salt and ground black pepper. Scatter with string cheese and pour the gravy over. Serve warm.

Peppery Brown Rice Fritters

Prep time: 10 minutes | Cook time: 8 to 10 minutes | Serves 4

◄ 1 (10 ounces / 284 g) bag frozen cooked brown rice, thawed
◄ 1 egg
◄ 3 tablespoons brown rice flour
◄ ⅓ cup finely grated carrots

◄ ⅓ cup minced red bell pepper
◄ 2 tablespoons minced fresh basil
◄ 3 tablespoons grated Parmesan cheese
◄ 2 teaspoons olive oil

1. Preheat the air fryer to 380ºF (193ºC). 2. In a small bowl, combine the thawed rice, egg, and flour and mix to blend. 3. Stir in the carrots, bell pepper, basil, and Parmesan cheese. 4. Form the mixture into 8 fritters and drizzle with the olive oil. 5. Put the fritters carefully into the air fryer basket. Air fry for 8 to 10 minutes, or until the fritters are golden brown and cooked through. 6. Serve immediately.

Indian-Style Sweet Potato Fries

Seasoning Mixture:
- ◄ ¾ teaspoon ground coriander
- ◄ ½ teaspoon garam masala
- ◄ ½ teaspoon garlic powder
- ◄ ½ teaspoon ground cumin
- ◄ ¼ teaspoon ground cayenne pepper

Fries:
- ◄ 2 large sweet potatoes, peeled
- ◄ 2 teaspoons olive oil

1. Preheat the air fryer to 400ºF (204ºC). 2. In a small bowl, combine the coriander, garam masala, garlic powder, cumin, and cayenne pepper. 3. Slice the sweet potatoes into ¼-inch-thick fries. 4. In a large bowl, toss the sliced sweet potatoes with the olive oil and the seasoning mixture. 5. Transfer the seasoned sweet potatoes to the air fryer basket and fry for 8 minutes, until crispy. 6. Serve warm.

Simple Cheesy Shrimps

- ◄ ⅔ cup grated Parmesan cheese
- ◄ 4 minced garlic cloves
- ◄ 1 teaspoon onion powder
- ◄ ½ teaspoon oregano
- ◄ 1 teaspoon basil
- ◄ 1 teaspoon ground black
- pepper
- ◄ 2 tablespoons olive oil
- ◄ 2 pounds (907 g) cooked large shrimps, peeled and deveined
- ◄ Lemon wedges, for topping
- ◄ Cooking spray

1. Preheat the air fryer to 350ºF (177ºC). Spritz the air fryer basket with cooking spray. 2. Combine all the ingredients, except for the shrimps, in a large bowl. Stir to mix well. 3. Dunk the shrimps in the mixture and toss to coat well. Shake the excess off. 4. Arrange the shrimps in the preheated air fryer. Air fry for 8 minutes or until opaque. Flip the shrimps halfway through. You may need to work in batches to avoid overcrowding. 5. Transfer the cooked shrimps on a large plate and squeeze the lemon wedges over before serving.

Lemony and Garlicky Asparagus

- ◄ 10 spears asparagus (about ½ pound / 227 g in total), snap the ends off
- ◄ 1 tablespoon lemon juice
- ◄ 2 teaspoons minced garlic
- ◄ ½ teaspoon salt
- ◄ ¼ teaspoon ground black pepper
- ◄ Cooking spray

1. Preheat the air fryer to 400ºF (204ºC). Line a parchment paper in the air fryer basket. 2. Put the asparagus spears in a large bowl. Drizzle with lemon juice and sprinkle with minced garlic, salt, and ground black pepper. Toss to coat well. 3. Transfer the asparagus in the preheated air fryer and spritz with cooking spray. Air fryer for 10 minutes or until wilted and soft. Flip the asparagus halfway through. 4. Serve immediately.

Simple and Easy Croutons

- ◄ 2 slices friendly bread
- ◄ 1 tablespoon olive oil
- ◄ Hot soup, for serving

1. Preheat the air fryer to 390ºF (199ºC). 2. Cut the slices of bread into medium-size chunks. 3. Brush the air fryer basket with the oil. 4. Place the chunks inside and air fry for at least 8 minutes. 5. Serve with hot soup.

Frico

- ◄ 1 cup shredded aged Manchego cheese
- ◄ 1 teaspoon all-purpose flour
- ◄ ½ teaspoon cumin seeds
- ◄ ¼ teaspoon cracked black pepper

1. Preheat the air fryer to 375ºF (191ºC). Line the air fryer basket with parchment paper. 2. Combine the cheese and flour in a bowl. Stir to mix well. Spread the mixture in the basket into a 4-inch round. 3. Combine the cumin and black pepper in a small bowl. Stir to mix well. Sprinkle the cumin mixture over the cheese round. 4. Air fry 5 minutes or until the cheese is lightly browned and frothy. 5. Use tongs to transfer the cheese wafer onto a plate and slice to serve.

Rosemary and Orange Roasted Chickpeas

- ◄ 4 cups cooked chickpeas
- ◄ 2 tablespoons vegetable oil
- ◄ 1 teaspoon kosher salt
- ◄ 1 teaspoon cumin
- ◄ 1 teaspoon paprika
- ◄ Zest of 1 orange
- ◄ 1 tablespoon chopped fresh rosemary

1. Preheat the air fryer to 400ºF (204ºC). 2. Make sure the chickpeas are completely dry prior to roasting. In a medium bowl, toss the chickpeas with oil, salt, cumin, and paprika. 3. Working in batches, spread the chickpeas in a single layer in the air fryer basket. Air fry for 10 to 12 minutes until crisp, shaking once halfway through. 4. Return the warm chickpeas to the bowl and toss with the orange zest and rosemary. Allow to cool completely. 5. Serve.

Chapter 4 Beef, Pork, and Lamb

Cinnamon-Beef Kofta

Prep time: 10 minutes | Cook time: 13 minutes per batch | Makes 12 koftas

- 1½ pounds (680 g) lean ground beef
- 1 teaspoon onion powder
- ¾ teaspoon ground cinnamon
- ¾ teaspoon ground dried turmeric
- 1 teaspoon ground cumin
- ¾ teaspoon salt
- ¼ teaspoon cayenne
- 12 (3½- to 4-inch-long) cinnamon sticks
- Cooking spray

1. Preheat the air fryer to 375ºF (191ºC). Spritz the air fryer basket with cooking spray. 2. Combine all the ingredients, except for the cinnamon sticks, in a large bowl. Toss to mix well. 3. Divide and shape the mixture into 12 balls, then wrap each ball around each cinnamon stick and leave a quarter of the length uncovered. 4. Arrange the beef-cinnamon sticks in the preheated air fryer and spritz with cooking spray. Work in batches to avoid overcrowding. 5. Air fry for 13 minutes or until the beef is browned. Flip the sticks halfway through. 6. Serve immediately.

Bacon Wrapped Pork with Apple Gravy

Prep time: 10 minutes | Cook time: 25 minutes | Serves 4

Pork:
- 1 tablespoons Dijon mustard
- 1 pork tenderloin

Apple Gravy:
- 3 tablespoons ghee, divided
- 1 small shallot, chopped
- 2 apples

- 3 strips bacon

- 1 tablespoon almond flour
- 1 cup vegetable broth
- ½ teaspoon Dijon mustard

1. Preheat the air fryer to 360ºF (182ºC). 2. Spread Dijon mustard all over tenderloin and wrap with strips of bacon. 3. Put into air fryer and air fry for 12 minutes. Use a meat thermometer to check for doneness. 4. To make sauce, heat 1 tablespoons of ghee in a pan and add shallots. Cook for 1 minute. 5. Then add apples, cooking for 4 minutes until softened. 6. Add flour and 2 tablespoons of ghee to make a roux. Add broth and mustard, stirring well to combine. 7. When sauce starts to bubble, add 1 cup of sautéed apples, cooking until sauce thickens. 8. Once pork tenderloin is cooked, allow to sit 8 minutes to rest before slicing. 9. Serve topped with apple gravy.

Bacon-Wrapped Vegetable Kebabs

Prep time: 10 minutes | Cook time: 10 to 12 minutes | Serves 4

- 4 ounces (113 g) mushrooms, sliced
- 1 small zucchini, sliced
- 12 grape tomatoes
- 4 ounces (113 g) sliced
- bacon, halved
- Avocado oil spray
- Sea salt and freshly ground black pepper, to taste

1. Stack 3 mushroom slices, 1 zucchini slice, and 1 grape tomato. Wrap a bacon strip around the vegetables and thread them onto a skewer. Repeat with the remaining vegetables and bacon. Spray with oil and sprinkle with salt and pepper. 2. Set the air fryer to 400ºF (204ºC). Place the skewers in the air fryer basket in a single layer, working in batches if necessary, and air fry for 5 minutes. Flip the skewers and cook for 5 to 7 minutes more, until the bacon is crispy and the vegetables are tender. 3. Serve warm.

Korean Beef Tacos

Prep time: 30 minutes | Cook time: 12 minutes | Serves 6

- 2 tablespoons gochujang (Korean red chile paste)
- 2 cloves garlic, minced
- 2 teaspoons minced fresh ginger
- 2 tablespoons toasted sesame oil
- 1 tablespoon soy sauce
- 2 tablespoons sesame seeds
- 2 teaspoons sugar
- ½ teaspoon kosher salt
- 1½ pounds (680 g) thinly sliced beef (chuck, rib eye, or sirloin)
- 1 medium red onion, sliced
- 12 (6-inch) flour tortillas, warmed; or lettuce leaves
- ½ cup chopped green onions
- ¼ cup chopped fresh cilantro (optional)
- ½ cup kimchi (optional)

1. In a small bowl, combine the gochujang, garlic, ginger, sesame oil, soy sauce, sesame seeds, sugar, and salt. Whisk until well combined. Place the beef and red onion in a resealable plastic bag and pour the marinade over. Seal the bag and massage to coat all of the meat and onion. Marinate at room temperature for 30 minutes or in the refrigerator for up to 24 hours. 2. Place the meat and onion in the air fryer basket, leaving behind as much of the marinade as possible; discard the marinade. Set the air fryer to 400ºF (204ºC) for 12 minutes, shaking halfway through the cooking time. 3. To serve, place meat and onion in the tortillas. Top with the green onions and the cilantro and kimchi, if using, and serve.

Beef Chuck Cheeseburgers

Prep time: 10 minutes | Cook time: 15 minutes | Serves 4

- ¾ pound (340 g) ground beef chuck
- 1 envelope onion soup mix
- Kosher salt and freshly ground black pepper, to
- taste
- 1 teaspoon paprika
- 4 slices Monterey Jack cheese
- 4 ciabatta rolls

1. In a bowl, stir together the ground chuck, onion soup mix, salt, black pepper, and paprika to combine well. 2. Preheat the air fryer to 385ºF (196ºC). 3. Take four equal portions of the mixture and mold each one into a patty. Transfer to the air fryer and air fry for 10 minutes. 4. Put the slices of cheese on the top of the burgers. 5. Air fry for another minute before serving on ciabatta rolls.

Air Fryer Chicken-Fried Steak

Prep time: 5 minutes | Cook time: 20 minutes | Serves 4

- 1 pound beef chuck sirloin steak
- 3 cups low-fat milk, divided
- 1 teaspoon dried thyme
- 1 teaspoon dried rosemary
- 2 medium egg whites
- 1 cup chickpea crumbs
- ½ cup coconut flour
- 1 tablespoon Creole seasoning

1. In a bowl, marinate the steak in 2 cups of milk for 30 to 45 minutes. 2. Remove the steak from milk, shake off the excess liquid, and season with the thyme and rosemary. Discard the milk. 3. In a shallow bowl, beat the egg whites with the remaining 1 cup of milk. 4. In a separate shallow bowl, combine the chickpea crumbs, coconut flour, and seasoning. 5. Dip the steak in the egg white mixture then dredge in the chickpea crumb mixture, coating well. 6. Place the steak in the basket of an air fryer. 7. Set the air fryer to 390ºF, close, and cook for 10 minutes. 8. Open the air fryer, turn the steaks, close, and cook for 10 minutes. Let rest for 5 minutes.

Kale and Beef Omelet

Prep time: 15 minutes | Cook time: 16 minutes | Serves 4

- ½ pound (227 g) leftover beef, coarsely chopped
- 2 garlic cloves, pressed
- 1 cup kale, torn into pieces and wilted
- 1 tomato, chopped
- ¼ teaspoon sugar
- 4 eggs, beaten
- 4 tablespoons heavy cream
- ½ teaspoon turmeric powder
- Salt and ground black pepper, to taste
- ⅛ teaspoon ground allspice
- Cooking spray

1. Preheat the air fryer to 360ºF (182ºC). Spritz four ramekins with cooking spray. 2. Put equal amounts of each of the ingredients into each ramekin and mix well. 3. Air fry for 16 minutes. Serve immediately.

New York Strip with Honey-Mustard Butter

Prep time: 5 minutes | Cook time: 14 minutes | Serves 4

- 2 pounds (907 g) New York Strip
- 1 teaspoon cayenne pepper
- 1 tablespoon honey
- 1 tablespoon Dijon mustard
- ½ stick butter, softened
- Sea salt and freshly ground black pepper, to taste
- Cooking spray

1. Preheat the air fryer to 400ºF (204ºC) and spritz with cooking spray. 2. Sprinkle the New York Strip with cayenne pepper, salt, and black pepper on a clean work surface. 3. Arrange the New York Strip in the preheated air fryer and spritz with cooking spray. 4. Air fry for 14 minutes or until browned and reach your desired doneness. Flip the New York Strip halfway through. 5. Meanwhile, combine the honey, mustard, and butter in a small bowl. Stir to mix well. 6. Transfer the air fried New York Strip onto a plate and baste with the honey-mustard butter before serving.

Avocado Buttered Flank Steak

Prep time: 5 minutes | Cook time: 12 minutes | Serves 1

- 1 flank steak
- Salt and ground black pepper, to taste
- 2 avocados
- 2 tablespoons butter, melted
- ½ cup chimichurri sauce

1. Rub the flank steak with salt and pepper to taste and leave to sit for 20 minutes. 2. Preheat the air fryer to 400ºF (204ºC). 3. Halve the avocados and take out the pits. Spoon the flesh into a bowl and mash with a fork. Mix in the melted butter and chimichurri sauce, making sure everything is well combined. 4. Put the steak in the air fryer basket and air fry for 6 minutes. Flip over and allow to air fry for another 6 minutes. 5. Serve the steak with the avocado butter.

Herb-Roasted Beef Tips with Onions

Prep time: 5 minutes | Cook time: 10 minutes | Serves 4

- 1 pound (454 g) rib eye steak, cubed
- 2 garlic cloves, minced
- 2 tablespoons olive oil
- 1 tablespoon fresh oregano
- 1 teaspoon salt
- ½ teaspoon black pepper
- 1 yellow onion, thinly sliced

1. Preheat the air fryer to 380ºF(193ºC). 2. In a medium bowl, combine the steak, garlic, olive oil, oregano, salt, pepper, and onion. Mix until all of the beef and onion are well coated. 3. Put the seasoned steak mixture into the air fryer basket. Roast for 5 minutes. Stir and roast for 5 minutes more. 4. Let rest for 5 minutes before serving with some favorite sides.

Sweet and Spicy Country-Style Ribs

Prep time: 10 minutes | Cook time: 25 minutes | Serves 4

- 2 tablespoons brown sugar
- 2 tablespoons smoked paprika
- 1 teaspoon garlic powder
- 1 teaspoon onion powder
- 1 teaspoon dry mustard
- 1 teaspoon ground cumin
- 1 teaspoon kosher salt
- 1 teaspoon black pepper
- ¼ to ½ teaspoon cayenne pepper
- 1½ pounds (680 g) boneless country-style pork ribs
- 1 cup barbecue sauce

1. In a small bowl, stir together the brown sugar, paprika, garlic powder, onion powder, dry mustard, cumin, salt, black pepper, and cayenne. Mix until well combined. 2. Pat the ribs dry with a paper towel. Generously sprinkle the rub evenly over both sides of the ribs and rub in with your fingers. 3. Place the ribs in the air fryer basket. Set the air fryer to 350ºF (177ºC) for 15 minutes. Turn the ribs and brush with ½ cup of the barbecue sauce. Cook for an additional 10 minutes. Use a meat thermometer to ensure the pork has reached an internal temperature of 145ºF (63ºC). 4. Serve with remaining barbecue sauce.

Bo Luc Lac

Prep time: 50 minutes | Cook time: 8 minutes | Serves 4

For the Meat:
- 2 teaspoons soy sauce
- 4 garlic cloves, minced
- 1 teaspoon kosher salt
- 2 teaspoons sugar
- ¼ teaspoon ground black pepper

For the Salad:
- 1 head Bibb lettuce, leaves separated and torn into large pieces
- ¼ cup fresh mint leaves
- ½ cup halved grape tomatoes
- ½ red onion, halved and thinly sliced
- 2 tablespoons apple cider

For Serving:
- Lime wedges, for garnish
- Coarse salt and freshly

- 1 teaspoon toasted sesame oil
- 1½ pounds (680 g) top sirloin steak, cut into 1-inch cubes
- Cooking spray

vinegar
- 1 garlic clove, minced
- 2 teaspoons sugar
- ¼ teaspoon kosher salt
- ¼ teaspoon ground black pepper
- 2 tablespoons vegetable oil

cracked black pepper, to taste

1. Combine the ingredients for the meat, except for the steak, in a large bowl. Stir to mix well. 2. Dunk the steak cubes in the bowl and press to coat. Wrap the bowl in plastic and marinate under room temperature for at least 30 minutes. 3. Preheat the air fryer to 450ºF (232ºC). Spritz the air fryer basket with cooking spray. 4. Discard the marinade and transfer the steak cubes in the preheated air fryer basket. You need to air fry in batches to avoid overcrowding. 5. Air fry for 4 minutes or until the steak cubes are lightly browned but still have a little pink. Shake the basket halfway through the cooking time. 6. Meanwhile, combine the ingredients for the salad

in a separate large bowl. Toss to mix well. 7. Pour the salad in a large serving bowl and top with the steak cubes. Squeeze the lime wedges over and sprinkle with salt and black pepper before serving.

Herb-Crusted Lamb Chops

Prep time: 10 minutes | Cook time: 5 minutes | Serves 2

- 1 large egg
- 2 cloves garlic, minced
- ¼ cup pork dust
- ¼ cup powdered Parmesan cheese
- 1 tablespoon chopped fresh oregano leaves
- 1 tablespoon chopped fresh rosemary leaves
- 1 teaspoon chopped fresh thyme leaves
- ½ teaspoon ground black pepper
- 4 (1-inch-thick) lamb chops
- For Garnish/Serving (Optional):
- Sprigs of fresh oregano
- Sprigs of fresh rosemary
- Sprigs of fresh thyme
- Lavender flowers
- Lemon slices

1. Spray the air fryer basket with avocado oil. Preheat the air fryer to 400ºF (204ºC). 2. Beat the egg in a shallow bowl, add the garlic, and stir well to combine. In another shallow bowl, mix together the pork dust, Parmesan, herbs, and pepper. 3. One at a time, dip the lamb chops into the egg mixture, shake off the excess egg, and then dredge them in the Parmesan mixture. Use your hands to coat the chops well in the Parmesan mixture and form a nice crust on all sides; if necessary, dip the chops again in both the egg and the Parmesan mixture. 4. Place the lamb chops in the air fryer basket, leaving space between them, and air fry for 5 minutes, or until the internal temperature reaches 145ºF (63ºC) for medium doneness. Allow to rest for 10 minutes before serving. 5. Garnish with sprigs of oregano, rosemary, and thyme, and lavender flowers, if desired. Serve with lemon slices, if desired. 6. Best served fresh. Store leftovers in an airtight container in the fridge for up to 4 days. Serve chilled over a salad, or reheat in a 350ºF (177ºC) air fryer for 3 minutes, or until heated through.

Beef Burger

Prep time: 20 minutes | Cook time: 12 minutes | Serves 4

- 1¼ pounds (567 g) lean ground beef
- 1 tablespoon coconut aminos
- 1 teaspoon Dijon mustard
- A few dashes of liquid smoke
- 1 teaspoon shallot powder
- 1 clove garlic, minced
- ½ teaspoon cumin powder
- ¼ cup scallions, minced
- ⅓ teaspoon sea salt flakes
- ⅓ teaspoon freshly cracked mixed peppercorns
- 1 teaspoon celery seeds
- 1 teaspoon parsley flakes

1. Mix all of the above ingredients in a bowl; knead until everything is well incorporated. 2. Shape the mixture into four patties. Next, make a shallow dip in the center of each patty to prevent them puffing up during air frying. 3. Spritz the patties on all sides using nonstick cooking spray. Cook approximately 12 minutes at 360ºF (182ºC). 4. Check for doneness, an instant-read thermometer should read 160ºF (71ºC). Bon appétit!

Cajun Bacon Pork Loin Fillet

Prep time: 30 minutes | Cook time: 20 minutes | Serves 6

◀ 1½ pounds (680 g) pork loin fillet or pork tenderloin
◀ 3 tablespoons olive oil
◀ 2 tablespoons Cajun spice
mix
◀ Salt, to taste
◀ 6 slices bacon
◀ Olive oil spray

1. Cut the pork in half so that it will fit in the air fryer basket. 2. Place both pieces of meat in a resealable plastic bag. Add the oil, Cajun seasoning, and salt to taste, if using. Seal the bag and massage to coat all of the meat with the oil and seasonings. Marinate in the refrigerator for at least 1 hour or up to 24 hours. 3. Remove the pork from the bag and wrap 3 bacon slices around each piece. Spray the air fryer basket with olive oil spray. Place the meat in the air fryer. Set the air fryer to 350ºF (177ºC) for 15 minutes. Increase the temperature to 400ºF (204ºC) for 5 minutes. Use a meat thermometer to ensure the meat has reached an internal temperature of 145ºF (63ºC). 4. Let the meat rest for 10 minutes. Slice into 6 medallions and serve.

Onion Pork Kebabs

Prep time: 22 minutes | Cook time: 18 minutes | Serves 3

◀ 2 tablespoons tomato purée
◀ ½ fresh serrano, minced
◀ ⅓ teaspoon paprika
◀ 1 pound (454 g) pork, ground
◀ ½ cup green onions, finely chopped
◀ 3 cloves garlic, peeled and finely minced
◀ 1 teaspoon ground black pepper, or more to taste
◀ 1 teaspoon salt, or more to taste

1. Thoroughly combine all ingredients in a mixing dish. Then form your mixture into sausage shapes. 2. Cook for 18 minutes at 355ºF (179ºC). Mound salad on a serving platter, top with air-fried kebabs and serve warm. Bon appétit!

Peppercorn-Crusted Beef Tenderloin

Prep time: 10 minutes | Cook time: 25 minutes | Serves 6

◀ 2 tablespoons salted butter, melted
◀ 2 teaspoons minced roasted garlic
◀ 3 tablespoons ground
4-peppercorn blend
◀ 1 (2 pounds / 907 g) beef tenderloin, trimmed of visible fat

1. In a small bowl, mix the butter and roasted garlic. Brush it over the beef tenderloin. 2. Place the ground peppercorns onto a plate and roll the tenderloin through them, creating a crust. Place tenderloin into the air fryer basket. 3. Adjust the temperature to 400ºF (204ºC) and roast for 25 minutes. 4. Turn the tenderloin

halfway through the cooking time. 5. Allow meat to rest 10 minutes before slicing.

Smothered Chops

Prep time: 20 minutes | Cook time: 30 minutes | Serves 4

◀ 4 bone-in pork chops (8 ounces / 227 g each)
◀ 2 teaspoons salt, divided
◀ 1½ teaspoons freshly ground black pepper, divided
◀ 1 teaspoon garlic powder
◀ 1 cup tomato purée
◀ 1½ teaspoons Italian
seasoning
◀ 1 tablespoon sugar
◀ 1 tablespoon cornstarch
◀ ½ cup chopped onion
◀ ½ cup chopped green bell pepper
◀ 1 to 2 tablespoons oil

1. Evenly season the pork chops with 1 teaspoon salt, 1 teaspoon pepper, and the garlic powder. 2. In a medium bowl, stir together the tomato purée, Italian seasoning, sugar, remaining 1 teaspoon of salt, and remaining ½ teaspoon of pepper. 3. In a small bowl, whisk ¾ cup water and the cornstarch until blended. Stir this slurry into the tomato purée, with the onion and green bell pepper. Transfer to a baking pan. 4. Preheat the air fryer to 350ºF (177ºC). 5. Place the sauce in the fryer and cook for 10 minutes. Stir and cook for 10 minutes more. Remove the pan and keep warm. 6. Increase the air fryer temperature to 400ºF (204ºC). Line the air fryer basket with parchment paper. 7. Place the pork chops on the parchment and spritz with oil. 8. Cook for 5 minutes. Flip and spritz the chops with oil and cook for 5 minutes more, until the internal temperature reaches 145ºF (63ºC). Serve with the tomato mixture spooned on top.

Cheese Pork Chops

Prep time: 15 minutes | Cook time: 9 to 14 minutes | Serves 4

◀ 2 large eggs
◀ ½ cup finely grated Parmesan cheese
◀ ½ cup finely ground blanched almond flour or finely crushed pork rinds
◀ 1 teaspoon paprika
◀ ½ teaspoon dried oregano
◀ ½ teaspoon garlic powder
◀ Salt and freshly ground black pepper, to taste
◀ 1¼ pounds (567 g) (1-inch-thick) boneless pork chops
◀ Avocado oil spray

1. Beat the eggs in a shallow bowl. In a separate bowl, combine the Parmesan cheese, almond flour, paprika, oregano, garlic powder, and salt and pepper to taste. 2. Dip the pork chops into the eggs, then coat them with the Parmesan mixture, gently pressing the coating onto the meat. Spray the breaded pork chops with oil. 3. Set the air fryer to 400ºF (204ºC). Place the pork chops in the air fryer basket in a single layer, working in batches if necessary. Cook for 6 minutes. Flip the chops and spray them with more oil. Cook for another 3 to 8 minutes, until an instant-read thermometer reads 145ºF (63ºC). 4. Allow the pork chops to rest for at least 5 minutes, then serve.

Dijon Porterhouse Steak

Prep time: 20 minutes | Cook time: 14 minutes | Serves 2

- ◄ 1 pound (454 g) porterhouse steak, cut meat from bones in 2 pieces
- ◄ ½ teaspoon ground black pepper
- ◄ 1 teaspoon cayenne pepper
- ◄ ½ teaspoon salt
- ◄ 1 teaspoon garlic powder
- ◄ ½ teaspoon dried thyme
- ◄ ½ teaspoon dried marjoram
- ◄ 1 teaspoon Dijon mustard
- ◄ 1 tablespoon butter, melted

1. Sprinkle the porterhouse steak with all the seasonings. 2. Spread the mustard and butter evenly over the meat. 3. Cook in the preheated air fryer at 390ºF (199ºC) for 12 to 14 minutes. 4. Taste for doneness with a meat thermometer and serve immediately.

Pigs in a Blanket

Prep time: 10 minutes | Cook time: 7 minutes | Serves 2

- ◄ ½ cup shredded Mozzarella cheese
- ◄ 2 tablespoons blanched finely ground almond flour
- ◄ 1 ounce (28 g) full-fat cream
- cheese
- ◄ 2 (2 ounces / 57 g) beef smoked sausages
- ◄ ½ teaspoon sesame seeds

1. Place Mozzarella, almond flour, and cream cheese in a large microwave-safe bowl. Microwave for 45 seconds and stir until smooth. Roll dough into a ball and cut in half. 2. Press each half out into a 4 × 5-inch rectangle. Roll one sausage up in each dough half and press seams closed. Sprinkle the top with sesame seeds. 3. Place each wrapped sausage into the air fryer basket. 4. Adjust the temperature to 400ºF (204ºC) and air fry for 7 minutes. 5. The outside will be golden when completely cooked. Serve immediately.

Hamburger Steak with Mushroom Gravy

Prep time: 20 minutes | Cook time: 29 to 34 minutes | Serves 4

Mushroom Gravy:
- ◄ 1 (1 ounce / 28 g) envelope dry onion soup mix

Hamburger Steak:
- ◄ 1 pound (454 g) ground beef (85% lean)
- ◄ ¾ cup minced onion
- ◄ ½ cup Italian-style bread crumbs
- ◄ 2 teaspoons Worcestershire
- ◄ ⅓ cup cornstarch
- ◄ 1 cup diced mushrooms

- sauce
- ◄ 1 teaspoon salt
- ◄ 1 teaspoon freshly ground black pepper
- ◄ 1 to 2 tablespoons oil

Make the Mushroom Gravy 1. In a metal bowl, whisk the soup mix, cornstarch, mushrooms, and 2 cups water until blended. 2.

Preheat the air fryer to 350ºF (177ºC). 3. Place the bowl in the air fryer basket. 4. Cook for 10 minutes. Stir and cook for 5 to 10 minutes more to your desired thickness. Make the Hamburger Steak 5. In a large bowl, mix the ground beef, onion, bread crumbs, Worcestershire sauce, salt, and pepper until blended. Shape the beef mixture into 4 patties. 6. Decrease the air fryer's temperature to 320ºF (160ºC). 7. Place the patties in the air fryer basket. 8. Cook for 7 minutes. Flip the patties, spritz them with oil, and cook for 7 minutes more, until the internal temperature reaches 145ºF (63ºC).

Smoky Pork Tenderloin

Prep time: 5 minutes | Cook time: 19 to 22 minutes | Serves 6

- ◄ 1½ pounds (680 g) pork tenderloin
- ◄ 1 tablespoon avocado oil
- ◄ 1 teaspoon chili powder
- ◄ 1 teaspoon smoked paprika
- ◄ 1 teaspoon garlic powder
- ◄ 1 teaspoon sea salt
- ◄ 1 teaspoon freshly ground black pepper

1. Pierce the tenderloin all over with a fork and rub the oil all over the meat. 2. In a small dish, stir together the chili powder, smoked paprika, garlic powder, salt, and pepper. 3. Rub the spice mixture all over the tenderloin. 4. Set the air fryer to 400ºF (204ºC). Place the pork in the air fryer basket and air fry for 10 minutes. Flip the tenderloin and cook for 9 to 12 minutes more, until an instant-read thermometer reads at least 145ºF (63ºC). 5. Allow the tenderloin to rest for 5 minutes, then slice and serve.

Lemon Pork with Marjoram

Prep time: 5 minutes | Cook time: 10 minutes | Serves 4

- ◄ 1 (1 pound / 454 g) pork tenderloin, cut into ½-inch-thick slices
- ◄ 1 tablespoon extra-virgin olive oil
- ◄ 1 tablespoon freshly squeezed lemon juice
- ◄ 1 tablespoon honey
- ◄ ½ teaspoon grated lemon zest
- ◄ ½ teaspoon dried marjoram leaves
- ◄ Pinch salt
- ◄ Freshly ground black pepper, to taste
- ◄ Cooking oil spray

1. Put the pork slices in a medium bowl. 2. In a small bowl, whisk the olive oil, lemon juice, honey, lemon zest, marjoram, salt, and pepper until combined. Pour this marinade over the tenderloin slices and gently massage with your hands to work it into the pork. 3. Insert the crisper plate into the basket and the basket into the unit. Preheat the unit by selecting AIR ROAST, setting the temperature to 400ºF (204ºC), and setting the time to 3 minutes. Select START/STOP to begin. 4. Once the unit is preheated, spray the crisper plate with cooking oil. Place the pork into the basket. 5. Select AIR ROAST, set the temperature to 400ºF (204ºC), and set the time to 10 minutes. Select START/STOP to begin. 6. When the cooking is complete, a food thermometer inserted into the pork should register at least 145ºF (63ºC). Let the pork stand for 5 minutes and serve.

Italian Sausage Links

Prep time: 10 minutes | Cook time: 24 minutes | Serves 4

- 1 bell pepper (any color), sliced
- 1 medium onion, sliced
- 1 tablespoon avocado oil
- 1 teaspoon Italian seasoning
- Sea salt and freshly ground black pepper, to taste
- 1 pound (454 g) Italian sausage links

1. Place the bell pepper and onion in a medium bowl, and toss with the avocado oil, Italian seasoning, and salt and pepper to taste. 2. Set the air fryer to 400°F (204°C). Put the vegetables in the air fryer basket and cook for 12 minutes. 3. Push the vegetables to the side of the basket and arrange the sausage links in the bottom of the basket in a single layer. Spoon the vegetables over the sausages. Cook for 12 minutes, tossing halfway through, until an instant-read thermometer inserted into the sausage reads 160°F (71°C).

Pork Meatballs

Prep time: 10 minutes | Cook time: 12 minutes | Makes 18 meatballs

- 1 pound (454 g) ground pork
- 1 large egg, whisked
- ½ teaspoon garlic powder
- ½ teaspoon salt
- ½ teaspoon ground ginger
- ¼ teaspoon crushed red pepper flakes
- 1 medium scallion, trimmed and sliced

1. Combine all ingredients in a large bowl. Spoon out 2 tablespoons mixture and roll into a ball. Repeat to form eighteen meatballs total. 2. Place meatballs into ungreased air fryer basket. Adjust the temperature to 400°F (204°C) and air fry for 12 minutes, shaking the basket three times throughout cooking. Meatballs will be browned and have an internal temperature of at least 145°F (63°C) when done. Serve warm.

Spicy Lamb Sirloin Chops

Prep time: 30 minutes | Cook time: 15 minutes | Serves 4

- ½ yellow onion, coarsely chopped
- 4 coin-size slices peeled fresh ginger
- 5 garlic cloves
- 1 teaspoon garam masala
- 1 teaspoon ground fennel
- 1 teaspoon ground cinnamon
- 1 teaspoon ground turmeric
- ½ to 1 teaspoon cayenne pepper
- ½ teaspoon ground cardamom
- 1 teaspoon kosher salt
- 1 pound (454 g) lamb sirloin chops

1. In a blender, combine the onion, ginger, garlic, garam masala, fennel, cinnamon, turmeric, cayenne, cardamom, and salt. Pulse until the onion is finely minced and the mixture forms a thick paste, 3 to 4 minutes. 2. Place the lamb chops in a large bowl. Slash the meat and fat with a sharp knife several times to allow the marinade to penetrate better. Add the spice paste to the bowl and toss the lamb to coat. Marinate at room temperature for 30 minutes or cover and refrigerate for up to 24 hours. 3. Place the lamb chops in a single layer in the air fryer basket. Set the air fryer to 325°F (163°C) for 15 minutes, turning the chops halfway through the cooking time. Use a meat thermometer to ensure the lamb has reached an internal temperature of 145°F (63°C) (medium-rare).

Greek Pork with Tzatziki Sauce

Prep time: 30 minutes | Cook time: 50 minutes | Serves 4

Greek Pork:
- 2 pounds (907 g) pork sirloin roast
- Salt and black pepper, to taste
- 1 teaspoon smoked paprika
- ½ teaspoon mustard seeds
- ½ teaspoon celery seeds
- 1 teaspoon fennel seeds
- 1 teaspoon Ancho chili powder
- 1 teaspoon turmeric powder
- ½ teaspoon ground ginger
- 2 tablespoons olive oil
- 2 cloves garlic, finely chopped

Tzatziki:
- ½ cucumber, finely chopped and squeezed
- 1 cup full-fat Greek yogurt
- 1 garlic clove, minced
- 1 tablespoon extra-virgin
- olive oil
- 1 teaspoon balsamic vinegar
- 1 teaspoon minced fresh dill
- A pinch of salt

1. Toss all ingredients for Greek pork in a large mixing bowl. Toss until the meat is well coated. 2. Cook in the preheated air fryer at 360°F (182°C) for 30 minutes; turn over and cook another 20 minutes. 3. Meanwhile, prepare the tzatziki by mixing all the tzatziki ingredients. Place in your refrigerator until ready to use. 4. Serve the pork sirloin roast with the chilled tzatziki on the side. Enjoy!

Blackened Cajun Pork Roast

Prep time: 20 minutes | Cook time: 33 minutes | Serves 4

- 2 pounds (907 g) bone-in pork loin roast
- 2 tablespoons oil
- ¼ cup Cajun seasoning
- ½ cup diced onion
- ½ cup diced celery
- ½ cup diced green bell pepper
- 1 tablespoon minced garlic

1. Cut 5 slits across the pork roast. Spritz it with oil, coating it completely. Evenly sprinkle the Cajun seasoning over the pork roast. 2. In a medium bowl, stir together the onion, celery, green bell pepper, and garlic until combined. Set aside. 3. Preheat the air fryer to 360°F (182°C). Line the air fryer basket with parchment paper. 4. Place the pork roast on the parchment and spritz with oil. 5. Cook for 5 minutes. Flip the roast and cook for 5 minutes more. Continue to flip and cook in 5-minute increments for a total cook time of 20 minutes. 6. Increase the air fryer temperature to 390°F (199°C). 7. Cook the roast for 8 minutes more and flip. Add the vegetable mixture to the basket and cook for a final 5 minutes. Let the roast sit for 5 minutes before serving.

Spaghetti Zoodles and Meatballs

Prep time: 30 minutes | Cook time: 11 to 13 minutes | Serves 6

- 1 pound (454 g) ground beef
- 1½ teaspoons sea salt, plus more for seasoning
- 1 large egg, beaten
- 1 teaspoon gelatin
- ¾ cup Parmesan cheese
- 2 teaspoons minced garlic
- 1 teaspoon Italian seasoning
- Freshly ground black pepper, to taste
- Avocado oil spray
- Keto-friendly marinara sauce, for serving
- 6 ounces (170 g) zucchini noodles, made using a spiralizer or store-bought

1. Place the ground beef in a large bowl, and season with the salt. 2. Place the egg in a separate bowl and sprinkle with the gelatin. Allow to sit for 5 minutes. 3. Stir the gelatin mixture, then pour it over the ground beef. Add the Parmesan, garlic, and Italian seasoning. Season with salt and pepper. 4. Form the mixture into 1½-inch meatballs and place them on a plate; cover with plastic wrap and refrigerate for at least 1 hour or overnight. 5. Spray the meatballs with oil. Set the air fryer to 400ºF (204ºC) and arrange the meatballs in a single layer in the air fryer basket. Air fry for 4 minutes. Flip the meatballs and spray them with more oil. Air fry for 4 minutes more, until an instant-read thermometer reads 160ºF (71ºC). Transfer the meatballs to a plate and allow them to rest. 6. While the meatballs are resting, heat the marinara in a saucepan on the stove over medium heat. 7. Place the zucchini noodles in the air fryer, and cook at 400ºF (204ºC) for 3 to 5 minutes. 8. To serve, place the zucchini noodles in serving bowls. Top with meatballs and warm marinara.

Five-Spice Pork Belly

Prep time: 10 minutes | Cook time: 17 minutes | Serves 4

- 1 pound (454 g) unsalted pork belly
Sauce:
- 1 tablespoon coconut oil
- 1 (1-inch) piece fresh ginger, peeled and grated
- 2 cloves garlic, minced
- ½ cup beef or chicken broth
- ¼ to ½ cup Swerve confectioners'-style sweetener or equivalent
- 2 teaspoons Chinese five-spice powder

  amount of liquid or powdered sweetener
- 3 tablespoons wheat-free tamari, or ½ cup coconut aminos
- 1 green onion, sliced, plus more for garnish

1. Spray the air fryer basket with avocado oil. Preheat the air fryer to 400ºF (204ºC). 2. Cut the pork belly into ½-inch-thick slices and season well on all sides with the five-spice powder. Place the slices in a single layer in the air fryer basket (if you're using a smaller air fryer, work in batches if necessary) and cook for 8 minutes, or until cooked to your liking, flipping halfway through. 3. While the pork belly cooks, make the sauce: Heat the coconut oil in a small saucepan over medium heat. Add the ginger and garlic and sauté for 1 minute, or until fragrant. Add the broth, sweetener, and tamari and simmer for 10 to 15 minutes, until thickened. Add the green onion

and cook for another minute, until the green onion is softened. Taste and adjust the seasoning to your liking. 4. Transfer the pork belly to a large bowl. Pour the sauce over the pork belly and coat well. Place the pork belly slices on a serving platter and garnish with sliced green onions. 5. Best served fresh. Store leftovers in an airtight container in the fridge for up to 4 days. Reheat in a preheated 400ºF (204ºC) air fryer for 3 minutes, or until heated through.

Barbecue Ribs

Prep time: 5 minutes | Cook time: 30 minutes | Serves 4

- 1 (2 pounds / 907 g) rack baby back ribs
- 1 teaspoon onion powder
- 1 teaspoon garlic powder
- 1 teaspoon light brown sugar
- 1 teaspoon dried oregano
- Salt and freshly ground black pepper, to taste
- Cooking oil spray
- ½ cup barbecue sauce

1. Use a sharp knife to remove the thin membrane from the back of the ribs. Cut the rack in half, or as needed, so the ribs fit in the air fryer basket. The best way to do this is to cut the ribs into 4- or 5-rib sections. 2. In a small bowl, stir together the onion powder, garlic powder, brown sugar, and oregano and season with salt and pepper. Rub the spice seasoning onto the front and back of the ribs. 3. Cover the ribs with plastic wrap or foil and let sit at room temperature for 30 minutes. 4. Insert the crisper plate into the basket and the basket into the unit. Preheat the unit by selecting AIR ROAST, setting the temperature to 360ºF (182ºC), and setting the time to 3 minutes. Select START/STOP to begin. 5. Once the unit is preheated, spray the crisper plate with cooking oil. Place the ribs into the basket. It is okay to stack them. 6. Select AIR ROAST, set the temperature to 360ºF (182ºC), and set the time to 30 minutes. Select START/STOP to begin. 7. After 15 minutes, flip the ribs. Resume cooking for 15 minutes, or until a food thermometer registers 190ºF (88ºC). 8. When the cooking is complete, transfer the ribs to a serving dish. Drizzle the ribs with the barbecue sauce and serve.

Mustard Herb Pork Tenderloin

Prep time: 5 minutes | Cook time: 20 minutes | Serves 6

- ¼ cup mayonnaise
- 2 tablespoons Dijon mustard
- ½ teaspoon dried thyme
- ¼ teaspoon dried rosemary
- 1 (1 pound / 454 g) pork
- tenderloin
- ½ teaspoon salt
- ¼ teaspoon ground black pepper

1. In a small bowl, mix mayonnaise, mustard, thyme, and rosemary. Brush tenderloin with mixture on all sides, then sprinkle with salt and pepper on all sides. 2. Place tenderloin into ungreased air fryer basket. Adjust the temperature to 400ºF (204ºC) and air fry for 20 minutes, turning tenderloin halfway through cooking. Tenderloin will be golden and have an internal temperature of at least 145ºF (63ºC) when done. Serve warm.

Kheema Burgers

Prep time: 15 minutes | Cook time: 12 minutes | Serves 4

Burgers:
- ◀ 1 pound (454 g) 85% lean ground beef or ground lamb
- ◀ 2 large eggs, lightly beaten
- ◀ 1 medium yellow onion, diced
- ◀ ¼ cup chopped fresh cilantro
- ◀ 1 tablespoon minced fresh ginger
- ◀ 3 cloves garlic, minced

- ◀ 2 teaspoons garam masala
- ◀ 1 teaspoon ground turmeric
- ◀ ½ teaspoon ground cinnamon
- ◀ ⅛ teaspoon ground cardamom
- ◀ 1 teaspoon kosher salt
- ◀ 1 teaspoon cayenne pepper

Raita Sauce:
- ◀ 1 cup grated cucumber
- ◀ ½ cup sour cream
- ◀ ¼ teaspoon kosher salt
- ◀ ¼ teaspoon black pepper

- ◀ For Serving:
- ◀ 4 lettuce leaves, hamburger buns, or naan breads

1. For the burgers: In a large bowl, combine the ground beef, eggs, onion, cilantro, ginger, garlic, garam masala, turmeric, cinnamon, cardamom, salt, and cayenne. Gently mix until ingredients are thoroughly combined. 2. Divide the meat into four portions and form into round patties. Make a slight depression in the middle of each patty with your thumb to prevent them from puffing up into a dome shape while cooking. 3. Place the patties in the air fryer basket. Set the air fryer to 350ºF (177ºC) for 12 minutes. Use a meat thermometer to ensure the burgers have reached an internal temperature of 160ºF / 71ºC (for medium). 4. Meanwhile, for the sauce: In a small bowl, combine the cucumber, sour cream, salt, and pepper. 5. To serve: Place the burgers on the lettuce, buns, or naan and top with the sauce.

Apple Cornbread Stuffed Pork Loin

Prep time: 15 minutes | Cook time: 1 hour | Serves 4 to 6

- ◀ 4 strips of bacon, chopped
- ◀ 1 Granny Smith apple, peeled, cored and finely chopped
- ◀ 2 teaspoons fresh thyme leaves
- ◀ ¼ cup chopped fresh parsley

Apple Gravy:
- ◀ 2 tablespoons butter
- ◀ 1 shallot, minced
- ◀ 1 Granny Smith apple, peeled, cored and finely chopped
- ◀ 3 sprigs fresh thyme

- ◀ 2 cups cubed cornbread
- ◀ ½ cup chicken stock
- ◀ Salt and freshly ground black pepper, to taste
- ◀ 1 (2 pounds / 907 g) boneless pork loin

- ◀ 2 tablespoons flour
- ◀ 1 cup chicken stock
- ◀ ½ cup apple cider
- ◀ Salt and freshly ground black pepper, to taste

1. Preheat the air fryer to 400ºF (204ºC). 2. Add the bacon to the air fryer and air fry for 6 to 8 minutes until crispy. While the bacon is cooking, combine the apple, fresh thyme, parsley and cornbread in a bowl and toss well. Moisten the mixture with the chicken stock and season to taste with salt and freshly ground black pepper. Add the cooked bacon to the mixture. 3. Butterfly the pork loin by holding it flat on the cutting board with one hand, while slicing into the pork loin parallel to the cutting board with the other. Slice into the longest side of the pork loin, but stop before you cut all the way through. You should then be able to open the pork loin up like a book, making it twice as wide as it was when you started. Season the inside of the pork with salt and freshly ground black pepper. 4. Spread the cornbread mixture onto the butterflied pork loin, leaving a one-inch border around the edge of the pork. Roll the pork loin up around the stuffing to enclose the stuffing, and tie the rolled pork in several places with kitchen twine or secure with toothpicks. Try to replace any stuffing that falls out of the roast as you roll it, by stuffing it into the ends of the rolled pork. Season the outside of the pork with salt and freshly ground black pepper. 5. Preheat the air fryer to 360ºF (182ºC). 6. Place the stuffed pork loin into the air fryer, seam side down. Air fry the pork loin for 15 minutes at 360ºF (182ºC). Turn the pork loin over and air fry for an additional 15 minutes. Turn the pork loin a quarter turn and air fry for an additional 15 minutes. Turn the pork loin over again to expose the fourth side, and air fry for an additional 10 minutes. The pork loin should register 155ºF (68ºC) on an instant read thermometer when it is finished. 7. While the pork is cooking, make the apple gravy. Preheat a saucepan over medium heat on the stovetop and melt the butter. Add the shallot, apple and thyme sprigs and sauté until the apple starts to soften and brown a little. Add the flour and stir for a minute or two. Whisk in the stock and apple cider vigorously to prevent the flour from forming lumps. Bring the mixture to a boil to thicken and season to taste with salt and pepper. 8. Transfer the pork loin to a resting plate and loosely tent with foil, letting the pork rest for at least 5 minutes before slicing and serving with the apple gravy poured over the top.

Panko Pork Chops

Prep time: 10 minutes | Cook time: 12 minutes | Serves 4

- ◀ 4 center-cut boneless pork chops, excess fat trimmed
- ◀ ¼ teaspoon salt
- ◀ 2 eggs
- ◀ 1½ cups panko bread crumbs
- ◀ 3 tablespoons grated Parmesan cheese

- ◀ 1½ teaspoons paprika
- ◀ ½ teaspoon granulated garlic
- ◀ ½ teaspoon onion powder
- ◀ 1 teaspoon chili powder
- ◀ ¼ teaspoon freshly ground black pepper
- ◀ Olive oil spray

1. Sprinkle the pork chops with salt on both sides and let them sit while you prepare the seasonings and egg wash. 2. In a shallow medium bowl, beat the eggs. 3. In another shallow medium bowl, stir together the panko, Parmesan cheese, paprika, granulated garlic, onion powder, chili powder, and pepper. 4. Dip the pork chops in the egg and in the panko mixture to coat. Firmly press the crumbs onto the chops. 5. Insert the crisper plate into the basket and the basket into the unit. Preheat the unit by selecting AIR ROAST, setting the temperature to 400ºF (204ºC), and setting the time to 3 minutes. Select START/STOP to begin. 6. Once the unit is preheated, spray the crisper plate with olive oil. Place the pork chops into the basket and spray them with olive oil. 7. Select AIR ROAST, set the temperature to 400ºF (204ºC), and set the time to 12 minutes. Select START/STOP to begin. 8. After 6 minutes, flip the pork chops and spray them with more olive oil. Resume cooking. 9. When the cooking is complete, the chops should be golden and crispy and a food thermometer should register 145ºF (63ºC). Serve immediately.

Chuck Kebab with Arugula

Prep time: 30 minutes | Cook time: 25 minutes | Serves 4

◄ ½ cup leeks, chopped
◄ 2 garlic cloves, smashed
◄ 2 pounds (907 g) ground chuck
◄ Salt, to taste
◄ ¼ teaspoon ground black pepper, or more to taste
◄ 1 teaspoon cayenne pepper
◄ ½ teaspoon ground sumac

◄ 3 saffron threads
◄ 2 tablespoons loosely packed fresh continental parsley leaves
◄ 4 tablespoons tahini sauce
◄ 4 ounces (113 g) baby arugula
◄ 1 tomato, cut into slices

1. In a bowl, mix the chopped leeks, garlic, ground chuck, and spices; knead with your hands until everything is well incorporated. 2. Now, mound the beef mixture around a wooden skewer into a pointed-ended sausage. 3. Cook in the preheated air fryer at 360ºF (182ºC) for 25 minutes. Serve your kebab with the tahini sauce, baby arugula and tomato. Enjoy!

Kheema Meatloaf

Prep time: 10 minutes | Cook time: 15 minutes | Serves 4

◄ 1 pound (454 g) 85% lean ground beef
◄ 2 large eggs, lightly beaten
◄ 1 cup diced yellow onion
◄ ¼ cup chopped fresh cilantro
◄ 1 tablespoon minced fresh ginger
◄ 1 tablespoon minced garlic

◄ 2 teaspoons garam masala
◄ 1 teaspoon kosher salt
◄ 1 teaspoon ground turmeric
◄ 1 teaspoon cayenne pepper
◄ ½ teaspoon ground cinnamon
◄ ⅛ teaspoon ground cardamom

1. In a large bowl, gently mix the ground beef, eggs, onion, cilantro, ginger, garlic, garam masala, salt, turmeric, cayenne, cinnamon, and cardamom until thoroughly combined. 2. Place the seasoned meat in a baking pan. Place the pan in the air fryer basket. Set the air fryer to 350ºF (177ºC) for 15 minutes. Use a meat thermometer to ensure the meat loaf has reached an internal temperature of 160ºF / 71ºC (medium). 3. Drain the fat and liquid from the pan and let stand for 5 minutes before slicing. 4. Slice and serve hot.

Garlic-Marinated Flank Steak

Prep time: 30 minutes | Cook time: 8 to 10 minutes | Serves 6

◄ ½ cup avocado oil
◄ ¼ cup coconut aminos
◄ 1 shallot, minced
◄ 1 tablespoon minced garlic
◄ 2 tablespoons chopped fresh oregano, or 2 teaspoons

dried
◄ 1½ teaspoons sea salt
◄ 1 teaspoon freshly ground black pepper
◄ ¼ teaspoon red pepper flakes
◄ 2 pounds (907 g) flank steak

1. In a blender, combine the avocado oil, coconut aminos, shallot, garlic, oregano, salt, black pepper, and red pepper flakes. Process until smooth. 2. Place the steak in a zip-top plastic bag or shallow dish with the marinade. Seal the bag or cover the dish and marinate in the refrigerator for at least 2 hours or overnight. 3. Remove the steak from the bag and discard the marinade. 4. Set the air fryer to 400ºF (204ºC). Place the steak in the air fryer basket (if needed, cut into sections and work in batches). Air fry for 4 to 6 minutes, flip the steak, and cook for another 4 minutes or until the internal temperature reaches 120ºF (49ºC) in the thickest part for medium-rare (or as desired).

Poblano Pepper Cheeseburgers

Prep time: 5 minutes | Cook time: 30 minutes | Serves 4

◄ 2 poblano chile peppers
◄ 1½ pounds (680 g) 85% lean ground beef
◄ 1 clove garlic, minced
◄ 1 teaspoon salt

◄ ½ teaspoon freshly ground black pepper
◄ 4 slices Cheddar cheese (about 3 ounces / 85 g)
◄ 4 large lettuce leaves

1. Preheat the air fryer to 400ºF (204ºC). 2. Arrange the poblano peppers in the basket of the air fryer. Pausing halfway through the cooking time to turn the peppers, air fry for 20 minutes, or until they are softened and beginning to char. Transfer the peppers to a large bowl and cover with a plate. When cool enough to handle, peel off the skin, remove the seeds and stems, and slice into strips. Set aside. 3. Meanwhile, in a large bowl, combine the ground beef with the garlic, salt, and pepper. Shape the beef into 4 patties. 4. Lower the heat on the air fryer to 360ºF (182ºC). Arrange the burgers in a single layer in the basket of the air fryer. Pausing halfway through the cooking time to turn the burgers, air fry for 10 minutes, or until a thermometer inserted into the thickest part registers 160ºF (71ºC). 5. Top the burgers with the cheese slices and continue baking for a minute or two, just until the cheese has melted. Serve the burgers on a lettuce leaf topped with the roasted poblano peppers.

Air Fried Crispy Venison

Prep time: 10 minutes | Cook time: 20 minutes | Serves 4

◄ 2 eggs
◄ ¼ cup milk
◄ 1 cup whole wheat flour
◄ ½ teaspoon salt
◄ ¼ teaspoon ground black

pepper
◄ 1 pound (454 g) venison backstrap, sliced
◄ Cooking spray

1. Preheat the air fryer to 360ºF (182ºC) and spritz with cooking spray. 2. Whisk the eggs with milk in a large bowl. Combine the flour with salt and ground black pepper in a shallow dish. 3. Dredge the venison in the flour first, then into the egg mixture. Shake the excess off and roll the venison back over the flour to coat well. 4. Arrange half of the venison in the preheated air fryer and spritz with cooking spray. 5. Air fry for 10 minutes or until the internal temperature of the venison reaches at least 145ºF (63ºC) for medium rare. Flip the venison halfway through. Repeat with remaining venison. 6. Serve immediately.

Easy Lamb Chops with Asparagus

Prep time: 10 minutes | Cook time: 15 minutes | Serves 4

◁ 4 asparagus spears, trimmed
◁ 2 tablespoons olive oil, divided
◁ 1 pound (454 g) lamb chops
◁ 1 garlic clove, minced
◁ 2 teaspoons chopped fresh thyme, for serving
◁ Salt and ground black pepper, to taste

1. Preheat the air fryer to 400ºF (204ºC). Spritz the air fryer basket with cooking spray. 2. On a large plate, brush the asparagus with 1 tablespoon olive oil, then sprinkle with salt. Set aside. 3. On a separate plate, brush the lamb chops with remaining olive oil and sprinkle with salt and ground black pepper. 4. Arrange the lamb chops in the preheated air fryer. Air fry for 10 minutes. 5. Flip the lamb chops and add the asparagus and garlic. Air fry for 5 more minutes or until the lamb is well browned and the asparagus is tender. 6. Serve them on a plate with thyme on top.

Mediterranean Beef Steaks

Prep time: 20 minutes | Cook time: 20 minutes | Serves 4

◁ 2 tablespoons coconut aminos
◁ 3 heaping tablespoons fresh chives
◁ 2 tablespoons olive oil
◁ 3 tablespoons dry white wine
◁ 4 small-sized beef steaks
◁ 2 teaspoons smoked cayenne pepper
◁ ½ teaspoon dried basil
◁ ½ teaspoon dried rosemary
◁ 1 teaspoon freshly ground black pepper
◁ 1 teaspoon sea salt, or more to taste

1. Firstly, coat the steaks with the cayenne pepper, black pepper, salt, basil, and rosemary. 2. Drizzle the steaks with olive oil, white wine, and coconut aminos. 3. Finally, roast in the air fryer for 20 minutes at 340ºF (171ºC). Serve garnished with fresh chives. Bon appétit!

Honey-Baked Pork Loin

Prep time: 30 minutes | Cook time: 22 to 25 minutes | Serves 6

◁ ¼ cup honey
◁ ¼ cup freshly squeezed lemon juice
◁ 2 tablespoons soy sauce
◁ 1 teaspoon garlic powder
◁ 1 (2 pounds / 907 g) pork loin
◁ 2 tablespoons vegetable oil

1. In a medium bowl, whisk together the honey, lemon juice, soy sauce, and garlic powder. Reserve half of the mixture for basting during cooking. 2. Cut 5 slits in the pork loin and transfer it to a resealable bag. Add the remaining honey mixture. Seal the bag and refrigerate to marinate for at least 2 hours. 3. Preheat the air fryer to 400ºF (204ºC). Line the air fryer basket with parchment paper. 4. Remove the pork from the marinade, and place it on the parchment. Spritz with oil, then baste with the reserved marinade. 5. Cook for 15 minutes. Flip the pork, baste with more marinade and spritz with oil again. Cook for 7 to 10 minutes more until the internal temperature reaches 145ºF (63ºC). Let rest for 5 minutes before serving.

Ham with Sweet Potatoes

Prep time: 20 minutes | Cook time: 15 to 17 minutes | Serves 4

◁ 1 cup freshly squeezed orange juice
◁ ½ cup packed light brown sugar
◁ 1 tablespoon Dijon mustard
◁ ½ teaspoon salt
◁ ½ teaspoon freshly ground
◁ black pepper
◁ 3 sweet potatoes, cut into small wedges
◁ 2 ham steaks (8 ounces / 227 g each), halved
◁ 1 to 2 tablespoons oil

1. In a large bowl, whisk the orange juice, brown sugar, Dijon, salt, and pepper until blended. Toss the sweet potato wedges with the brown sugar mixture. 2. Preheat the air fryer to 400ºF (204ºC). Line the air fryer basket with parchment paper and spritz with oil. 3. Place the sweet potato wedges on the parchment. 4. Cook for 10 minutes. 5. Place ham steaks on top of the sweet potatoes and brush everything with more of the orange juice mixture. 6. Cook for 3 minutes. Flip the ham and cook or 2 to 4 minutes more until the sweet potatoes are soft and the glaze has thickened. Cut the ham steaks in half to serve.

Herbed Lamb Steaks

Prep time: 30 minutes | Cook time: 15 minutes | Serves 4

◁ ½ medium onion
◁ 2 tablespoons minced garlic
◁ 2 teaspoons ground ginger
◁ 1 teaspoon ground cinnamon
◁ 1 teaspoon onion powder
◁ 1 teaspoon cayenne pepper
◁ 1 teaspoon salt
◁ 4 (6 ounces / 170 g) boneless lamb sirloin steaks
◁ Oil, for spraying

1. In a blender, combine the onion, garlic, ginger, cinnamon, onion powder, cayenne pepper, and salt and pulse until the onion is minced. 2. Place the lamb steaks in a large bowl or zip-top plastic bag and sprinkle the onion mixture over the top. Turn the steaks until they are evenly coated. Cover with plastic wrap or seal the bag and refrigerate for 30 minutes. 3. Preheat the air fryer to 330ºF (166ºC). Line the air fryer basket with parchment and spray lightly with oil. 4. Place the lamb steaks in a single layer in the prepared basket, making sure they don't overlap. You may need to work in batches, depending on the size of your air fryer. 5. Cook for 8 minutes, flip, and cook for another 7 minutes, or until the internal temperature reaches 155ºF (68ºC).

Mojito Lamb Chops

Prep time: 30 minutes | Cook time: 5 minutes | Serves 2

Marinade:
- 2 teaspoons grated lime zest
- ½ cup lime juice
- ¼ cup avocado oil
- ¼ cup chopped fresh mint leaves
- 4 cloves garlic, roughly chopped
- 2 teaspoons fine sea salt
- ½ teaspoon ground black pepper
- 4 (1-inch-thick) lamb chops
- Sprigs of fresh mint, for garnish (optional)
- Lime slices, for serving (optional)

1. Make the marinade: Place all the ingredients for the marinade in a food processor or blender and purée until mostly smooth with a few small chunks. Transfer half of the marinade to a shallow dish and set the other half aside for serving. Add the lamb to the shallow dish, cover, and place in the refrigerator to marinate for at least 2 hours or overnight. 2. Spray the air fryer basket with avocado oil. Preheat the air fryer to 390ºF (199ºC). 3. Remove the chops from the marinade and place them in the air fryer basket. Air fry for 5 minutes, or until the internal temperature reaches 145ºF (63ºC) for medium doneness. 4. Allow the chops to rest for 10 minutes before serving with the rest of the marinade as a sauce. Garnish with fresh mint leaves and serve with lime slices, if desired. Best served fresh.

Lamb and Cucumber Burgers

Prep time: 8 minutes | Cook time: 15 to 18 minutes | Serves 4

- 1 teaspoon ground ginger
- ½ teaspoon ground coriander
- ¼ teaspoon freshly ground white pepper
- ½ teaspoon ground cinnamon
- ½ teaspoon dried oregano
- ¼ teaspoon ground allspice
- ¼ teaspoon ground turmeric
- ½ cup low-fat plain Greek yogurt
- 1 pound (454 g) ground lamb
- 1 teaspoon garlic paste
- ¼ teaspoon salt
- ¼ teaspoon freshly ground black pepper
- Cooking oil spray
- 4 hamburger buns
- ½ cucumber, thinly sliced

1. In a small bowl, stir together the ginger, coriander, white pepper, cinnamon, oregano, allspice, and turmeric. 2. Put the yogurt in a small bowl and add half the spice mixture. Mix well and refrigerate. 3. Insert the crisper plate into the basket and the basket into the unit. Preheat the unit by selecting AIR FRY, setting the temperature to 360ºF (182ºC), and setting the time to 3 minutes. Select START/STOP to begin. 4. In a large bowl, combine the lamb, garlic paste, remaining spice mix, salt, and pepper. Gently but thoroughly mix the ingredients with your hands. Form the meat into 4 patties. 5. Once the unit is preheated, spray the crisper plate with cooking oil, and place the patties into the basket. 6. Select AIR FRY, set the temperature to 360ºF (182ºC), and set the time to 18 minutes. Select START/STOP to begin. 7. After 15 minutes, check the burgers. If a food thermometer inserted into the burgers registers 160ºF (71ºC), the burgers are done. If not, resume cooking. 8. When the cooking is complete, assemble the burgers on the buns with cucumber slices and a dollop of the yogurt dip.

Pork Milanese

Prep time: 10 minutes | Cook time: 12 minutes | Serves 4

- 4 (1-inch) boneless pork chops
- Fine sea salt and ground black pepper, to taste
- 2 large eggs
- ¾ cup powdered Parmesan cheese
- Chopped fresh parsley, for garnish
- Lemon slices, for serving

1. Spray the air fryer basket with avocado oil. Preheat the air fryer to 400ºF (204ºC). 2. Place the pork chops between 2 sheets of plastic wrap and pound them with the flat side of a meat tenderizer until they're ¼ inch thick. Lightly season both sides of the chops with salt and pepper. 3. Lightly beat the eggs in a shallow bowl. Divide the Parmesan cheese evenly between 2 bowls and set the bowls in this order: Parmesan, eggs, Parmesan. Dredge a chop in the first bowl of Parmesan, then dip it in the eggs, and then dredge it again in the second bowl of Parmesan, making sure both sides and all edges are well coated. Repeat with the remaining chops. 4. Place the chops in the air fryer basket and air fry for 12 minutes, or until the internal temperature reaches 145ºF (63ºC), flipping halfway through. 5. Garnish with fresh parsley and serve immediately with lemon slices. Store leftovers in an airtight container in the refrigerator for up to 3 days. Reheat in a preheated 390ºF (199ºC) air fryer for 5 minutes, or until warmed through.

Pork Kebab with Yogurt Sauce

Prep time: 25 minutes | Cook time: 12 minutes | Serves 4

- 2 teaspoons olive oil
- ½ pound (227 g) ground pork
- ½ pound (227 g) ground beef
- 1 egg, whisked
- Sea salt and ground black pepper, to taste
- 1 teaspoon paprika
- 2 garlic cloves, minced
- 1 teaspoon dried marjoram
- 1 teaspoon mustard seeds
- ½ teaspoon celery seeds
- Yogurt Sauce:
- 2 tablespoons olive oil
- 2 tablespoons fresh lemon juice
- Sea salt, to taste
- ¼ teaspoon red pepper flakes, crushed
- ½ cup full-fat yogurt
- 1 teaspoon dried dill weed

1. Spritz the sides and bottom of the air fryer basket with 2 teaspoons of olive oil. 2. In a mixing dish, thoroughly combine the ground pork, beef, egg, salt, black pepper, paprika, garlic, marjoram, mustard seeds, and celery seeds. 3. Form the mixture into kebabs and transfer them to the greased basket. Cook at 365ºF (185ºC) for 11 to 12 minutes, turning them over once or twice. In the meantime, mix all the sauce ingredients and place in the refrigerator until ready to serve. Serve the pork kebabs with the yogurt sauce on the side. Enjoy!

Chapter 5 Poultry

Barbecue Chicken

Prep time: 10 minutes | Cook time: 18 to 20 minutes | Serves 4

- ◀ ⅓ cup no-salt-added tomato sauce
- ◀ 2 tablespoons low-sodium grainy mustard
- ◀ 2 tablespoons apple cider vinegar
- ◀ 1 tablespoon honey
- ◀ 2 garlic cloves, minced
- ◀ 1 jalapeño pepper, minced
- ◀ 3 tablespoons minced onion
- ◀ 4 (5 ounces / 142 g) low-sodium boneless, skinless chicken breasts

1. Preheat the air fryer to 370°F (188°C). 2. In a small bowl, stir together the tomato sauce, mustard, cider vinegar, honey, garlic, jalapeño, and onion. 3. Brush the chicken breasts with some sauce and air fry for 10 minutes. 4. Remove the air fryer basket and turn the chicken; brush with more sauce. Air fry for 5 minutes more. 5. Remove the air fryer basket and turn the chicken again; brush with more sauce. Air fry for 3 to 5 minutes more, or until the chicken reaches an internal temperature of 165°F (74°C) on a meat thermometer. Discard any remaining sauce. Serve immediately.

Tandoori Chicken

Prep time: 30 minutes | Cook time: 15 minutes | Serves 4

- ◀ 1 pound (454 g) chicken tenders, halved crosswise
- ◀ ¼ cup plain Greek yogurt
- ◀ 1 tablespoon minced fresh ginger
- ◀ 1 tablespoon minced garlic
- ◀ ¼ cup chopped fresh cilantro or parsley
- ◀ 1 teaspoon kosher salt
- ◀ ½ to 1 teaspoon cayenne pepper
- ◀ 1 teaspoon ground turmeric
- ◀ 1 teaspoon garam masala
- ◀ 1 teaspoon sweet smoked paprika
- ◀ 1 tablespoon vegetable oil or melted ghee
- ◀ 2 teaspoons fresh lemon juice
- ◀ 2 tablespoons chopped fresh cilantro

1. In a large glass bowl, toss together the chicken, yogurt, ginger, garlic, cilantro, salt, cayenne, turmeric, garam masala, and paprika to coat. Marinate at room temperature for 30 minutes, or cover and refrigerate for up to 24 hours. 2. Place the chicken in a single layer in the air fryer basket. (Discard remaining marinade.) Spray the chicken with oil. Set the air fryer to 350°F (177°C) for 15 minutes. Halfway through the cooking time, spray the chicken with more vegetable oil spray, and toss gently to coat. Cook for 5 minutes more. 3. Transfer the chicken to a serving platter. Sprinkle with lemon juice and toss to coat. Sprinkle with the cilantro and serve.

Smoky Chicken Leg Quarters

Prep time: 30 minutes | Cook time: 23 to 27 minutes | Serves 6

- ◀ ½ cup avocado oil
- ◀ 2 teaspoons smoked paprika
- ◀ 1 teaspoon sea salt
- ◀ 1 teaspoon garlic powder
- ◀ ½ teaspoon dried rosemary
- ◀ ½ teaspoon dried thyme
- ◀ ½ teaspoon freshly ground black pepper
- ◀ 2 pounds (907 g) bone-in, skin-on chicken leg quarters

1. In a blender or small bowl, combine the avocado oil, smoked paprika, salt, garlic powder, rosemary, thyme, and black pepper. 2. Place the chicken in a shallow dish or large zip-top bag. Pour the marinade over the chicken, making sure all the legs are coated. Cover and marinate for at least 2 hours or overnight. 3. Place the chicken in a single layer in the air fryer basket, working in batches if necessary. Set the air fryer to 400°F (204°C) and air fry for 15 minutes. Flip the chicken legs, then reduce the temperature to 350°F (177°C). Cook for 8 to 12 minutes more, until an instant-read thermometer reads 160°F (71°C) when inserted into the thickest piece of chicken. 4. Allow to rest for 5 to 10 minutes before serving.

Crispy Dill Chicken Strips

Prep time: 30 minutes | Cook time: 10 minutes | Serves 4

- ◀ 2 whole boneless, skinless chicken breasts (about 1 pound / 454 g each), halved lengthwise
- ◀ 1 cup Italian dressing
- ◀ 3 cups finely crushed potato
- chips
- ◀ 1 tablespoon dried dill weed
- ◀ 1 tablespoon garlic powder
- ◀ 1 large egg, beaten
- ◀ 1 to 2 tablespoons oil

1. In a large resealable bag, combine the chicken and Italian dressing. Seal the bag and refrigerate to marinate at least 1 hour. 2. In a shallow dish, stir together the potato chips, dill, and garlic powder. Place the beaten egg in a second shallow dish. 3. Remove the chicken from the marinade. Roll the chicken pieces in the egg and the potato chip mixture, coating thoroughly. 4. Preheat the air fryer to 325°F (163°C). Line the air fryer basket with parchment paper. 5. Place the coated chicken on the parchment and spritz with oil. 6. Cook for 5 minutes. Flip the chicken, spritz it with oil, and cook for 5 minutes more until the outsides are crispy and the insides are no longer pink.

Bruschetta Chicken

Prep time: 10 minutes | Cook time: 20 minutes | Serves 4

Bruschetta Stuffing:
- 1 tomato, diced
- 3 tablespoons balsamic vinegar
- 1 teaspoon Italian seasoning
- 2 tablespoons chopped fresh basil
- 3 garlic cloves, minced
- 2 tablespoons extra-virgin olive oil

Chicken:
- 4 (4 ounces / 113 g) boneless, skinless chicken breasts, cut 4 slits each
- 1 teaspoon Italian seasoning
- Chicken seasoning or rub, to taste
- Cooking spray

1. Preheat the air fryer to 370ºF (188ºC). Spritz the air fryer basket with cooking spray. 2. Combine the ingredients for the bruschetta stuffing in a bowl. Stir to mix well. Set aside. 3. Rub the chicken breasts with Italian seasoning and chicken seasoning on a clean work surface. 4. Arrange the chicken breasts, slits side up, in a single layer in the air fryer basket and spritz with cooking spray. You may need to work in batches to avoid overcrowding. 5. Air fry for 7 minutes, then open the air fryer and fill the slits in the chicken with the bruschetta stuffing. Cook for another 3 minutes or until the chicken is well browned. 6. Serve immediately.

Crunchy Chicken with Roasted Carrots

Prep time: 10 minutes | Cook time: 22 minutes | Serves 4

- 4 bone-in, skin-on chicken thighs
- 2 carrots, cut into 2-inch pieces
- 2 tablespoons extra-virgin olive oil
- 2 teaspoons poultry spice
- 1 teaspoon sea salt, divided
- 2 teaspoons chopped fresh rosemary leaves
- Cooking oil spray
- 2 cups cooked white rice

1. Brush the chicken thighs and carrots with olive oil. Sprinkle both with the poultry spice, salt, and rosemary. 2. Insert the crisper plate into the basket and the basket into the unit. Preheat the unit by selecting AIR FRY, setting the temperature to 400ºF (204ºC), and setting the time to 3 minutes. Select START/STOP to begin. 3. Once the unit is preheated, spray the crisper plate with cooking oil. Place the carrots into the basket. Add the wire rack and arrange the chicken thighs on the rack. 4. Select AIR FRY, set the temperature to 400ºF (204ºC), and set the time to 20 minutes. Select START/STOP to begin. 5. When the cooking is complete, check the chicken temperature. If a food thermometer inserted into the chicken registers 165ºF (74ºC), remove the chicken from the air fryer, place it on a clean plate, and cover with aluminum foil to keep warm. Otherwise, resume cooking for 1 to 2 minutes longer. 6. The carrots can cook for 18 to 22 minutes and will be tender and caramelized; cooking time isn't as crucial for root vegetables. 7. Serve the chicken and carrots with the hot cooked rice.

Korean Honey Wings

Prep time: 10 minutes | Cook time: 25 minutes per batch | Serves 4

- ¼ cup gochujang, or red pepper paste
- ¼ cup mayonnaise
- 2 tablespoons honey
- 1 tablespoon sesame oil
- 2 teaspoons minced garlic
- 1 tablespoon sugar
- 2 teaspoons ground ginger
- 3 pounds (1.4 kg) whole chicken wings
- Olive oil spray
- 1 teaspoon salt
- ½ teaspoon freshly ground black pepper

1. In a large bowl, whisk the gochujang, mayonnaise, honey, sesame oil, garlic, sugar, and ginger. Set aside. 2. Insert the crisper plate into the basket and the basket into the unit. Preheat the unit by selecting AIR FRY, setting the temperature to 400ºF (204ºC), and setting the time to 3 minutes. Select START/STOP to begin. 3. To prepare the chicken wings, cut the wings in half. The meatier part is the drumette. Cut off and discard the wing tip from the flat part (or save the wing tips in the freezer to make chicken stock). 4. Once the unit is preheated, spray the crisper plate with olive oil. Working in batches, place half the chicken wings into the basket, spray them with olive oil, and sprinkle with the salt and pepper. 5. Select AIR FRY, set the temperature to 400ºF (204ºC), and set the time to 20 minutes. Select START/STOP to begin. 6. After 10 minutes, remove the basket, flip the wings, and spray them with more olive oil. Reinsert the basket to resume cooking. 7. Cook the wings to an internal temperature of 165ºF (74ºC), then transfer them to the bowl with the prepared sauce and toss to coat. 8. Repeat steps 4, 5, 6, and 7 for the remaining chicken wings. 9. Return the coated wings to the basket and air fry for 4 to 6 minutes more until the sauce has glazed the wings and the chicken is crisp. After 3 minutes, check the wings to make sure they aren't burning. Serve hot.

Ham Chicken with Cheese

Prep time: 15 minutes | Cook time: 25 minutes | Serves 4

- ¼ cup unsalted butter, softened
- 4 ounces (113 g) cream cheese, softened
- 1½ teaspoons Dijon mustard
- 2 tablespoons white wine vinegar
- ¼ cup water
- 2 cups shredded cooked chicken
- ¼ pound (113 g) ham, chopped
- 4 ounces (113 g) sliced Swiss or Provolone cheese

1. Preheat the air fryer to 380ºF (193ºC). Lightly coat a casserole dish that will fit in the air fryer, such as an 8-inch round pan, with olive oil and set aside. 2. In a large bowl and using an electric mixer, combine the butter, cream cheese, Dijon mustard, and vinegar. With the motor running at low speed, slowly add the water and beat until smooth. Set aside. 3. Arrange an even layer of chicken in the bottom of the prepared pan, followed by the ham. Spread the butter and cream cheese mixture on top of the ham, followed by the cheese slices on the top layer. Air fry for 20 to 25 minutes until warmed through and the cheese has browned.

Chicken Schnitzel

Prep time: 15 minutes | Cook time: 5 minutes | Serves 4

- ½ cup all-purpose flour
- 1 teaspoon marjoram
- ½ teaspoon thyme
- 1 teaspoon dried parsley flakes
- ½ teaspoon salt
- 1 egg
- 1 teaspoon lemon juice
- 1 teaspoon water
- 1 cup breadcrumbs
- 4 chicken tenders, pounded thin, cut in half lengthwise
- Cooking spray

1. Preheat the air fryer to 390°F (199°C) and spritz with cooking spray. 2. Combine the flour, marjoram, thyme, parsley, and salt in a shallow dish. Stir to mix well. 3. Whisk the egg with lemon juice and water in a large bowl. Pour the breadcrumbs in a separate shallow dish. 4. Roll the chicken halves in the flour mixture first, then in the egg mixture, and then roll over the breadcrumbs to coat well. Shake the excess off. 5. Arrange the chicken halves in the preheated air fryer and spritz with cooking spray on both sides. 6. Air fry for 5 minutes or until the chicken halves are golden brown and crispy. Flip the halves halfway through. 7. Serve immediately.

Spinach and Feta Stuffed Chicken Breasts

Prep time: 10 minutes | Cook time: 27 minutes | Serves 4

- 1 (10 ounces / 283 g) package frozen spinach, thawed and drained well
- 1 cup feta cheese, crumbled
- ½ teaspoon freshly ground
- black pepper
- 4 boneless chicken breasts
- Salt and freshly ground black pepper, to taste
- 1 tablespoon olive oil

1. Prepare the filling. Squeeze out as much liquid as possible from the thawed spinach. Rough chop the spinach and transfer it to a mixing bowl with the feta cheese and the freshly ground black pepper. 2. Prepare the chicken breast. Place the chicken breast on a cutting board and press down on the chicken breast with one hand to keep it stabilized. Make an incision about 1-inch long in the fattest side of the breast. Move the knife up and down inside the chicken breast, without poking through either the top or the bottom, or the other side of the breast. The inside pocket should be about 3-inches long, but the opening should only be about 1-inch wide. If this is too difficult, you can make the incision longer, but you will have to be more careful when cooking the chicken breast since this will expose more of the stuffing. 3. Once you have prepared the chicken breasts, use your fingers to stuff the filling into each pocket, spreading the mixture down as far as you can. 4. Preheat the air fryer to 380°F (193°C). 5. Lightly brush or spray the air fryer basket and the chicken breasts with olive oil. Transfer two of the stuffed chicken breasts to the air fryer. Air fry for 12 minutes, turning the chicken breasts over halfway through the cooking time. Remove the chicken to a resting plate and air fry the second two breasts for 12 minutes. Return the first batch of chicken to the air fryer with the second batch and air fry for 3 more minutes. When the chicken is cooked, an instant read thermometer should register 165°F (74°C) in the thickest part of the chicken, as well as in the stuffing. 6.

Remove the chicken breasts and let them rest on a cutting board for 2 to 3 minutes. Slice the chicken on the bias and serve with the slices fanned out.

Pecan-Crusted Chicken Tenders

Prep time: 10 minutes | Cook time: 12 minutes | Serves 4

- 2 tablespoons mayonnaise
- 1 teaspoon Dijon mustard
- 1 pound (454 g) boneless, skinless chicken tenders
- ½ teaspoon salt
- ¼ teaspoon ground black pepper
- ½ cup chopped roasted pecans, finely ground

1. In a small bowl, whisk mayonnaise and mustard until combined. Brush mixture onto chicken tenders on both sides, then sprinkle tenders with salt and pepper. 2. Place pecans in a medium bowl and press each tender into pecans to coat each side. 3. Place tenders into ungreased air fryer basket in a single layer, working in batches if needed. Adjust the temperature to 375°F (191°C) and roast for 12 minutes, turning tenders halfway through cooking. Tenders will be golden brown and have an internal temperature of at least 165°F (74°C) when done. Serve warm.

Taco Chicken

Prep time: 10 minutes | Cook time: 23 minutes | Serves 4

- 2 large eggs
- 1 tablespoon water
- Fine sea salt and ground black pepper, to taste
- 1 cup pork dust
- 1 teaspoon ground cumin
- 1 teaspoon smoked paprika
- 4 (5 ounces / 142 g) boneless, skinless chicken
- breasts or thighs, pounded to ¼ inch thick
- 1 cup salsa
- 1 cup shredded Monterey Jack cheese (about 4 ounces / 113 g) (omit for dairy-free)
- Sprig of fresh cilantro, for garnish (optional)

1. Spray the air fryer basket with avocado oil. Preheat the air fryer to 400°F (204°C). 2. Crack the eggs into a shallow baking dish, add the water and a pinch each of salt and pepper, and whisk to combine. In another shallow baking dish, stir together the pork dust, cumin, and paprika until well combined. 3. Season the chicken breasts well on both sides with salt and pepper. Dip 1 chicken breast in the eggs and let any excess drip off, then dredge both sides of the chicken breast in the pork dust mixture. Spray the breast with avocado oil and place it in the air fryer basket. Repeat with the remaining 3 chicken breasts. 4. Air fry the chicken in the air fryer for 20 minutes, or until the internal temperature reaches 165°F (74°C) and the breading is golden brown, flipping halfway through. 5. Dollop each chicken breast with ¼ cup of the salsa and top with ¼ cup of the cheese. Return the breasts to the air fryer and cook for 3 minutes, or until the cheese is melted. Garnish with cilantro before serving, if desired. 6. Store leftovers in an airtight container in the refrigerator for up to 4 days. Reheat in a preheated 400°F (204°C) air fryer for 5 minutes, or until warmed through.

Indian Fennel Chicken

Prep time: 30 minutes | Cook time: 15 minutes | Serves 4

- ◀ 1 pound (454 g) boneless, skinless chicken thighs, cut crosswise into thirds
- ◀ 1 yellow onion, cut into 1½-inch-thick slices
- ◀ 1 tablespoon coconut oil, melted
- ◀ 2 teaspoons minced fresh ginger
- ◀ 2 teaspoons minced garlic
- ◀ 1 teaspoon smoked paprika
- ◀ 1 teaspoon ground fennel
- ◀ 1 teaspoon garam masala
- ◀ 1 teaspoon ground turmeric
- ◀ 1 teaspoon kosher salt
- ◀ ½ to 1 teaspoon cayenne pepper
- ◀ Vegetable oil spray
- ◀ 2 teaspoons fresh lemon juice

¼ cup chopped fresh cilantro or parsley

1. Use a fork to pierce the chicken all over to allow the marinade to penetrate better. 2. In a large bowl, combine the onion, coconut oil, ginger, garlic, paprika, fennel, garam masala, turmeric, salt, and cayenne. Add the chicken, toss to combine, and marinate at room temperature for 30 minutes, or cover and refrigerate for up to 24 hours. 3. Place the chicken and onion in the air fryer basket. (Discard remaining marinade.) Spray with some vegetable oil spray. Set the air fryer to 350ºF (177ºC) for 15 minutes. Halfway through the cooking time, remove the basket, spray the chicken and onion with more vegetable oil spray, and toss gently to coat. At the end of the cooking time, use a meat thermometer to ensure the chicken has reached an internal temperature of 165ºF (74ºC). 4. Transfer the chicken and onion to a serving platter. Sprinkle with the lemon juice and cilantro and serve.

Pomegranate glazed Chicken with Couscous Salad

Prep time: 25 minutes | Cook time: 20 minutes | Serves 4

- ◀ 3 tablespoons plus 2 teaspoons pomegranate molasses
- ◀ ½ teaspoon ground cinnamon
- ◀ 1 teaspoon minced fresh thyme
- ◀ Salt and ground black pepper, to taste
- ◀ 2 (12 ounces / 340 g) bone-in split chicken breasts, trimmed
- ◀ ¼ cup chicken broth
- ◀ ¼ cup water
- ◀ ½ cup couscous
- ◀ 1 tablespoon minced fresh parsley
- ◀ 2 ounces (57 g) cherry tomatoes, quartered
- ◀ 1 scallion, white part minced, green part sliced thin on bias
- ◀ 1 tablespoon extra-virgin olive oil
- ◀ 1 ounce (28 g) feta cheese, crumbled
- ◀ Cooking spray

1. Preheat the air fryer to 350ºF (177ºC). Spritz the air fryer basket with cooking spray. 2. Combine 3 tablespoons of pomegranate molasses, cinnamon, thyme, and ⅛ teaspoon of salt in a small bowl. Stir to mix well. Set aside. 3. Place the chicken breasts in the preheated air fryer, skin side down, and spritz with cooking spray. Sprinkle with salt and ground black pepper. 4. Air fry the chicken for 10 minutes, then brush the chicken with half of pomegranate

molasses mixture and flip. Air fry for 5 more minutes. 5. Brush the chicken with remaining pomegranate molasses mixture and flip. Air fry for another 5 minutes or until the internal temperature of the chicken breasts reaches at least 165ºF (74ºC). 6. Meanwhile, pour the broth and water in a pot and bring to a boil over medium-high heat. Add the couscous and sprinkle with salt. Cover and simmer for 7 minutes or until the liquid is almost absorbed. 7. Combine the remaining ingredients, except for the cheese, with cooked couscous in a large bowl. Toss to mix well. Scatter with the feta cheese. 8. When the air frying is complete, remove the chicken from the air fryer and allow to cool for 10 minutes. Serve with vegetable and couscous salad.

Ginger Turmeric Chicken Thighs

Prep time: 5 minutes | Cook time: 25 minutes | Serves 4

- ◀ 4 (4 ounces / 113 g) boneless, skin-on chicken thighs
- ◀ 2 tablespoons coconut oil, melted
- ◀ ½ teaspoon ground turmeric
- ◀ ½ teaspoon salt
- ◀ ½ teaspoon garlic powder
- ◀ ½ teaspoon ground ginger
- ◀ ¼ teaspoon ground black pepper

1. Place chicken thighs in a large bowl and drizzle with coconut oil. Sprinkle with remaining ingredients and toss to coat both sides of thighs. 2. Place thighs skin side up into ungreased air fryer basket. Adjust the temperature to 400ºF (204ºC) and air fry for 25 minutes. After 10 minutes, turn thighs. When 5 minutes remain, flip thighs once more. Chicken will be done when skin is golden brown and the internal temperature is at least 165ºF (74ºC). Serve warm.

Wild Rice and Kale Stuffed Chicken Thighs

Prep time: 10 minutes | Cook time: 22 minutes | Serves 4

- ◀ 4 boneless, skinless chicken thighs
- ◀ 1 cup cooked wild rice
- ◀ ½ cup chopped kale
- ◀ 2 garlic cloves, minced
- ◀ 1 teaspoon salt
- ◀ Juice of 1 lemon
- ◀ ½ cup crumbled feta
- ◀ Olive oil cooking spray
- ◀ 1 tablespoon olive oil

1. Preheat the air fryer to 380°F(193ºC). 2. Place the chicken thighs between two pieces of plastic wrap, and using a meat mallet or a rolling pin, pound them out to about ¼-inch thick. 3. In a medium bowl, combine the rice, kale, garlic, salt, and lemon juice and mix well. 4. Place a quarter of the rice mixture into the middle of each chicken thigh, then sprinkle 2 tablespoons of feta over the filling. 5. Spray the air fryer basket with olive oil cooking spray. 6. Fold the sides of the chicken thigh over the filling, and then gently place each of them seam-side down into the air fryer basket. Brush each stuffed chicken thigh with olive oil. 7. Roast the stuffed chicken thighs for 12 minutes, then turn them over and cook for an additional 10 minutes, or until the internal temperature reaches 165°F(74ºC).

Jalapeño Popper Hasselback Chicken

Prep time: 10 minutes | Cook time: 19 minutes | Serves 2

- ◀ Oil, for spraying
- ◀ 2 (8 ounces / 227 g) boneless, skinless chicken breasts
- ◀ 2 ounces (57 g) cream cheese, softened
- ◀ ¼ cup bacon bits
- ◀ ¼ cup chopped pickled jalapeños
- ◀ ½ cup shredded Cheddar cheese, divided

1. Line the air fryer basket with parchment and spray lightly with oil. 2. Make multiple cuts across the top of each chicken breast, cutting only halfway through. 3. In a medium bowl, mix together the cream cheese, bacon bits, jalapeños, and ¼ cup of Cheddar cheese. Spoon some of the mixture into each cut. 4. Place the chicken in the prepared basket. 5. Air fry at 350ºF (177ºC) for 14 minutes. Scatter the remaining ¼ cup of cheese on top of the chicken and cook for another 2 to 5 minutes, or until the cheese is melted and the internal temperature reaches 165ºF (74ºC).

General Tso's Chicken

Prep time: 10 minutes | Cook time: 14 minutes | Serves 4

- ◀ 1 tablespoon sesame oil
- ◀ 1 teaspoon minced garlic
- ◀ ½ teaspoon ground ginger
- ◀ 1 cup chicken broth
- ◀ 4 tablespoons soy sauce, divided
- ◀ ½ teaspoon sriracha, plus more for serving
- ◀ 2 tablespoons hoisin sauce
- ◀ 4 tablespoons cornstarch, divided
- ◀ 4 boneless, skinless chicken breasts, cut into 1-inch pieces
- ◀ Olive oil spray
- ◀ 2 medium scallions, sliced, green parts only
- ◀ Sesame seeds, for garnish

1. In a small saucepan over low heat, combine the sesame oil, garlic, and ginger and cook for 1 minute. 2. Add the chicken broth, 2 tablespoons of soy sauce, the sriracha, and hoisin. Whisk to combine. 3. Whisk in 2 tablespoons of cornstarch and continue cooking over low heat until the sauce starts to thicken, about 5 minutes. Remove the pan from the heat, cover it, and set aside. 4. Insert the crisper plate into the basket and the basket into the unit. Preheat the unit by selecting BAKE, setting the temperature to 400ºF (204ºC), and setting the time to 3 minutes. Select START/STOP to begin. 5. In a medium bowl, toss together the chicken, remaining 2 tablespoons of soy sauce, and remaining 2 tablespoons of cornstarch. 6. Once the unit is preheated, spray the crisper plate with olive oil. Place the chicken into the basket and spray it with olive oil. 7. Select BAKE, set the temperature to 400ºF (204ºC), and set the time to 9 minutes. Select START/STOP to begin. 8. After 5 minutes, remove the basket, shake, and spray the chicken with more olive oil. Reinsert the basket to resume cooking. 9. When the cooking is complete, a food thermometer inserted into the chicken should register at least 165ºF (74ºC). Transfer the chicken to a large bowl and toss it with the sauce. Garnish with the scallions and sesame seeds and serve.

African Piri-Piri Chicken Drumsticks

Prep time: 30 minutes | Cook time: 20 minutes | Serves 2

Chicken:
- ◀ 1 tablespoon chopped fresh thyme leaves
- ◀ 1 tablespoon minced fresh ginger
- ◀ 1 small shallot, finely chopped
- ◀ 2 garlic cloves, minced
- ◀ ⅓ cup piri-piri sauce or hot

Glaze:
- ◀ 2 tablespoons butter or ghee
- ◀ 1 teaspoon chopped fresh thyme leaves
- ◀ 1 garlic clove, minced
- sauce
- ◀ 3 tablespoons extra-virgin olive oil
- ◀ Zest and juice of 1 lemon
- ◀ 1 teaspoon smoked paprika
- ◀ ½ teaspoon kosher salt
- ◀ ½ teaspoon black pepper
- ◀ 4 chicken drumsticks

- ◀ 1 tablespoon piri-piri sauce
- ◀ 1 tablespoon fresh lemon juice

1. For the chicken: In a small bowl, stir together all the ingredients except the chicken. Place the chicken and the marinade in a gallon-size resealable plastic bag. Seal the bag and massage to coat. Refrigerate for at least 2 hours or up to 24 hours, turning the bag occasionally. 2. Place the chicken legs in the air fryer basket. Set the air fryer to 400ºF (204ºC) for 20 minutes, turning the chicken halfway through the cooking time. 3. Meanwhile, for the glaze: Melt the butter in a small saucepan over medium-high heat. Add the thyme and garlic. Cook, stirring, until the garlic just begins to brown, 1 to 2 minutes. Add the piri-piri sauce and lemon juice. Reduce the heat to medium-low and simmer for 1 to 2 minutes. 4. Transfer the chicken to a serving platter. Pour the glaze over the chicken. Serve immediately.

Apricot Chicken

Prep time: 15 minutes | Cook time: 10 to 12 minutes | Serves 4

- ◀ ⅔ cup apricot preserves
- ◀ 2 tablespoons freshly squeezed lemon juice
- ◀ 1 teaspoon soy sauce
- ◀ ¼ teaspoon salt
- ◀ ¾ cup panko bread crumbs
- ◀ 2 whole boneless, skinless chicken breasts (1 pound / 454 g each), halved
- ◀ 1 to 2 tablespoons oil

1. In a shallow bowl, stir together the apricot preserves, lemon juice, soy sauce, and salt. Place the bread crumbs in a second shallow bowl. 2. Roll the chicken in the preserves mixture and then the bread crumbs, coating thoroughly. 3. Preheat the air fryer to 350ºF (177ºC). Line the air fryer basket with parchment paper. 4. Place the coated chicken on the parchment and spritz with oil. 5. Cook for 5 minutes. Flip the chicken, spritz it with oil, and cook for 5 to 7 minutes more until the internal temperature reaches 165ºF (74ºC) and the chicken is no longer pink inside. Let sit for 5 minutes.

Celery Chicken

Prep time: 10 minutes | Cook time: 15 minutes | Serves 4

- ½ cup soy sauce
- 2 tablespoons hoisin sauce
- 4 teaspoons minced garlic
- 1 teaspoon freshly ground black pepper
- 8 boneless, skinless chicken tenderloins
- 1 cup chopped celery
- 1 medium red bell pepper, diced
- Olive oil spray

1. Preheat the air fryer to 375ºF (191ºC). Spray the air fryer basket lightly with olive oil spray. 2. In a large bowl, mix together the soy sauce, hoisin sauce, garlic, and black pepper to make a marinade. Add the chicken, celery, and bell pepper and toss to coat. 3. Shake the excess marinade off the chicken, place it and the vegetables in the air fryer basket, and lightly spray with olive oil spray. You may need to cook them in batches. Reserve the remaining marinade. 4. Air fry for 8 minutes. Turn the chicken over and brush with some of the remaining marinade. Air fry for an additional 5 to 7 minutes, or until the chicken reaches an internal temperature of at least 165ºF (74ºC). Serve.

Crispy Duck with Cherry Sauce

Prep time: 10 minutes | Cook time: 33 minutes | Serves 2 to 4

- 1 whole duck (up to 5 pounds / 2.3 kg), split in half, back and rib bones removed

Cherry Sauce:
- 1 tablespoon butter
- 1 shallot, minced
- ½ cup sherry
- ¾ cup cherry preserves
- 1 cup chicken stock
- 1 teaspoon white wine
- 1 teaspoon olive oil
- Salt and freshly ground black pepper, to taste

- vinegar
- 1 teaspoon fresh thyme leaves
- Salt and freshly ground black pepper, to taste

1. Preheat the air fryer to 400ºF (204ºC). 2. Trim some of the fat from the duck. Rub olive oil on the duck and season with salt and pepper. Place the duck halves in the air fryer basket, breast side up and facing the center of the basket. 3. Air fry the duck for 20 minutes. Turn the duck over and air fry for another 6 minutes. 4. While duck is air frying, make the cherry sauce. Melt the butter in a large sauté pan. Add the shallot and sauté until it is just starting to brown, about 2 to 3 minutes. Add the sherry and deglaze the pan by scraping up any brown bits from the bottom of the pan. Simmer the liquid for a few minutes, until it has reduced by half. Add the cherry preserves, chicken stock and white wine vinegar. Whisk well to combine all the ingredients. Simmer the sauce until it thickens and coats the back of a spoon, about 5 to 7 minutes. Season with salt and pepper and stir in the fresh thyme leaves. 5. When the air fryer timer goes off, spoon some cherry sauce over the duck and continue to air fry at 400ºF (204ºC) for 4 more minutes. Then, turn the duck halves back over so that the breast side is facing up. Spoon more cherry sauce over the top of the duck, covering the skin completely.

Air fry for 3 more minutes and then remove the duck to a plate to rest for a few minutes. 6. Serve the duck in halves, or cut each piece in half again for a smaller serving. Spoon any additional sauce over the duck or serve it on the side.

Chicken and Broccoli Casserole

Prep time: 5 minutes | Cook time: 20 to 25 minutes | Serves 4

- ½ pound (227 g) broccoli, chopped into florets
- 2 cups shredded cooked chicken
- 4 ounces (113 g) cream cheese
- ⅓ cup heavy cream
- 1½ teaspoons Dijon mustard
- ½ teaspoon garlic powder
- Salt and freshly ground black pepper, to taste
- 2 tablespoons chopped fresh basil
- 1 cup shredded Cheddar cheese

1. Preheat the air fryer to 390ºF (199ºC). Lightly coat a casserole dish that will fit in air fryer, with olive oil and set aside. 2. Place the broccoli in a large glass bowl with 1 tablespoon of water and cover with a microwavable plate. Microwave on high for 2 to 3 minutes until the broccoli is bright green but not mushy. Drain if necessary and add to another large bowl along with the shredded chicken. 3. In the same glass bowl used to microwave the broccoli, combine the cream cheese and cream. Microwave for 30 seconds to 1 minute on high and stir until smooth. Add the mustard and garlic powder and season to taste with salt and freshly ground black pepper. Whisk until the sauce is smooth. 4. Pour the warm sauce over the broccoli and chicken mixture and then add the basil. Using a silicone spatula, gently fold the mixture until thoroughly combined. 5. Transfer the chicken mixture to the prepared casserole dish and top with the cheese. Air fry for 20 to 25 minutes until warmed through and the cheese has browned.

Jerk Chicken Kebabs

Prep time: 10 minutes | Cook time: 14 minutes | Serves 4

- 8 ounces (227 g) boneless, skinless chicken thighs, cut into 1-inch cubes
- 2 tablespoons jerk seasoning
- 2 tablespoons coconut oil
- ½ medium red bell pepper, seeded and cut into 1-inch pieces
- ¼ medium red onion, peeled and cut into 1-inch pieces
- ½ teaspoon salt

1. Place chicken in a medium bowl and sprinkle with jerk seasoning and coconut oil. Toss to coat on all sides. 2. Using eight (6-inch) skewers, build skewers by alternating chicken, pepper, and onion pieces, about three repetitions per skewer. 3. Sprinkle salt over skewers and place into ungreased air fryer basket. Adjust the temperature to 370ºF (188ºC) and air fry for 14 minutes, turning skewers halfway through cooking. Chicken will be golden and have an internal temperature of at least 165ºF (74ºC) when done. Serve warm.

Easy Chicken Fingers

Prep time: 20 minutes | Cook time: 30 minutes | Makes 12 chicken fingers

- ½ cup all-purpose flour
- 2 cups panko breadcrumbs
- 2 tablespoons canola oil
- 1 large egg
- 3 boneless and skinless chicken breasts, each cut
- into 4 strips
- Kosher salt and freshly ground black pepper, to taste
- Cooking spray

1. Preheat the air fryer to 360°F (182°C). Spritz the air fryer basket with cooking spray. 2. Pour the flour in a large bowl. Combine the panko and canola oil on a shallow dish. Whisk the egg in a separate bowl. 3. Rub the chicken strips with salt and ground black pepper on a clean work surface, then dip the chicken in the bowl of flour. Shake the excess off and dunk the chicken strips in the bowl of whisked egg, then roll the strips over the panko to coat well. 4. Arrange 4 strips in the air fryer basket each time and air fry for 10 minutes or until crunchy and lightly browned. Flip the strips halfway through. Repeat with remaining ingredients. 5. Serve immediately.

Spicy Chicken Thighs and Gold Potatoes

Prep time: 5 minutes | Cook time: 25 minutes | Serves 4

- 4 bone-in, skin-on chicken thighs
- ½ teaspoon kosher salt or ¼ teaspoon fine salt
- 2 tablespoons melted unsalted butter
- 2 teaspoons Worcestershire sauce
- 2 teaspoons curry powder
- 1 teaspoon dried oregano
- leaves
- ½ teaspoon dry mustard
- ½ teaspoon granulated garlic
- ¼ teaspoon paprika
- ¼ teaspoon hot pepper sauce
- Cooking oil spray
- 4 medium Yukon gold potatoes, chopped
- 1 tablespoon extra-virgin olive oil

1. Sprinkle the chicken thighs on both sides with salt. 2. In a medium bowl, stir together the melted butter, Worcestershire sauce, curry powder, oregano, dry mustard, granulated garlic, paprika, and hot pepper sauce. Add the thighs to the sauce and stir to coat. 3. Insert the crisper plate into the basket and the basket into the unit. Preheat the unit by selecting AIR FRY, setting the temperature to 400°F (204°C), and setting the time to 3 minutes. Select START/STOP to begin. 4. Once the unit is preheated, spray the crisper plate with cooking oil. In the basket, combine the potatoes and olive oil and toss to coat. 5. Add the wire rack to the air fryer and place the chicken thighs on top. 6. Select AIR FRY, set the temperature to 400°F (204°C), and set the time to 25 minutes. Select START/STOP to begin. 7. After 19 minutes check the chicken thighs. If a food thermometer inserted into the chicken registers 165°F (74°C), transfer them to a clean plate, and cover with aluminum foil to keep warm. If they aren't cooked to 165°F (74°C), resume cooking for another 1 to 2 minutes until they are done. Remove them from the unit along with the rack. 8. Remove the basket and shake it to distribute the potatoes. Reinsert the basket to resume cooking for 3 to 6 minutes, or until the potatoes are crisp and golden brown. 9. When the cooking is complete, serve the chicken with the potatoes.

Cilantro Chicken Kebabs

Prep time: 30 minutes | Cook time: 10 minutes | Serves 4

Chutney:
- ½ cup unsweetened shredded coconut
- ½ cup hot water
- 2 cups fresh cilantro leaves, roughly chopped
- ¼ cup fresh mint leaves, roughly chopped
- 6 cloves garlic, roughly chopped
- 1 jalapeño, seeded and roughly chopped
- ¼ to ¾ cup water, as needed
- Juice of 1 lemon

Chicken:
- 1 pound (454 g) boneless, skinless chicken thighs, cut
- crosswise into thirds
- Olive oil spray

1. For the chutney: In a blender or food processor, combine the coconut and hot water; set aside to soak for 5 minutes. 2. To the processor, add the cilantro, mint, garlic, and jalapeño, along with ¼ cup water. Blend at low speed, stopping occasionally to scrape down the sides. Add the lemon juice. With the blender or processor running, add only enough additional water to keep the contents moving. Turn the blender to high once the contents are moving freely and blend until the mixture is puréed. 3. For the chicken: Place the chicken pieces in a large bowl. Add ¼ cup of the chutney and mix well to coat. Set aside the remaining chutney to use as a dip. Marinate the chicken for 15 minutes at room temperature. 4. Spray the air fryer basket with olive oil spray. Arrange the chicken in the air fryer basket. Set the air fryer to 350°F (177°C) for 10 minutes. Use a meat thermometer to ensure that the chicken has reached an internal temperature of 165°F (74°C). 5. Serve the chicken with the remaining chutney.

Italian Chicken Thighs

Prep time: 5 minutes | Cook time: 20 minutes | Serves 2

- 4 bone-in, skin-on chicken thighs
- 2 tablespoons unsalted butter, melted
- 1 teaspoon dried parsley
- 1 teaspoon dried basil
- ½ teaspoon garlic powder
- ¼ teaspoon onion powder
- ¼ teaspoon dried oregano

1. Brush chicken thighs with butter and sprinkle remaining ingredients over thighs. Place thighs into the air fryer basket. 2. Adjust the temperature to 380°F (193°C) and roast for 20 minutes. 3. Halfway through the cooking time, flip the thighs. 4. When fully cooked, internal temperature will be at least 165°F (74°C) and skin will be crispy. Serve warm.

Chicken Paillard

Prep time: 10 minutes | Cook time: 10 minutes | Serves 2

- 2 large eggs, room temperature
- 1 tablespoon water
- ½ cup powdered Parmesan cheese (about 1½ ounces / 43 g) or pork dust
- 2 teaspoons dried thyme

Lemon Butter Sauce:
- 2 tablespoons unsalted butter, melted
- 2 teaspoons lemon juice
- ¼ teaspoon finely chopped

leaves
- 1 teaspoon ground black pepper
- 2 (5 ounces / 142 g) boneless, skinless chicken breasts, pounded to ½ inch thick

fresh thyme leaves, plus more for garnish
- ⅛ teaspoon fine sea salt
- Lemon slices, for serving

1. Spray the air fryer basket with avocado oil. Preheat the air fryer to 390ºF (199ºC). 2. Beat the eggs in a shallow dish, then add the water and stir well. 3. In a separate shallow dish, mix together the Parmesan, thyme, and pepper until well combined. 4. One at a time, dip the chicken breasts in the eggs and let any excess drip off, then dredge both sides of the chicken in the Parmesan mixture. As you finish, set the coated chicken in the air fryer basket. 5. Roast the chicken in the air fryer for 5 minutes, then flip the chicken and cook for another 5 minutes, or until cooked through and the internal temperature reaches 165ºF (74ºC). 6. While the chicken cooks, make the lemon butter sauce: In a small bowl, mix together all the sauce ingredients until well combined. 7. Plate the chicken and pour the sauce over it. Garnish with chopped fresh thyme and serve with lemon slices. 8. Store leftovers in an airtight container in the refrigerator for up to 4 days. Reheat in a preheated 390ºF (199ºC) air fryer for 5 minutes, or until heated through.

Chicken Jalfrezi

Prep time: 15 minutes | Cook time: 15 minutes | Serves 4

Chicken:
- 1 pound (454 g) boneless, skinless chicken thighs, cut into 2 or 3 pieces each
- 1 medium onion, chopped
- 1 large green bell pepper, stemmed, seeded, and chopped

Sauce:
- ¼ cup tomato sauce
- 1 tablespoon water
- 1 teaspoon garam masala
- ½ teaspoon kosher salt

- 2 tablespoons olive oil
- 1 teaspoon ground turmeric
- 1 teaspoon garam masala
- 1 teaspoon kosher salt
- ½ to 1 teaspoon cayenne pepper

- ½ teaspoon cayenne pepper
- Side salad, rice, or naan bread, for serving

1. For the chicken: In a large bowl, combine the chicken, onion, bell pepper, oil, turmeric, garam masala, salt, and cayenne. Stir and toss until well combined. 2. Place the chicken and vegetables in the air fryer basket. Set the air fryer to 350ºF (177ºC) for 15 minutes, stirring and tossing halfway through the cooking time.

Use a meat thermometer to ensure the chicken has reached an internal temperature of 165ºF (74ºC). 3. Meanwhile, for the sauce: In a small microwave-safe bowl, combine the tomato sauce, water, garam masala, salt, and cayenne. Microwave on high for 1 minute. Remove and stir. Microwave for another minute; set aside. 4. When the chicken is cooked, remove and place chicken and vegetables in a large bowl. Pour the sauce over all. Stir and toss to coat the chicken and vegetables evenly. 5. Serve with rice, naan, or a side salad.

Turkey Meatloaf

Prep time: 10 minutes | Cook time: 50 minutes | Serves 4

- 8 ounces (227 g) sliced mushrooms
- 1 small onion, coarsely chopped
- 2 cloves garlic
- 1½ pounds (680 g) 85% lean ground turkey
- 2 eggs, lightly beaten

- 1 tablespoon tomato paste
- ¼ cup almond meal
- 2 tablespoons almond milk
- 1 tablespoon dried oregano
- 1 teaspoon salt
- ½ teaspoon freshly ground black pepper
- 1 Roma tomato, thinly sliced

1. Preheat the air fryer to 350ºF (177ºC). Lightly coat a round pan with olive oil and set aside. 2. In a food processor fitted with a metal blade, combine the mushrooms, onion, and garlic. Pulse until finely chopped. Transfer the vegetables to a large mixing bowl. 3. Add the turkey, eggs, tomato paste, almond meal, milk, oregano, salt, and black pepper. Mix gently until thoroughly combined. Transfer the mixture to the prepared pan and shape into a loaf. Arrange the tomato slices on top. 4. Air fry for 50 minutes or until the meatloaf is nicely browned and a thermometer inserted into the thickest part registers 165ºF (74ºC). Remove from the air fryer and let rest for about 10 minutes before slicing.

Golden Chicken Cutlets

Prep time: 15 minutes | Cook time: 15 minutes | Serves 4

- 2 tablespoons panko breadcrumbs
- ¼ cup grated Parmesan cheese
- ⅛ tablespoon paprika
- ½ tablespoon garlic powder

- 2 large eggs
- 4 chicken cutlets
- 1 tablespoon parsley
- Salt and ground black pepper, to taste
- Cooking spray

1. Preheat air fryer to 400ºF (204ºC). Spritz the air fryer basket with cooking spray. 2. Combine the breadcrumbs, Parmesan, paprika, garlic powder, salt, and ground black pepper in a large bowl. Stir to mix well. Beat the eggs in a separate bowl. 3. Dredge the chicken cutlets in the beaten eggs, then roll over the breadcrumbs mixture to coat well. Shake the excess off. 4. Transfer the chicken cutlets in the preheated air fryer and spritz with cooking spray. 5. Air fry for 15 minutes or until crispy and golden brown. Flip the cutlets halfway through. 6. Serve with parsley on top.

Chicken with Lettuce

Prep time: 15 minutes | Cook time: 14 minutes | Serves 4

- 1 pound (454 g) chicken breast tenders, chopped into bite-size pieces
- ½ onion, thinly sliced
- ½ red bell pepper, seeded and thinly sliced
- ½ green bell pepper, seeded and thinly sliced
- 1 tablespoon olive oil
- 1 tablespoon fajita seasoning
- 1 teaspoon kosher salt
- Juice of ½ lime
- 8 large lettuce leaves
- 1 cup prepared guacamole

1. Preheat the air fryer to 400°F (204°C). 2. In a large bowl, combine the chicken, onion, and peppers. Drizzle with the olive oil and toss until thoroughly coated. Add the fajita seasoning and salt and toss again. 3. Working in batches if necessary, arrange the chicken and vegetables in a single layer in the air fryer basket. Pausing halfway through the cooking time to shake the basket, air fry for 14 minutes, or until the vegetables are tender and a thermometer inserted into the thickest piece of chicken registers 165°F (74°C). 4. Transfer the mixture to a serving platter and drizzle with the fresh lime juice. Serve with the lettuce leaves and top with the guacamole.

Chicken Legs with Leeks

Prep time: 30 minutes | Cook time: 18 minutes | Serves 6

- 2 leeks, sliced
- 2 large-sized tomatoes, chopped
- 3 cloves garlic, minced
- ½ teaspoon dried oregano
- 6 chicken legs, boneless and skinless
- ½ teaspoon smoked cayenne pepper
- 2 tablespoons olive oil
- A freshly ground nutmeg

1. In a mixing dish, thoroughly combine all ingredients, minus the leeks. Place in the refrigerator and let it marinate overnight. 2. Lay the leeks onto the bottom of the air fryer basket. Top with the chicken legs. 3. Roast chicken legs at 375°F (191°C) for 18 minutes, turning halfway through. Serve with hoisin sauce.

Nacho Chicken Fries

Prep time: 20 minutes | Cook time: 6 to 7 minutes per batch | Serves 4 to 6

- 1 pound (454 g) chicken tenders
- Salt, to taste
- ¼ cup flour
- 2 eggs
- ¾ cup panko bread crumbs
- ¾ cup crushed organic nacho cheese tortilla chips
- Oil for misting or cooking spray
- Seasoning Mix:
- 1 tablespoon chili powder
- 1 teaspoon ground cumin
- ½ teaspoon garlic powder
- ½ teaspoon onion powder

1. Stir together all seasonings in a small cup and set aside. 2. Cut chicken tenders in half crosswise, then cut into strips no wider than about ½ inch. 3. Preheat the air fryer to 390°F (199°C). 4. Salt chicken to taste. Place strips in large bowl and sprinkle with 1 tablespoon of the seasoning mix. Stir well to distribute seasonings. 5. Add flour to chicken and stir well to coat all sides. 6. Beat eggs together in a shallow dish. 7. In a second shallow dish, combine the panko, crushed chips, and the remaining 2 teaspoons of seasoning mix. 8. Dip chicken strips in eggs, then roll in crumbs. Mist with oil or cooking spray. 9. Chicken strips will cook best if done in two batches. They can be crowded and overlapping a little but not stacked in double or triple layers. 10. Cook for 4 minutes. Shake basket, mist with oil, and cook 2 to 3 more minutes, until chicken juices run clear and outside is crispy. 11. Repeat step 10 to cook remaining chicken fries.

Chipotle Drumsticks

Prep time: 5 minutes | Cook time: 25 minutes | Serves 4

- 1 tablespoon tomato paste
- ½ teaspoon chipotle powder
- ¼ teaspoon apple cider vinegar
- ¼ teaspoon garlic powder
- 8 chicken drumsticks
- ½ teaspoon salt
- ⅛ teaspoon ground black pepper

1. In a small bowl, combine tomato paste, chipotle powder, vinegar, and garlic powder. 2. Sprinkle drumsticks with salt and pepper, then place into a large bowl and pour in tomato paste mixture. Toss or stir to evenly coat all drumsticks in mixture. 3. Place drumsticks into ungreased air fryer basket. Adjust the temperature to 400°F (204°C) and air fry for 25 minutes, turning drumsticks halfway through cooking. Drumsticks will be dark red with an internal temperature of at least 165°F (74°C) when done. Serve warm.

Chicken Manchurian

Prep time: 10 minutes | Cook time: 20 minutes | Serves 2

- 1 pound (454 g) boneless, skinless chicken breasts, cut into 1-inch pieces
- ¼ cup ketchup
- 1 tablespoon tomato-based chili sauce, such as Heinz
- 1 tablespoon soy sauce
- 1 tablespoon rice vinegar
- 2 teaspoons vegetable oil
- 1 teaspoon hot sauce, such as Tabasco
- ½ teaspoon garlic powder
- ¼ teaspoon cayenne pepper
- 2 scallions, thinly sliced
- Cooked white rice, for serving

1. Preheat the air fryer to 350°F (177°C). 2. In a bowl, combine the chicken, ketchup, chili sauce, soy sauce, vinegar, oil, hot sauce, garlic powder, cayenne, and three-quarters of the scallions and toss until evenly coated. 3. Scrape the chicken and sauce into a metal cake pan and place the pan in the air fryer. Bake until the chicken is cooked through and the sauce is reduced to a thick glaze, about 20 minutes, flipping the chicken pieces halfway through. 4. Remove the pan from the air fryer. Spoon the chicken and sauce over rice and top with the remaining scallions. Serve immediately.

Sesame Chicken

Prep time: 10 minutes | Cook time: 18 minutes | Serves 6

- Oil, for spraying
- 2 (6 ounces / 170 g) boneless, skinless chicken breasts, cut into bite-size pieces
- ½ cup cornstarch, plus 1 tablespoon
- ¼ cup soy sauce
- 2 tablespoons packed light brown sugar
- 2 tablespoons pineapple juice
- 1 tablespoon molasses
- ½ teaspoon ground ginger
- 1 tablespoon water
- 2 teaspoons sesame seeds

1. Line the air fryer basket with parchment and spray lightly with oil. 2. Place the chicken and ½ cup of cornstarch in a zip-top plastic bag, seal, and shake well until evenly coated. 3. Place the chicken in an even layer in the prepared basket and spray liberally with oil. You may need to work in batches, depending on the size of your fryer. 4. Air fry at 390ºF (199ºC) for 9 minutes, flip, spray with more oil, and cook for another 8 to 9 minutes, or until the internal temperature reaches 165ºF (74ºC). 5. In a small saucepan, combine the soy sauce, brown sugar, pineapple juice, molasses, and ginger over medium heat and cook, stirring frequently, until the brown sugar has dissolved. 6. In a small bowl, mix together the water and remaining 1 tablespoon of cornstarch. Pour it into the soy sauce mixture. 7. Bring the mixture to a boil, stirring frequently, until the sauce thickens. Remove from the heat. 8. Transfer the chicken to a large bowl, add the sauce, and toss until evenly coated. Sprinkle with the sesame seeds and serve.

Hawaiian Huli Huli Chicken

Prep time: 30 minutes | Cook time: 15 minutes | Serves 4

- 4 boneless, skinless chicken thighs (about 1½ pounds / 680 g)
- 1 (8 ounces / 227 g) can pineapple chunks in juice, drained, ¼ cup juice reserved
- ¼ cup soy sauce
- ¼ cup sugar
- 2 tablespoons ketchup
- 1 tablespoon minced fresh ginger
- 1 tablespoon minced garlic
- ¼ cup chopped scallions

1. Use a fork to pierce the chicken all over to allow the marinade to penetrate better. Place the chicken in a large bowl or large resealable plastic bag. 2. Set the drained pineapple chunks aside. In a small microwave-safe bowl, combine the pineapple juice, soy sauce, sugar, ketchup, ginger, and garlic. Pour half the sauce over the chicken; toss to coat. Reserve the remaining sauce. Marinate the chicken at room temperature for 30 minutes, or cover and refrigerate for up to 24 hours. 3. Place the chicken in the air fryer basket. (Discard marinade.) Set the air fryer to 350ºF (177ºC) for 15 minutes, turning halfway through the cooking time. 4. Meanwhile, microwave the reserved sauce on high for 45 to 60 seconds, stirring every 15 seconds, until the sauce has the consistency of a thick glaze. 5. At the end of the cooking time, use a meat thermometer to ensure the chicken has reached an internal temperature of 165ºF (74ºC). 6. Transfer the chicken to a serving platter. Pour the sauce over the chicken. Garnish with the pineapple chunks and scallions.

Tortilla Crusted Chicken Breast

Prep time: 10 minutes | Cook time: 12 minutes | Serves 2

- ⅓ cup flour
- 1 teaspoon salt
- 1½ teaspoons chili powder
- 1 teaspoon ground cumin
- Freshly ground black pepper, to taste
- 1 egg, beaten
- ¾ cup coarsely crushed yellow corn tortilla chips
- 2 (3 to 4 ounces / 85 to 113 g) boneless chicken breasts
- Vegetable oil
- ½ cup salsa
- ½ cup crumbled queso fresco
- Fresh cilantro leaves
- Sour cream or guacamole (optional)

1. Set up a dredging station with three shallow dishes. Combine the flour, salt, chili powder, cumin and black pepper in the first shallow dish. Beat the egg in the second shallow dish. Place the crushed tortilla chips in the third shallow dish. 2. Dredge the chicken in the spiced flour, covering all sides of the breast. Then dip the chicken into the egg, coating the chicken completely. Finally, place the chicken into the tortilla chips and press the chips onto the chicken to make sure they adhere to all sides of the breast. Spray the coated chicken breasts on both sides with vegetable oil. 3. Preheat the air fryer to 380ºF (193ºC). 4. Air fry the chicken for 6 minutes. Then turn the chicken breasts over and air fry for another 6 minutes. (Increase the cooking time if you are using chicken breasts larger than 3 to 4 ounces / 85 to 113 g.) 5. When the chicken has finished cooking, serve each breast with a little salsa, the crumbled queso fresco and cilantro as the finishing touch. Serve some sour cream and/or guacamole at the table, if desired.

Coconut Chicken Meatballs

Prep time: 10 minutes | Cook time: 14 minutes | Serves 4

- 1 pound (454 g) ground chicken
- 2 scallions, finely chopped
- 1 cup chopped fresh cilantro leaves
- ¼ cup unsweetened shredded coconut
- 1 tablespoon hoisin sauce
- 1 tablespoon soy sauce
- 2 teaspoons Sriracha or other hot sauce
- 1 teaspoon toasted sesame oil
- ½ teaspoon kosher salt
- 1 teaspoon black pepper

1. In a large bowl, gently mix the chicken, scallions, cilantro, coconut, hoisin, soy sauce, Sriracha, sesame oil, salt, and pepper until thoroughly combined (the mixture will be wet and sticky). 2. Place a sheet of parchment paper in the air fryer basket. Using a small scoop or teaspoon, drop rounds of the mixture in a single layer onto the parchment paper. 3. Set the air fryer to 350ºF (177ºC) for 10 minutes, turning the meatballs halfway through the cooking time. Raise the air fryer temperature to 400ºF (204ºC) and cook for 4 minutes more to brown the outsides of the meatballs. Use a meat thermometer to ensure the meatballs have reached an internal temperature of 165ºF (74ºC). 4. Transfer the meatballs to a serving platter. Repeat with any remaining chicken mixture.

Cornish Hens with Honey-Lime Glaze

Prep time: 15 minutes | Cook time: 25 to 30 minutes | Serves 2 to 3

- ◀ 1 Cornish game hen (1½ to 2 pounds / 680 to 907 g)
- ◀ 1 tablespoon honey
- ◀ 1 tablespoon lime juice
- ◀ 1 teaspoon poultry seasoning
- ◀ Salt and pepper, to taste
- ◀ Cooking spray

1. To split the hen into halves, cut through breast bone and down one side of the backbone. 2. Mix the honey, lime juice, and poultry seasoning together and brush or rub onto all sides of the hen. Season to taste with salt and pepper. 3. Spray the air fryer basket with cooking spray and place hen halves in the basket, skin-side down. 4. Air fry at 330ºF (166ºC) for 25 to 30 minutes. Hen will be done when juices run clear when pierced at leg joint with a fork. Let hen rest for 5 to 10 minutes before cutting.

Teriyaki Chicken Legs

Prep time: 12 minutes | Cook time: 18 to 20 minutes | Serves 2

- ◀ 4 tablespoons teriyaki sauce
- ◀ 1 tablespoon orange juice
- ◀ 1 teaspoon smoked paprika
- ◀ 4 chicken legs
- ◀ Cooking spray

1. Mix together the teriyaki sauce, orange juice, and smoked paprika. Brush on all sides of chicken legs. 2. Spray the air fryer basket with nonstick cooking spray and place chicken in basket. 3. Air fry at 360ºF (182ºC) for 6 minutes. Turn and baste with sauce. Cook for 6 more minutes, turn and baste. Cook for 6 to 8 minutes more, until juices run clear when chicken is pierced with a fork.

African Merguez Meatballs

Prep time: 30 minutes | Cook time: 10 minutes | Serves 4

- ◀ 1 pound (454 g) ground chicken
- ◀ 2 garlic cloves, finely minced
- ◀ 1 tablespoon sweet Hungarian paprika
- ◀ 1 teaspoon kosher salt
- ◀ 1 teaspoon sugar
- ◀ 1 teaspoon ground cumin
- ◀ ½ teaspoon black pepper
- ◀ ½ teaspoon ground fennel
- ◀ ½ teaspoon ground coriander
- ◀ ½ teaspoon cayenne pepper
- ◀ ¼ teaspoon ground allspice

1. In a large bowl, gently mix the chicken, garlic, paprika, salt, sugar, cumin, black pepper, fennel, coriander, cayenne, and allspice until all the ingredients are incorporated. Let stand for 30 minutes at room temperature, or cover and refrigerate for up to 24 hours. 2.

Form the mixture into 16 meatballs. Arrange them in a single layer in the air fryer basket. Set the air fryer to 400ºF (204ºC) for 10 minutes, turning the meatballs halfway through the cooking time. Use a meat thermometer to ensure the meatballs have reached an internal temperature of 165ºF (74ºC).

Turkish Chicken Kebabs

Prep time: 30 minutes | Cook time: 15 minutes | Serves 4

- ◀ ¼ cup plain Greek yogurt
- ◀ 1 tablespoon minced garlic
- ◀ 1 tablespoon tomato paste
- ◀ 1 tablespoon fresh lemon juice
- ◀ 1 tablespoon vegetable oil
- ◀ 1 teaspoon kosher salt
- ◀ 1 teaspoon ground cumin
- ◀ 1 teaspoon sweet Hungarian paprika
- ◀ ½ teaspoon ground cinnamon
- ◀ ½ teaspoon black pepper
- ◀ ½ teaspoon cayenne pepper
- ◀ 1 pound (454 g) boneless, skinless chicken thighs, quartered crosswise

1. In a large bowl, combine the yogurt, garlic, tomato paste, lemon juice, vegetable oil, salt, cumin, paprika, cinnamon, black pepper, and cayenne. Stir until the spices are blended into the yogurt. 2. Add the chicken to the bowl and toss until well coated. Marinate at room temperature for 30 minutes, or cover and refrigerate for up to 24 hours. 3. Arrange the chicken in a single layer in the air fryer basket. Set the air fryer to 375ºF (191ºC) for 10 minutes. Turn the chicken and cook for 5 minutes more. Use a meat thermometer to ensure the chicken has reached an internal temperature of 165ºF (74ºC).

Apricot glazed Chicken Drumsticks

Prep time: 15 minutes | Cook time: 30 minutes | Makes 6 drumsticks

For the Glaze:
- ◀ ½ cup apricot preserves
- ◀ ½ teaspoon tamari
- ◀ ¼ teaspoon chili powder
- ◀ 2 teaspoons Dijon mustard

For the Chicken:
- ◀ 6 chicken drumsticks
- ◀ ½ teaspoon seasoning salt
- ◀ 1 teaspoon salt
- ◀ ½ teaspoon ground black pepper
- ◀ Cooking spray

Make the glaze: 1. Combine the ingredients for the glaze in a saucepan, then heat over low heat for 10 minutes or until thickened. 2. Turn off the heat and sit until ready to use. Make the Chicken: 1. Preheat the air fryer to 370ºF (188ºC). Spritz the air fryer basket with cooking spray. 2. Combine the seasoning salt, salt, and pepper in a small bowl. Stir to mix well. 3. Place the chicken drumsticks in the preheated air fryer. Spritz with cooking spray and sprinkle with the salt mixture on both sides. 4. Air fry for 20 minutes or until well browned. Flip the chicken halfway through. 5. Baste the chicken with the glaze and air fryer for 2 more minutes or until the chicken tenderloin is glossy. 6. Serve immediately.

Ethiopian Chicken with Cauliflower

Prep time: 15 minutes | Cook time: 28 minutes | Serves 6

- 2 handful fresh Italian parsley, roughly chopped
- ½ cup fresh chopped chives
- 2 sprigs thyme
- 6 chicken drumsticks
- 1½ small-sized head cauliflower, broken into large-sized florets
- 2 teaspoons mustard powder
- ⅓ teaspoon porcini powder
- 1½teaspoons berbere spice
- ⅓ teaspoon sweet paprika
- ½ teaspoon shallot powder
- 1teaspoon granulated garlic
- 1 teaspoon freshly cracked pink peppercorns
- ½ teaspoon sea salt

1. Simply combine all items for the berbere spice rub mix. After that, coat the chicken drumsticks with this rub mix on all sides. Transfer them to the baking dish. 2. Now, lower the cauliflower onto the chicken drumsticks. Add thyme, chives and Italian parsley and spritz everything with a pan spray. Transfer the baking dish to the preheated air fryer. 3. Next step, set the timer for 28 minutes; roast at 355°F (179°C), turning occasionally. Bon appétit!

Peruvian Chicken with Green Herb Sauce

Prep time: 30 minutes | Cook time: 15 minutes | Serves 4

Chicken:
- 4 boneless, skinless chicken thighs (about 1½ pounds / 680 g)
- 2 teaspoons grated lemon zest
- 2 tablespoons fresh lemon juice
- 1 tablespoon extra-virgin

Sauce:
- 1 cup fresh cilantro leaves
- 1 jalapeño, seeded and coarsely chopped
- 1 garlic clove, minced
- 1 tablespoon extra-virgin

- olive oil
- 1 serrano chile, seeded and minced
- 1 teaspoon ground cumin
- ½ teaspoon dried oregano, crushed
- ½ teaspoon kosher salt

- olive oil
- 2½ teaspoons fresh lime juice
- ¼ teaspoon kosher salt
- ⅓ cup mayonnaise

1. For the chicken: Use a fork to pierce the chicken all over to allow the marinade to penetrate better. In a small bowl, combine the lemon zest, lemon juice, olive oil, serrano, cumin, oregano, and salt. Place the chicken in a large bowl or large resealable plastic bag. Pour the marinade over the chicken. Toss to coat. Marinate at room temperature for 30 minutes, or cover and refrigerate for up to 24 hours. 2. Place the chicken in the air fryer basket. (Discard remaining marinade.) Set the air fryer to 350°F (177°C) for 15 minutes, turning halfway through the cooking time. 3. Meanwhile, for the sauce: Combine the cilantro, jalapeño, garlic, olive oil, lime juice, and salt in a blender. Blend until combined. Add the mayonnaise and blend until puréed. Transfer to a small bowl. Cover and chill until ready to serve. 4. At the end of the cooking time, use a meat thermometer to ensure the chicken has reached an internal temperature of 165°F (74°C). Serve the chicken with the sauce.

Curried Orange Honey Chicken

Prep time: 10 minutes | Cook time: 16 to 19 minutes | Serves 4

- ¾ pound (340 g) boneless, skinless chicken thighs, cut into 1-inch pieces
- 1 yellow bell pepper, cut into 1½-inch pieces
- 1 small red onion, sliced
- Olive oil for misting
- ¼ cup chicken stock
- 2 tablespoons honey
- ¼ cup orange juice
- 1 tablespoon cornstarch
- 2 to 3 teaspoons curry powder

1. Preheat the air fryer to 370°F (188°C). 2. Put the chicken thighs, pepper, and red onion in the air fryer basket and mist with olive oil. 3. Roast for 12 to 14 minutes or until the chicken is cooked to 165°F (74°C), shaking the basket halfway through cooking time. 4. Remove the chicken and vegetables from the air fryer basket and set aside. 5. In a metal bowl, combine the stock, honey, orange juice, cornstarch, and curry powder, and mix well. Add the chicken and vegetables, stir, and put the bowl in the basket. 6. Return the basket to the air fryer and roast for 2 minutes. Remove and stir, then roast for 2 to 3 minutes or until the sauce is thickened and bubbly. 7. Serve warm.

Chicken Parmesan

Prep time: 15 minutes | Cook time: 10 minutes | Serves 4

- Oil, for spraying
- 2 (8 ounces / 227 g) boneless, skinless chicken breasts
- 1 cup Italian-style bread crumbs
- ¼ cup grated Parmesan cheese, plus ½ cup shredded
- 4 tablespoons unsalted butter, melted
- ½ cup marinara sauce

1. Preheat the air fryer to 360°F (182°C). Line the air fryer basket with parchment and spray lightly with oil. 2. Cut each chicken breast in half through its thickness to make 4 thin cutlets. Using a meat tenderizer, pound each cutlet until it is about ¾ inch thick. 3. On a plate, mix together the bread crumbs and grated Parmesan cheese. 4. Lightly brush the chicken with the melted butter, then dip into the bread crumb mixture. 5. Place the chicken in the prepared basket and spray lightly with oil. You may need to work in batches, depending on the size of your air fryer. 6. Cook for 6 minutes. Top the chicken with the marinara and shredded Parmesan cheese, dividing evenly. Cook for another 3 to 4 minutes, or until golden brown, crispy, and the internal temperature reaches 165°F (74°C).

Chapter 6 Fish and Seafood

Tandoori Shrimp

Prep time: 25 minutes | Cook time: 6 minutes | Serves 4

- 1 pound (454 g) jumbo raw shrimp (21 to 25 count), peeled and deveined
- 1 tablespoon minced fresh ginger
- 3 cloves garlic, minced
- ¼ cup chopped fresh cilantro or parsley, plus more for garnish
- 1 teaspoon ground turmeric
- 1 teaspoon garam masala
- 1 teaspoon smoked paprika
- 1 teaspoon kosher salt
- ½ to 1 teaspoon cayenne pepper
- 2 tablespoons olive oil (for Paleo) or melted ghee
- 2 teaspoons fresh lemon juice

1. In a large bowl, combine the shrimp, ginger, garlic, cilantro, turmeric, garam masala, paprika, salt, and cayenne. Toss well to coat. Add the oil or ghee and toss again. Marinate at room temperature for 15 minutes, or cover and refrigerate for up to 8 hours. 2. Place the shrimp in a single layer in the air fryer basket. Set the air fryer to 325ºF (163ºC) for 6 minutes. Transfer the shrimp to a serving platter. Cover and let the shrimp finish cooking in the residual heat, about 5 minutes. 3. Sprinkle the shrimp with the lemon juice and toss to coat. Garnish with additional cilantro and serve.

New Orleans-Style Crab Cakes

Prep time: 10 minutes | Cook time: 8 to 10 minutes | Serves 4

- 1¼ cups bread crumbs
- 2 teaspoons Creole Seasoning
- 1 teaspoon dry mustard
- 1 teaspoon salt
- 1 teaspoon freshly ground black pepper
- 1½ cups crab meat
- 2 large eggs, beaten
- 1 teaspoon butter, melted
- ⅓ cup minced onion
- Cooking spray
- Pecan Tartar Sauce, for serving

1. Preheat the air fryer to 350ºF (177ºC). Line the air fryer basket with parchment paper. 2. In a medium bowl, whisk the bread crumbs, Creole Seasoning, dry mustard, salt, and pepper until blended. Add the crab meat, eggs, butter, and onion. Stir until blended. Shape the crab mixture into 8 patties. 3. Place the crab cakes on the parchment and spritz with oil. 4. Air fry for 4 minutes. Flip the cakes, spritz them with oil, and air fry for 4 to 6 minutes more until the outsides are firm and a fork inserted into the center comes out clean. Serve with the Pecan Tartar Sauce.

Baked Grouper with Tomatoes and Garlic

Prep time: 5 minutes | Cook time: 12 minutes | Serves 4

- 4 grouper fillets
- ½ teaspoon salt
- 3 garlic cloves, minced
- 1 tomato, sliced
- ¼ cup sliced Kalamata
- olives
- ¼ cup fresh dill, roughly chopped
- Juice of 1 lemon
- ¼ cup olive oil

1. Preheat the air fryer to 380ºF(193ºC). 2. Season the grouper fillets on all sides with salt, then place into the air fryer basket and top with the minced garlic, tomato slices, olives, and fresh dill. 3. Drizzle the lemon juice and olive oil over the top of the grouper, then bake for 10 to 12 minutes, or until the internal temperature reaches 145ºF(63ºC).

Calamari with Hot Sauce

Prep time: 10 minutes | Cook time: 6 minutes | Serves 2

- 10 ounces (283 g) calamari, trimmed
- 2 tablespoons keto hot sauce
- 1 tablespoon avocado oil

1. Slice the calamari and sprinkle with avocado oil. 2. Put the calamari in the air fryer and cook at 400ºF (204ºC) for 3 minutes per side. 3. Then transfer the calamari in the serving plate and sprinkle with hot sauce.

Tuna Cakes

Prep time: 10 minutes | Cook time: 10 minutes | Serves 4

- 4 (3 ounces / 85 g) pouches tuna, drained
- 1 large egg, whisked
- 2 tablespoons peeled and
- chopped white onion
- ½ teaspoon Old Bay seasoning

1. In a large bowl, mix all ingredients together and form into four patties. 2. Place patties into ungreased air fryer basket. Adjust the temperature to 400ºF (204ºC) and air fry for 10 minutes. Patties will be browned and crispy when done. Let cool 5 minutes before serving.

Jalea

Prep time: 20 minutes | Cook time: 10 minutes | Serves 4

Salsa Criolla:
- ½ red onion, thinly sliced
- 2 tomatoes, diced
- 1 serrano or jalapeño pepper, deseeded and diced

Fried Seafood:
- 1 pound (454 g) firm, white-fleshed fish such as cod (add an extra ½ pound /227 g fish if not using shrimp)
- 20 large or jumbo shrimp, shelled and deveined
- ¼ cup all-purpose flour
- ¼ cup cornstarch
- 1 teaspoon garlic powder

- 1 clove garlic, minced
- ¼ cup chopped fresh cilantro
- Pinch of kosher salt
- 3 limes

- 1 teaspoon kosher salt
- ¼ teaspoon cayenne pepper
- 2 cups panko bread crumbs
- 2 eggs, beaten with 2 tablespoons water
- Vegetable oil, for spraying
- Mayonnaise or tartar sauce, for serving (optional)

1. To make the Salsa Criolla, combine the red onion, tomatoes, pepper, garlic, cilantro, and salt in a medium bowl. Add the juice and zest of 2 of the limes. Refrigerate the salad while you make the fish. 2. To make the seafood, cut the fish fillets into strips approximately 2 inches long and 1 inch wide. Place the flour, cornstarch, garlic powder, salt, and cayenne pepper on a plate and whisk to combine. Place the panko on a separate plate. Dredge the fish strips in the seasoned flour mixture, shaking off any excess. Dip the strips in the egg mixture, coating them completely, then dredge in the panko, shaking off any excess. Place the fish strips on a plate or rack. Repeat with the shrimp, if using. 3. Spray the air fryer basket with oil, and preheat the air fryer to 400ºF (204ºC). Working in 2 or 3 batches, arrange the fish and shrimp in a single layer in the basket, taking care not to crowd the basket. Spray with oil. Air fry for 5 minutes, then flip and air fry for another 4 to 5 minutes until the outside is brown and crisp and the inside of the fish is opaque and flakes easily with a fork. Repeat with the remaining seafood. 4. Place the fried seafood on a platter. Use a slotted spoon to remove the salsa criolla from the bowl, leaving behind any liquid that has accumulated. Place the salsa criolla on top of the fried seafood. Serve immediately with the remaining lime, cut into wedges, and mayonnaise or tartar sauce as desired.

Cripsy Shrimp with Cilantro

Prep time: 40 minutes | Cook time: 10 minutes | Serves 4

- 1 pound (454 g) raw large shrimp, peeled and deveined with tails on or off
- ½ cup chopped fresh cilantro
- Juice of 1 lime
- ½ cup all-purpose flour

- 1 egg
- ¾ cup bread crumbs
- Salt and freshly ground black pepper, to taste
- Cooking oil spray
- 1 cup cocktail sauce

1. Place the shrimp in a resealable plastic bag and add the cilantro and lime juice. Seal the bag. Shake it to combine. Marinate the shrimp in the refrigerator for 30 minutes. 2. Place the flour in a small bowl. 3. In another small bowl, beat the egg. 4. Place the bread crumbs in a third small bowl, season with salt and pepper,

and stir to combine. 5. Insert the crisper plate into the basket and the basket into the unit. Preheat the unit by selecting AIR FRY, setting the temperature to 400ºF (204ºC), and setting the time to 3 minutes. Select START/STOP to begin. 6. Remove the shrimp from the plastic bag. Dip each in the flour, the egg, and the bread crumbs to coat. Gently press the crumbs onto the shrimp. 7. Once the unit is preheated, spray the crisper plate and the basket with cooking oil. Place the shrimp in the basket. It is okay to stack them. Spray the shrimp with the cooking oil. 8. Select AIR FRY, set the temperature to 400ºF (204ºC), and set the time to 8 minutes. Select START/STOP to begin. 9. After 4 minutes, remove the basket and flip the shrimp one at a time. Reinsert the basket to resume cooking. 10. When the cooking is complete, the shrimp should be crisp. Let cool for 5 minutes. Serve with cocktail sauce.

Golden Shrimp

Prep time: 20 minutes | Cook time: 7 minutes | Serves 4

- 2 egg whites
- ½ cup coconut flour
- 1 cup Parmigiano-Reggiano, grated
- ½ teaspoon celery seeds
- ½ teaspoon porcini powder
- ½ teaspoon onion powder

- 1 teaspoon garlic powder
- ½ teaspoon dried rosemary
- ½ teaspoon sea salt
- ½ teaspoon ground black pepper
- 1½ pounds (680 g) shrimp, deveined

1. Whisk the egg with coconut flour and Parmigiano-Reggiano. Add in seasonings and mix to combine well. 2. Dip your shrimp in the batter. Roll until they are covered on all sides. 3. Cook in the preheated air fryer at 390ºF (199ºC) for 5 to 7 minutes or until golden brown. Work in batches. Serve with lemon wedges if desired.

Cajun and Lemon Pepper Cod

Prep time: 5 minutes | Cook time: 12 minutes | Makes 2 cod fillets

- 1 tablespoon Cajun seasoning
- 1 teaspoon salt
- ½ teaspoon lemon pepper
- ½ teaspoon freshly ground black pepper
- 2 (8 ounces / 227 g) cod

fillets, cut to fit into the air fryer basket
- Cooking spray
- 2 tablespoons unsalted butter, melted
- 1 lemon, cut into 4 wedges

1. Preheat the air fryer to 360ºF (182ºC). Spritz the air fryer basket with cooking spray. 2. Thoroughly combine the Cajun seasoning, salt, lemon pepper, and black pepper in a small bowl. Rub this mixture all over the cod fillets until completely coated. 3. Put the fillets in the air fryer basket and brush the melted butter over both sides of each fillet. 4. Bake in the preheated air fryer for 12 minutes, flipping the fillets halfway through, or until the fish flakes easily with a fork. 5. Remove the fillets from the basket and serve with fresh lemon wedges.

Chili Lime Shrimp

Prep time: 5 minutes | Cook time: 5 minutes | Serves 4

◁ 1 pound (454 g) medium shrimp, peeled and deveined
◁ 1 tablespoon salted butter, melted
◁ 2 teaspoons chili powder
◁ ¼ teaspoon garlic powder
◁ ¼ teaspoon salt
◁ ¼ teaspoon ground black pepper
◁ ½ small lime, zested and juiced, divided

1. In a medium bowl, toss shrimp with butter, then sprinkle with chili powder, garlic powder, salt, pepper, and lime zest. 2. Place shrimp into ungreased air fryer basket. Adjust the temperature to 400°F (204°C) and air fry for 5 minutes. Shrimp will be firm and form a "C" shape when done. 3. Transfer shrimp to a large serving dish and drizzle with lime juice. Serve warm.

Air Fryer Fish Fry

Prep time: 5 minutes | Cook time: 15 minutes | Serves 4

◁ 2 cups low-fat buttermilk
◁ ½ teaspoon garlic powder
◁ ½ teaspoon onion powder
◁ 4 (4 ounces) flounder fillets
◁ ½ cup plain yellow cornmeal
◁ ½ cup chickpea flour
◁ ¼ teaspoon cayenne pepper
◁ Freshly ground black pepper

1. In a large bowl, combine the buttermilk, garlic powder, and onion powder. 2. Add the flounder, turning until well coated, and set aside to marinate for 20 minutes. 3. In a shallow bowl, stir the cornmeal, chickpea flour, cayenne, and pepper together. 4. Dredge the fillets in the meal mixture, turning until well coated. Place in the basket of an air fryer. 5. Set the air fryer to 380°F, close, and cook for 12 minutes.

One-Pot Shrimp Fried Rice

Prep time: 10 minutes | Cook time: 25 minutes | Serves 4

Shrimp:
◁ 1 teaspoon cornstarch
◁ ½ teaspoon kosher salt
◁ ¼ teaspoon black pepper
Rice:
◁ 2 cups cold cooked rice
◁ 1 cup frozen peas and carrots, thawed
◁ ¼ cup chopped green onions (white and green parts)
Eggs:
◁ 2 large eggs, beaten
◁ ¼ teaspoon kosher salt
◁ 1 pound (454 g) jumbo raw shrimp (21 to 25 count), peeled and deveined
◁ 3 tablespoons toasted sesame oil
◁ 1 tablespoon soy sauce
◁ ½ teaspoon kosher salt
◁ 1 teaspoon black pepper
◁ ¼ teaspoon black pepper

1. For the shrimp: In a small bowl, whisk together the cornstarch, salt, and pepper until well combined. Place the shrimp in a large bowl and sprinkle the seasoned cornstarch over. Toss until well coated; set aside. 2. For the rice: In a baking pan, combine the rice, peas and carrots, green onions, sesame oil, soy sauce, salt, and pepper. Toss and stir until well combined. 3. Place the pan in the air fryer basket. Set the air fryer to 350°F (177°C) for 15 minutes, stirring and tossing the rice halfway through the cooking time. 4. Place the shrimp on top of the rice. Set the air fryer to 350°F (177°C) for 5 minutes. 5. Meanwhile, for the eggs: In a medium bowl, beat the eggs with the salt and pepper. 6. Open the air fryer and pour the eggs over the shrimp and rice mixture. Set the air fryer to 350°F (177°C) for 5 minutes. 7. Remove the pan from the air fryer. Stir to break up the rice and mix in the eggs and shrimp.

Fried Catfish with Dijon Sauce

Prep time: 20 minutes | Cook time: 7 minutes | Serves 4

◁ 4 tablespoons butter, melted
◁ 2 teaspoons Worcestershire sauce, divided
◁ 1 teaspoon lemon pepper
◁ 1 cup panko bread crumbs
◁ 4 (4 ounces / 113 g) catfish fillets
◁ Cooking spray
◁ ½ cup sour cream
◁ 1 tablespoon Dijon mustard

1. In a shallow bowl, stir together the melted butter, 1 teaspoon of Worcestershire sauce, and the lemon pepper. Place the bread crumbs in another shallow bowl. 2. One at a time, dip both sides of the fillets in the butter mixture, then the bread crumbs, coating thoroughly. 3. Preheat the air fryer to 300°F (149°C). Line the air fryer basket with parchment paper. 4. Place the coated fish on the parchment and spritz with oil. 5. Bake for 4 minutes. Flip the fish, spritz it with oil, and bake for 3 to 6 minutes more, depending on the thickness of the fillets, until the fish flakes easily with a fork. 6. In a small bowl, stir together the sour cream, Dijon, and remaining 1 teaspoon of Worcestershire sauce. This sauce can be made 1 day in advance and refrigerated before serving. Serve with the fried fish.

Salmon on Bed of Fennel and Carrot

Prep time: 15 minutes | Cook time: 13 to 14 minutes | Serves 2

◁ 1 fennel bulb, thinly sliced
◁ 1 large carrot, peeled and sliced
◁ 1 small onion, thinly sliced
◁ ¼ cup low-fat sour cream
◁ ¼ teaspoon coarsely ground pepper
◁ 2 (5 ounces / 142 g) salmon fillets

1. Combine the fennel, carrot, and onion in a bowl and toss. 2. Put the vegetable mixture into a baking pan. Roast in the air fryer at 400°F (204°C) for 4 minutes or until the vegetables are crisp-tender. 3. Remove the pan from the air fryer. Stir in the sour cream and sprinkle the vegetables with the pepper. 4. Top with the salmon fillets. 5. Return the pan to the air fryer. Roast for another 9 to 10 minutes or until the salmon just barely flakes when tested with a fork.

Sole and Asparagus Bundles

Prep time: 10 minutes | Cook time: 14 minutes | Serves 2

- ◄ 8 ounces (227 g) asparagus, trimmed
- ◄ 1 teaspoon extra-virgin olive oil, divided
- ◄ Salt and pepper, to taste
- ◄ 4 (3 ounces / 85 g) skinless sole or flounder fillets, ⅛ to ¼ inch thick
- ◄ 4 tablespoons unsalted butter, softened
- ◄ 1 small shallot, minced
- ◄ 1 tablespoon chopped fresh tarragon
- ◄ ¼ teaspoon lemon zest plus ½ teaspoon juice
- ◄ Vegetable oil spray

1. Preheat the air fryer to 300ºF (149ºC). 2. Toss asparagus with ½ teaspoon oil, pinch salt, and pinch pepper in a bowl. Cover and microwave until bright green and just tender, about 3 minutes, tossing halfway through microwaving. Uncover and set aside to cool slightly. 3. Make foil sling for air fryer basket by folding 1 long sheet of aluminum foil so it is 4 inches wide. Lay sheet of foil widthwise across basket, pressing foil into and up sides of basket. Fold excess foil as needed so that edges of foil are flush with top of basket. Lightly spray foil and basket with vegetable oil spray. 4. Pat sole dry with paper towels and season with salt and pepper. Arrange fillets skinned side up on cutting board, with thicker ends closest to you. Arrange asparagus evenly across base of each fillet, then tightly roll fillets away from you around asparagus to form tidy bundles. 5. Rub bundles evenly with remaining ½ teaspoon oil and arrange seam side down on sling in prepared basket. Bake until asparagus is tender and sole flakes apart when gently prodded with a paring knife, 14 to 18 minutes, using a sling to rotate bundles halfway through cooking. 6. Combine butter, shallot, tarragon, and lemon zest and juice in a bowl. Using sling, carefully remove sole bundles from air fryer and transfer to individual plates. Top evenly with butter mixture and serve.

Sole and Cauliflower Fritters

Prep time: 5 minutes | Cook time: 24 minutes | Serves 2

- ◄ ½ pound (227 g) sole fillets
- ◄ ½ pound (227 g) mashed cauliflower
- ◄ ½ cup red onion, chopped
- ◄ 1 bell pepper, finely chopped
- ◄ 1 egg, beaten
- ◄ 2 garlic cloves, minced
- ◄ 2 tablespoons fresh parsley, chopped
- ◄ 1 tablespoon olive oil
- ◄ 1 tablespoon coconut aminos
- ◄ ½ teaspoon scotch bonnet pepper, minced
- ◄ ½ teaspoon paprika
- ◄ Salt and white pepper, to taste
- ◄ Cooking spray

1. Preheat the air fryer to 395ºF (202ºC). Spray the air fryer basket with cooking spray. 2. Place the sole fillets in the basket and air fry for 10 minutes, flipping them halfway through. 3. When the fillets are done, transfer them to a large bowl. Mash the fillets into flakes. Add the remaining ingredients and stir to combine. 4. Make the fritters: Scoop out 2 tablespoons of the fish mixture and shape into a patty about ½ inch thick with your hands. Repeat with the remaining fish mixture. 5. Arrange the patties in the air fryer basket and bake for 14 minutes, flipping the patties halfway through, or until they are golden brown and cooked through. 6. Cool for 5 minutes and serve on a plate.

Cod with Creamy Mustard Sauce

Prep time: 10 minutes | Cook time: 10 minutes | Serves 4

Fish:
- ◄ Oil, for spraying
- ◄ 1 pound (454 g) cod fillets
- ◄ 2 tablespoons olive oil
- ◄ 1 tablespoon lemon juice
- ◄ 1 teaspoon salt
- ◄ ½ teaspoon freshly ground black pepper

Mustard Sauce:
- ◄ ½ cup heavy cream
- ◄ 3 tablespoons Dijon mustard
- ◄ 1 tablespoon unsalted butter
- ◄ 1 teaspoon salt

Make the Fish 1. Line the air fryer basket with parchment and spray lightly with oil. 2. Rub the cod with the olive oil and lemon juice. Season with the salt and black pepper. 3. Place the cod in the prepared basket. You may need to work in batches, depending on the size of your air fryer. 4. Roast at 350ºF (177ºC) for 5 minutes. Increase the temperature to 400ºF (204ºC) and cook for another 5 minutes, until flaky and the internal temperature reaches 145ºF (63ºC). Make the Mustard Sauce 5. In a small saucepan, mix together the heavy cream, mustard, butter, and salt and bring to a simmer over low heat. Cook for 3 to 4 minutes, or until the sauce starts to thicken. 6. Transfer the cod to a serving plate and drizzle with the mustard sauce. Serve immediately.

Pesto Fish Pie

Prep time: 15 minutes | Cook time: 15 minutes | Serves 4

- ◄ 2 tablespoons prepared pesto
- ◄ ¼ cup half-and-half
- ◄ ¼ cup grated Parmesan cheese
- ◄ 1 teaspoon kosher salt
- ◄ 1 teaspoon black pepper
- ◄ Vegetable oil spray
- ◄ 1 (10 ounces / 283 g) package frozen chopped spinach, thawed and
- squeezed dry
- ◄ 1 pound (454 g) firm white fish, cut into 2-inch chunks
- ◄ ½ cup cherry tomatoes, quartered
- ◄ All-purpose flour
- ◄ ½ sheet frozen puff pastry (from a 17.3 ounces / 490 g package), thawed

1. In a small bowl, combine the pesto, half-and-half, Parmesan, salt, and pepper. Stir until well combined; set aside. 2. Spray a baking pan with vegetable oil spray. Arrange the spinach evenly across the bottom of the pan. Top with the fish and tomatoes. Pour the pesto mixture evenly over everything. 3. On a lightly floured surface, roll the puff pastry sheet into a circle. Place the pastry on top of the pan and tuck it in around the edges of the pan. (Or, do what I do and stretch it with your hands and then pat it into place.) 4. Place the pan in the air fryer basket. Set the air fryer to 400ºF (204ºC) for 15 minutes, or until the pastry is well browned. Let stand 5 minutes before serving.

Shrimp Scampi

Prep time: 8 minutes | Cook time: 8 minutes | Serves 4

◄ 4 tablespoons (½ stick) salted butter or ghee
◄ 1 tablespoon fresh lemon juice
◄ 1 tablespoon minced garlic
◄ 2 teaspoons red pepper flakes
◄ 1 pound (454 g) shrimp (21 to 25 count), peeled and deveined
◄ 2 tablespoons chicken broth or dry white wine
◄ 2 tablespoons chopped fresh basil, plus more for sprinkling, or 1 teaspoon dried
◄ 1 tablespoon chopped fresh chives, or 1 teaspoon dried

1. Place a baking pan in the air fryer basket. Set the air fryer to 325ºF (163ºC) for 8 minutes (this will preheat the pan so the butter will melt faster). 2. Carefully remove the pan from the fryer and add the butter, lemon juice, garlic, and red pepper flakes. Place the pan back in the fryer. 3. Cook for 2 minutes, stirring once, until the butter has melted. (Do not skip this step; this is what infuses the butter with garlic flavor, which is what makes it all taste so good.) 4. Carefully remove the pan from the fryer and add the shrimp, broth, basil, and chives. Stir gently until the ingredients are well combined. 5. Return the pan to the air fryer and cook for 5 minutes, stirring once. 6. Thoroughly stir the shrimp mixture and let it rest for 1 minute on a wire rack. (This is so the shrimp cooks in the residual heat rather than getting overcooked and rubbery.) 7. Stir once more, sprinkle with additional chopped fresh basil, and serve.

Crunchy Air Fried Cod Fillets

Prep time: 10 minutes | Cook time: 12 minutes | Serves 2

◄ ⅓ cup panko bread crumbs
◄ 1 teaspoon vegetable oil
◄ 1 small shallot, minced
◄ 1 small garlic clove, minced
◄ ½ teaspoon minced fresh thyme
◄ Salt and pepper, to taste
◄ 1 tablespoon minced fresh parsley
◄ 1 tablespoon mayonnaise
◄ 1 large egg yolk
◄ ¼ teaspoon grated lemon zest, plus lemon wedges for serving
◄ 2 (8 ounces / 227 g) skinless cod fillets, 1¼ inches thick
◄ Vegetable oil spray

1. Preheat the air fryer to 300ºF (149ºC). 2. Make foil sling for air fryer basket by folding 1 long sheet of aluminum foil so it is 4 inches wide. Lay sheet of foil widthwise across basket, pressing foil into and up sides of basket. Fold excess foil as needed so that edges of foil are flush with top of basket. Lightly spray the foil and basket with vegetable oil spray. 3. Toss the panko with the oil in a bowl until evenly coated. Stir in the shallot, garlic, thyme, ¼ teaspoon salt, and ⅛ teaspoon pepper. Microwave, stirring frequently, until the panko is light golden brown, about 2 minutes. Transfer to a shallow dish and let cool slightly; stir in the parsley. Whisk the mayonnaise, egg yolk, lemon zest, and ⅛ teaspoon pepper together in another bowl. 4. Pat the cod dry with paper towels and season with salt and pepper. Arrange the fillets, skinned-side down, on plate and brush tops evenly with mayonnaise mixture. (Tuck thinner tail ends of fillets under themselves as needed to create uniform pieces.) Working with 1 fillet at a time, dredge the coated side in panko mixture, pressing gently to adhere. Arrange the fillets, crumb-side up, on sling in the prepared basket, spaced evenly apart. 5. Bake for 12 to 16 minutes, using a sling to rotate fillets halfway through cooking. Using a sling, carefully remove cod from air fryer. Serve with the lemon wedges.

Shrimp Curry

Prep time: 30 minutes | Cook time: 10 minutes | Serves 4

◄ ¾ cup unsweetened full-fat coconut milk
◄ ¼ cup finely chopped yellow onion
◄ 2 teaspoons garam masala
◄ 1 tablespoon minced fresh ginger
◄ 1 tablespoon minced garlic
◄ 1 teaspoon ground turmeric
◄ 1 teaspoon salt
◄ ¼ to ½ teaspoon cayenne pepper
◄ 1 pound (454 g) raw shrimp (21 to 25 count), peeled and deveined
◄ 2 teaspoons chopped fresh cilantro

1. In a large bowl, stir together the coconut milk, onion, garam masala, ginger, garlic, turmeric, salt and cayenne, until well blended. 2. Add the shrimp and toss until coated with sauce on all sides. Marinate at room temperature for 30 minutes. 3. Transfer the shrimp and marinade to a baking pan. Place the pan in the air fryer basket. Set the air fryer to 375ºF (191ºC) for 10 minutes, stirring halfway through the cooking time. 4. Transfer the shrimp to a serving bowl or platter. Sprinkle with the cilantro and serve.

Browned Shrimp Patties

Prep time: 15 minutes | Cook time: 10 to 12 minutes | Serves 4

◄ ½ pound (227 g) raw shrimp, shelled, deveined, and chopped finely
◄ 2 cups cooked sushi rice
◄ ¼ cup chopped red bell pepper
◄ ¼ cup chopped celery
◄ ¼ cup chopped green onion
◄ 2 teaspoons Worcestershire sauce
◄ ½ teaspoon salt
◄ ½ teaspoon garlic powder
◄ ½ teaspoon Old Bay seasoning
◄ ½ cup plain bread crumbs
◄ Cooking spray

1. Preheat the air fryer to 390ºF (199ºC). 2. Put all the ingredients except the bread crumbs and oil in a large bowl and stir to incorporate. 3. Scoop out the shrimp mixture and shape into 8 equal-sized patties with your hands, no more than ½-inch thick. Roll the patties in the bread crumbs on a plate and spray both sides with cooking spray. 4. Place the patties in the air fryer basket. You may need to work in batches to avoid overcrowding. 5. Air fry for 10 to 12 minutes, flipping the patties halfway through, or until the outside is crispy brown. 6. Divide the patties among four plates and serve warm.

Salmon with Provolone Cheese

Prep time: 5 minutes | Cook time: 15 minutes | Serves 4

◀ 1 pound (454 g) salmon fillet, chopped
◀ 2 ounces (57 g) Provolone, grated
◀ 1 teaspoon avocado oil
◀ ¼ teaspoon ground paprika

1. Sprinkle the salmon fillets with avocado oil and put in the air fryer. 2. Then sprinkle the fish with ground paprika and top with Provolone cheese. 3. Cook the fish at 360ºF (182ºC) for 15 minutes

Lemon-Dill Salmon Burgers

Prep time: 10 minutes | Cook time: 8 minutes | Serves 4

◀ 2 (6 ounces / 170 g) fillets of salmon, finely chopped by hand or in a food processor
◀ 1 cup fine bread crumbs
◀ 1 teaspoon freshly grated lemon zest
◀ 2 tablespoons chopped fresh dill weed
◀ 1 teaspoon salt
◀ Freshly ground black pepper, to taste
◀ 2 eggs, lightly beaten
◀ 4 brioche or hamburger buns
◀ Lettuce, tomato, red onion, avocado, mayonnaise or mustard, for serving

1. Preheat the air fryer to 400ºF (204ºC). 2. Combine all the ingredients in a bowl. Mix together well and divide into four balls. Flatten the balls into patties, making an indentation in the center of each patty with your thumb (this will help the burger stay flat as it cooks) and flattening the sides of the burgers so that they fit nicely into the air fryer basket. 3. Transfer the burgers to the air fryer basket and air fry for 4 minutes. Flip the burgers over and air fry for another 3 to 4 minutes, until nicely browned and firm to the touch. 4. Serve on soft brioche buns with your choice of topping: lettuce, tomato, red onion, avocado, mayonnaise or mustard

Parmesan Lobster Tails

Prep time: 5 minutes | Cook time: 7 minutes | Serves 4

◀ 4 (4 ounces / 113 g) lobster tails
◀ 2 tablespoons salted butter, melted
◀ 1½ teaspoons Cajun seasoning, divided
◀ ¼ teaspoon salt
◀ ¼ teaspoon ground black pepper
◀ ¼ cup grated Parmesan cheese
◀ ½ ounce (14 g) plain pork rinds, finely crushed

1. Cut lobster tails open carefully with a pair of scissors and gently pull meat away from shells, resting meat on top of shells. 2. Brush lobster meat with butter and sprinkle with 1 teaspoon Cajun seasoning, ¼ teaspoon per tail. 3. In a small bowl, mix remaining Cajun seasoning, salt, pepper, Parmesan, and pork rinds. Gently press ¼ mixture onto meat on each lobster tail. 4. Carefully place tails into ungreased air fryer basket. Adjust the temperature to 400ºF (204ºC) and air fry for 7 minutes. Lobster tails will be crispy

and golden on top and have an internal temperature of at least 145ºF (63ºC) when done. Serve warm.

Mediterranean-Style Cod

Prep time: 5 minutes | Cook time: 12 minutes | Serves 4

◀ 4 (6 ounces / 170 g) cod fillets
◀ 3 tablespoons fresh lemon juice
◀ 1 tablespoon olive oil
◀ ¼ teaspoon salt
◀ 6 cherry tomatoes, halved
◀ ¼ cup pitted and sliced kalamata olives

1. Place cod into an ungreased round nonstick baking dish. Pour lemon juice into dish and drizzle cod with olive oil. Sprinkle with salt. Place tomatoes and olives around baking dish in between fillets. 2. Place dish into air fryer basket. Adjust the temperature to 350ºF (177ºC) and bake for 12 minutes, carefully turning cod halfway through cooking. Fillets will be lightly browned, easily flake, and have an internal temperature of at least 145ºF (63ºC) when done. Serve warm.

Balsamic Tilapia

Prep time: 5 minutes | Cook time: 15 minutes | Serves 4

◀ 4 tilapia fillets, boneless
◀ 2 tablespoons balsamic vinegar
◀ 1 teaspoon avocado oil
◀ 1 teaspoon dried basil

1. Sprinkle the tilapia fillets with balsamic vinegar, avocado oil, and dried basil. 2. Then put the fillets in the air fryer basket and cook at 365ºF (185ºC) for 15 minutes.

Almond-Crusted Fish

Prep time: 15 minutes | Cook time: 10 minutes | Serves 4

◀ 4 (4 ounces / 113 g) fish fillets
◀ ¾ cup bread crumbs
◀ ¼ cup sliced almonds, crushed
◀ 2 tablespoons lemon juice
◀ ⅛ teaspoon cayenne
◀ Salt and pepper, to taste
◀ ¾ cup flour
◀ 1 egg, beaten with 1 tablespoon water
◀ Oil for misting or cooking spray

1. Split fish fillets lengthwise down the center to create 8 pieces. 2. Mix bread crumbs and almonds together and set aside. 3. Mix the lemon juice and cayenne together. Brush on all sides of fish. 4. Season fish to taste with salt and pepper. 5. Place the flour on a sheet of wax paper. 6. Roll fillets in flour, dip in egg wash, and roll in the crumb mixture. 7. Mist both sides of fish with oil or cooking spray. 8. Spray the air fryer basket and lay fillets inside. 9. Roast at 390ºF (199ºC) for 5 minutes, turn fish over, and cook for an additional 5 minutes or until fish is done and flakes easily.

Cornmeal-Crusted Trout Fingers

Prep time: 15 minutes | Cook time: 6 minutes | Serves 2

◁ ½ cup yellow cornmeal, medium or finely ground (not coarse)
◁ ⅓ cup all-purpose flour
◁ 1½ teaspoons baking powder
◁ 1 teaspoon kosher salt, plus more as needed
◁ ½ teaspoon freshly ground black pepper, plus more as needed
◁ ⅛ teaspoon cayenne pepper
◁ ¾ pound (340 g) skinless

trout fillets, cut into strips 1 inch wide and 3 inches long
◁ 3 large eggs, lightly beaten
◁ Cooking spray
◁ ½ cup mayonnaise
◁ 2 tablespoons capers, rinsed and finely chopped
◁ 1 tablespoon fresh tarragon
◁ 1 teaspoon fresh lemon juice, plus lemon wedges, for serving

1. Preheat the air fryer to 400ºF (204ºC). 2. In a large bowl, whisk together the cornmeal, flour, baking powder, salt, black pepper, and cayenne. Dip the trout strips in the egg, then toss them in the cornmeal mixture until fully coated. Transfer the trout to a rack set over a baking sheet and liberally spray all over with cooking spray. 3. Transfer half the fish to the air fryer and air fry until the fish is cooked through and golden brown, about 6 minutes. Transfer the fish sticks to a plate and repeat with the remaining fish. 4. Meanwhile, in a bowl, whisk together the mayonnaise, capers, tarragon, and lemon juice. Season the tartar sauce with salt and black pepper. 5. Serve the trout fingers hot along with the tartar sauce and lemon wedges.

Fish Tacos with Jalapeño-Lime Sauce

Prep time: 25 minutes | Cook time: 7 to 10 minutes | Serves 4

Fish Tacos:
◁ 1 pound (454 g) fish fillets
◁ ¼ teaspoon cumin
◁ ¼ teaspoon coriander
◁ ⅛ teaspoon ground red pepper
◁ 1 tablespoon lime zest
Jalapeño-Lime Sauce:
◁ ½ cup sour cream
◁ 1 tablespoon lime juice
◁ ¼ teaspoon grated lime zest
◁ ½ teaspoon minced jalapeño (flesh only)
◁ ¼ teaspoon cumin

◁ ¼ teaspoon smoked paprika
◁ 1 teaspoon oil
◁ Cooking spray
◁ 6 to 8 corn or flour tortillas (6-inch size)

◁ Napa Cabbage Garnish:
◁ 1 cup shredded Napa cabbage
◁ ¼ cup slivered red or green bell pepper
◁ ¼ cup slivered onion

1. Slice the fish fillets into strips approximately ½-inch thick. 2. Put the strips into a sealable plastic bag along with the cumin, coriander, red pepper, lime zest, smoked paprika, and oil. Massage seasonings into the fish until evenly distributed. 3. Spray the air fryer basket with nonstick cooking spray and place seasoned fish

inside. 4. Air fry at 390ºF (199ºC) for approximately 5 minutes. Shake basket to distribute fish. Cook an additional 2 to 5 minutes, until fish flakes easily. 5. While the fish is cooking, prepare the Jalapeño-Lime Sauce by mixing the sour cream, lime juice, lime zest, jalapeño, and cumin together to make a smooth sauce. Set aside. 6. Mix the cabbage, bell pepper, and onion together and set aside. 7. To warm refrigerated tortillas, wrap in damp paper towels and microwave for 30 to 60 seconds. 8. To serve, spoon some of fish into a warm tortilla. Add one or two tablespoons Napa Cabbage Garnish and drizzle with Jalapeño-Lime Sauce.

Crab and Bell Pepper Cakes

Prep time: 5 minutes | Cook time: 10 minutes | Serves 4

◁ 8 ounces (227 g) jumbo lump crabmeat
◁ 1 tablespoon Old Bay seasoning
◁ ⅓ cup bread crumbs
◁ ¼ cup diced red bell pepper
◁ ¼ cup diced green bell

pepper
◁ 1 egg
◁ ¼ cup mayonnaise
◁ Juice of ½ lemon
◁ 1 teaspoon all-purpose flour
◁ Cooking oil spray

1. Sort through the crabmeat, picking out any bits of shell or cartilage. 2. In a large bowl, stir together the Old Bay seasoning, bread crumbs, red and green bell peppers, egg, mayonnaise, and lemon juice. Gently stir in the crabmeat. 3. Insert the crisper plate into the basket and the basket into the unit. Preheat the unit by selecting AIR FRY, setting the temperature to 375ºF (191ºC), and setting the time to 3 minutes. Select START/STOP to begin. 4. Form the mixture into 4 patties. Sprinkle ¼ teaspoon of flour on top of each patty. 5. Once the unit is preheated, spray the crisper plate with cooking oil. Place the crab cakes into the basket and spray them with cooking oil. 6. Select AIR FRY, set the temperature to 375ºF (191ºC), and set the time to 10 minutes. Select START/STOP to begin. 7. When the cooking is complete, the crab cakes will be golden brown and firm.

Tilapia Almondine

Prep time: 10 minutes | Cook time: 10 minutes | Serves 2

◁ ½ cup almond flour or fine dried bread crumbs
◁ 2 tablespoons salted butter or ghee, melted
◁ 1 teaspoon black pepper

◁ ½ teaspoon kosher salt
◁ ¼ cup mayonnaise
◁ 2 tilapia fillets
◁ ½ cup thinly sliced almonds
◁ Vegetable oil spray

1. In a small bowl, mix together the almond flour, butter, pepper and salt. 2. Spread the mayonnaise on both sides of each fish fillet. Dredge the fillets in the almond flour mixture. Spread the sliced almonds on one side of each fillet, pressing lightly to adhere. 3. Spray the air fryer basket with vegetable oil spray. Place the fish fillets in the basket. Set the air fryer to 325ºF (163ºC) for 10 minutes, or until the fish flakes easily with a fork.

Snapper Scampi

- ◄ 4 (6 ounces / 170 g) skinless snapper or arctic char fillets
- ◄ 1 tablespoon olive oil
- ◄ 3 tablespoons lemon juice, divided
- ◄ ½ teaspoon dried basil
- ◄ Pinch salt
- ◄ Freshly ground black pepper, to taste
- ◄ 2 tablespoons butter
- ◄ 2 cloves garlic, minced

1. Rub the fish fillets with olive oil and 1 tablespoon of the lemon juice. Sprinkle with the basil, salt, and pepper, and place in the air fryer basket. 2. Air fry the fish at 380ºF (193ºC) for 7 to 8 minutes or until the fish just flakes when tested with a fork. Remove the fish from the basket and put on a serving plate. Cover to keep warm. 3. In a baking pan, combine the butter, remaining 2 tablespoons lemon juice, and garlic. Bake in the air fryer for 1 to 2 minutes or until the garlic is sizzling. Pour this mixture over the fish and serve

Almond Pesto Salmon

- ◄ ¼ cup pesto
- ◄ ¼ cup sliced almonds, roughly chopped
- ◄ 2 (1½-inch-thick) salmon
- fillets (about 4 ounces / 113 g each)
- ◄ 2 tablespoons unsalted butter, melted

1. In a small bowl, mix pesto and almonds. Set aside. 2. Place fillets into a round baking dish. 3. Brush each fillet with butter and place half of the pesto mixture on the top of each fillet. Place dish into the air fryer basket. 4. Adjust the temperature to 390ºF (199ºC) and set the timer for 12 minutes. 5. Salmon will easily flake when fully cooked and reach an internal temperature of at least 145ºF (63ºC). Serve warm.

Tandoori-Spiced Salmon and Potatoes

- ◄ 1 pound (454 g) fingerling potatoes
- ◄ 2 tablespoons vegetable oil, divided
- ◄ Kosher salt and freshly ground black pepper, to taste
- ◄ 1 teaspoon ground turmeric
- ◄ 1 teaspoon ground cumin
- ◄ 1 teaspoon ground ginger
- ◄ ½ teaspoon smoked paprika
- ◄ ¼ teaspoon cayenne pepper
- ◄ 2 (6 ounces / 170 g) skin-on salmon fillets

1. Preheat the air fryer to 375ºF (191ºC). 2. In a bowl, toss the potatoes with 1 tablespoon of the oil until evenly coated. Season with salt and pepper. Transfer the potatoes to the air fryer and air fry for 20 minutes. 3. Meanwhile, in a bowl, combine the remaining

1 tablespoon oil, the turmeric, cumin, ginger, paprika, and cayenne. Add the salmon fillets and turn in the spice mixture until fully coated all over. 4. After the potatoes have cooked for 20 minutes, place the salmon fillets, skin-side up, on top of the potatoes, and continue cooking until the potatoes are tender, the salmon is cooked, and the salmon skin is slightly crisp. 5. Transfer the salmon fillets to two plates and serve with the potatoes while both are warm.

Fish Gratin

- ◄ 1 tablespoon avocado oil
- ◄ 1 pound (454 g) hake fillets
- ◄ 1 teaspoon garlic powder
- ◄ Sea salt and ground white pepper, to taste
- ◄ 2 tablespoons shallots, chopped
- ◄ 1 bell pepper, seeded and
- chopped
- ◄ ½ cup Cottage cheese
- ◄ ½ cup sour cream
- ◄ 1 egg, well whisked
- ◄ 1 teaspoon yellow mustard
- ◄ 1 tablespoon lime juice
- ◄ ½ cup Swiss cheese, shredded

1. Brush the bottom and sides of a casserole dish with avocado oil. Add the hake fillets to the casserole dish and sprinkle with garlic powder, salt, and pepper. 2. Add the chopped shallots and bell peppers. 3. In a mixing bowl, thoroughly combine the Cottage cheese, sour cream, egg, mustard, and lime juice. Pour the mixture over fish and spread evenly. 4. Cook in the preheated air fryer at 370ºF (188ºC) for 10 minutes. 5. Top with the Swiss cheese and cook an additional 7 minutes. Let it rest for 10 minutes before slicing and serving. Bon appétit!

Tuna Patties with Spicy Sriracha Sauce

- ◄ 2 (6 ounces / 170 g) cans tuna packed in oil, drained
- ◄ 3 tablespoons almond flour
- ◄ 2 tablespoons mayonnaise
- ◄ 1 teaspoon dried dill
- ◄ ½ teaspoon onion powder
- ◄ Pinch of salt and pepper
- ◄ Spicy Sriracha Sauce:
- ◄ ¼ cup mayonnaise
- ◄ 1 tablespoon Sriracha sauce
- ◄ 1 teaspoon garlic powder

1. Preheat the air fryer to 380ºF (193ºC). Line the basket with parchment paper. 2. In a large bowl, combine the tuna, almond flour, mayonnaise, dill, and onion powder. Season to taste with salt and freshly ground black pepper. Use a fork to stir, mashing with the back of the fork as necessary, until thoroughly combined. 3. Use an ice cream scoop to form the tuna mixture patties. Place the patties in a single layer on the parchment paper in the air fryer basket. Press lightly with the bottom of the scoop to flatten into a circle about ½ inch thick. Pausing halfway through the cooking time to turn the patties, air fry for 10 minutes until lightly browned. 4. To make the Sriracha sauce: In a small bowl, combine the mayonnaise, Sriracha, and garlic powder. Serve the tuna patties topped with the Sriracha sauce.

Crab Cakes

Prep time: 10 minutes | Cook time: 10 minutes | Serves 4

- ◄ 2 (6 ounces / 170 g) cans lump crab meat
- ◄ ¼ cup blanched finely ground almond flour
- ◄ 1 large egg
- ◄ 2 tablespoons full-fat mayonnaise
- ◄ ½ teaspoon Dijon mustard
- ◄ ½ tablespoon lemon juice
- ◄ ½ medium green bell pepper, seeded and chopped
- ◄ ¼ cup chopped green onion
- ◄ ½ teaspoon Old Bay seasoning

1. In a large bowl, combine all ingredients. Form into four balls and flatten into patties. Place patties into the air fryer basket. 2. Adjust the temperature to 350°F (177°C) and air fry for 10 minutes. 3. Flip patties halfway through the cooking time. Serve warm.

Sesame-Crusted Tuna Steak

Prep time: 5 minutes | Cook time: 8 minutes | Serves 2

- ◄ 2 (6 ounces / 170 g) tuna steaks
- ◄ 1 tablespoon coconut oil, melted
- ◄ ½ teaspoon garlic powder
- ◄ 2 teaspoons white sesame seeds
- ◄ 2 teaspoons black sesame seeds

1. Brush each tuna steak with coconut oil and sprinkle with garlic powder. 2. In a large bowl, mix sesame seeds and then press each tuna steak into them, covering the steak as completely as possible. Place tuna steaks into the air fryer basket. 3. Adjust the temperature to 400°F (204°C) and air fry for 8 minutes. 4. Flip the steaks halfway through the cooking time. Steaks will be well-done at 145°F (63°C) internal temperature. Serve warm.

Crab Cakes with Sriracha Mayonnaise

Prep time: 15 minutes | Cook time: 10 minutes | Serves 4

Sriracha Mayonnaise:
- ◄ 1 cup mayonnaise
- ◄ 1 tablespoon sriracha
Crab Cakes:
- ◄ 1 teaspoon extra-virgin olive oil
- ◄ ¼ cup finely diced red bell pepper
- ◄ ¼ cup diced onion
- ◄ ¼ cup diced celery
- ◄ 1 pound (454 g) lump crab meat
- ◄ 1½ teaspoons freshly squeezed lemon juice
- ◄ 1 teaspoon Old Bay seasoning
- ◄ 1 egg
- ◄ 1½ teaspoons freshly squeezed lemon juice
- ◄ 1¾ cups panko bread crumbs, divided
- ◄ Vegetable oil, for spraying

1. Mix the mayonnaise, sriracha, and lemon juice in a small bowl.

Place ⅔ cup of the mixture in a separate bowl to form the base of the crab cakes. Cover the remaining sriracha mayonnaise and refrigerate. (This will become dipping sauce for the crab cakes once they are cooked.) 2. Heat the olive oil in a heavy-bottomed, medium skillet over medium-high heat. Add the bell pepper, onion, and celery and sauté for 3 minutes. Transfer the vegetables to the bowl with the reserved ⅔ cup of sriracha mayonnaise. Mix in the crab, Old Bay seasoning, egg, and lemon juice. Add 1 cup of the panko. Form the crab mixture into 8 cakes. Dredge the cakes in the remaining ¾ cup of panko, turning to coat. Place on a baking sheet. Cover and refrigerate for at least 1 hour and up to 8 hours. 3. Preheat the air fryer to 375°F (191°C). Spray the air fryer basket with oil. Working in batches as needed so as not to overcrowd the basket, place the chilled crab cakes in a single layer in the basket. Spray the crab cakes with oil. Bake until golden brown, 8 to 10 minutes, carefully turning halfway through cooking. Remove to a platter and keep warm. Repeat with the remaining crab cakes as needed. Serve the crab cakes immediately with sriracha mayonnaise dipping sauce.

Tilapia Sandwiches with Tartar Sauce

Prep time: 8 minutes | Cook time: 17 minutes | Serves 4

- ◄ ¾ cup mayonnaise
- ◄ 2 tablespoons dried minced onion
- ◄ 1 dill pickle spear, finely chopped
- ◄ 2 teaspoons pickle juice
- ◄ ¼ teaspoon salt
- ◄ ⅛ teaspoon freshly ground black pepper
- ◄ ⅓ cup all-purpose flour
- ◄ 1 egg, lightly beaten
- ◄ 1¾ cups panko bread crumbs
- ◄ 2 teaspoons lemon pepper
- ◄ 4 (6 ounces / 170 g) tilapia fillets
- ◄ Olive oil spray
- ◄ 4 hoagie rolls
- ◄ 4 butter lettuce leaves

1. To make the tartar sauce, in a small bowl, whisk the mayonnaise, dried onion, pickle, pickle juice, salt, and pepper until blended. Refrigerate while you make the fish. 2. Scoop the flour onto a plate; set aside. 3. Put the beaten egg in a medium shallow bowl. 4. On another plate, stir together the panko and lemon pepper. 5. Insert the crisper plate into the basket and the basket into the unit. Preheat the unit by selecting AIR FRY, setting the temperature to 400°F (204°C), and setting the time to 3 minutes. Select START/STOP to begin. 6. Dredge the tilapia fillets in the flour, in the egg, and press into the panko mixture to coat. 7. Once the unit is preheated, spray the crisper plate with olive oil and place a parchment paper liner into the basket. Place the prepared fillets on the liner in a single layer. Lightly spray the fillets with olive oil. 8. Select AIR FRY, set the temperature to 400°F (204°C), and set the time to 17 minutes. Select START/STOP to begin. 9. After 8 minutes, remove the basket, carefully flip the fillets, and spray them with more olive oil. Reinsert the basket to resume cooking. 10. When the cooking is complete, the fillets should be golden and crispy and a food thermometer should register 145°F (63°C). Place each cooked fillet in a hoagie roll, top with a little bit of tartar sauce and lettuce, and serve.

Dukkah-Crusted Halibut

Prep time: 15 minutes | Cook time: 17 minutes | Serves 2

Dukkah:
- ◀ 1 tablespoon coriander seeds
- ◀ 1 tablespoon sesame seeds
- ◀ 1½ teaspoons cumin seeds

Fish:
- ◀ 2 (5 ounces / 142 g) halibut fillets
- ◀ 2 tablespoons mayonnaise

- ◀ ⅓ cup roasted mixed nuts
- ◀ ¼ teaspoon kosher salt
- ◀ ¼ teaspoon black pepper

- ◀ Vegetable oil spray
- ◀ Lemon wedges, for serving

1. For the dukkah: Combine the coriander, sesame seeds, and cumin in a small baking pan. Place the pan in the air fryer basket. Set the air fryer to 400ºF (204ºC) for 5 minutes. Toward the end of the cooking time, you will hear the seeds popping. Transfer to a plate and let cool for 5 minutes. 2. Transfer the toasted seeds to a food processor or spice grinder and add the mixed nuts. Pulse until coarsely chopped. Add the salt and pepper and stir well. 3. For the fish: Spread each fillet with 1 tablespoon of the mayonnaise. Press a heaping tablespoon of the dukkah into the mayonnaise on each fillet, pressing lightly to adhere. 4. Spray the air fryer basket with vegetable oil spray. Place the fish in the basket. Set the air fryer to 400ºF (204ºC) for 12 minutes, or until the fish flakes easily with a fork. 5. Serve the fish with lemon wedges.

Panko-Crusted Fish Sticks

Prep time: 10 minutes | Cook time: 15 minutes | Serves 4

Tartar Sauce:
- ◀ 2 cups mayonnaise
- ◀ 2 tablespoons dill pickle relish

Fish Sticks:
- ◀ Oil, for spraying
- ◀ 1 pound (454 g) tilapia fillets
- ◀ ½ cup all-purpose flour
- ◀ 2 cups panko bread crumbs
- ◀ 2 tablespoons Creole seasoning

- ◀ 1 tablespoon dried minced onions

- ◀ 2 teaspoons granulated garlic
- ◀ 1 teaspoon onion powder
- ◀ ½ teaspoon salt
- ◀ ¼ teaspoon freshly ground black pepper
- ◀ 1 large egg

Make the Tartar Sauce 1. In a small bowl, whisk together the mayonnaise, pickle relish, and onions. Cover with plastic wrap and refrigerate until ready to serve. You can make this sauce ahead of time; the flavors will intensify as it chills. Make the Fish Sticks 2. Preheat the air fryer to 350ºF (177ºC). Line the air fryer basket with parchment and spray lightly with oil. 3. Cut the fillets into equal-size sticks and place them in a zip-top plastic bag. 4. Add the flour to the bag, seal, and shake well until evenly coated. 5. In a shallow bowl, mix together the bread crumbs, Creole seasoning, garlic, onion powder, salt, and black pepper. 6. In a small bowl, whisk the egg. 7. Dip the fish sticks in the egg, then dredge in the bread crumb mixture until completely coated. 8. Place the fish sticks in the prepared basket. You may need to work in batches, depending on the size of your air fryer. Do not overcrowd. Spray lightly with

oil. 9. Cook for 12 to 15 minutes, or until browned and cooked through. Serve with the tartar sauce.

Salmon Spring Rolls

Prep time: 20 minutes | Cook time: 8 to 10 minutes | Serves 4

- ◀ ½ pound (227 g) salmon fillet
- ◀ 1 teaspoon toasted sesame oil
- ◀ 1 onion, sliced
- ◀ 8 rice paper wrappers

- ◀ 1 yellow bell pepper, thinly sliced
- ◀ 1 carrot, shredded
- ◀ ⅓ cup chopped fresh flat-leaf parsley
- ◀ ¼ cup chopped fresh basil

1. Put the salmon in the air fryer basket and drizzle with the sesame oil. Add the onion. Air fry at 370ºF (188ºC) for 8 to 10 minutes, or until the salmon just flakes when tested with a fork and the onion is tender. 2. Meanwhile, fill a small shallow bowl with warm water. One at a time, dip the rice paper wrappers into the water and place on a work surface. 3. Top each wrapper with one-eighth each of the salmon and onion mixture, yellow bell pepper, carrot, parsley, and basil. Roll up the wrapper, folding in the sides, to enclose the ingredients. 4. If you like, bake in the air fryer at 380ºF (193ºC) for 7 to 9 minutes, until the rolls are crunchy. Cut the rolls in half to serve.

Chinese Ginger-Scallion Fish

Prep time: 15 minutes | Cook time: 15 minutes | Serves 2

Bean Sauce:
- ◀ 2 tablespoons soy sauce
- ◀ 1 tablespoon rice wine
- ◀ 1 tablespoon doubanjiang (Chinese black bean paste)

Vegetables and Fish:
- ◀ 1 tablespoon peanut oil
- ◀ ¼ cup julienned green onions (white and green parts)
- ◀ ¼ cup chopped fresh cilantro

- ◀ 1 teaspoon minced fresh ginger
- ◀ 1 clove garlic, minced

- ◀ 2 tablespoons julienned fresh ginger
- ◀ 2 (6 ounces / 170 g) white fish fillets, such as tilapia

1. For the sauce: In a small bowl, combine all the ingredients and stir until well combined; set aside. 2. For the vegetables and fish: In a medium bowl, combine the peanut oil, green onions, cilantro, and ginger. Toss to combine. 3. Cut two squares of parchment large enough to hold one fillet and half of the vegetables. Place one fillet on each parchment square, top with the vegetables, and pour over the sauce. Fold over the parchment paper and crimp the sides in small, tight folds to hold the fish, vegetables, and sauce securely inside the packet. 4. Place the packets in a single layer in the air fryer basket. Set fryer to 350ºF (177ºC) for 15 minutes. 5. Transfer each packet to a dinner plate. Cut open with scissors just before serving.

.

Blackened Salmon

Prep time: 10 minutes | Cook time: 8 minutes | Serves 2

- 10 ounces (283 g) salmon fillet
- ½ teaspoon ground coriander
- 1 teaspoon ground cumin
- 1 teaspoon dried basil
- 1 tablespoon avocado oil

1. In the shallow bowl, mix ground coriander, ground cumin, and dried basil. 2. Then coat the salmon fillet in the spices and sprinkle with avocado oil. 3. Put the fish in the air fryer basket and cook at 395ºF (202ºC) for 4 minutes per side.

Foil-Packet Lobster Tail

Prep time: 15 minutes | Cook time: 12 minutes | Serves 2

- 2 (6 ounces / 170 g) lobster tails, halved
- 2 tablespoons salted butter, melted
- ½ teaspoon Old Bay seasoning
- Juice of ½ medium lemon
- 1 teaspoon dried parsley

1. Place the two halved tails on a sheet of aluminum foil. Drizzle with butter, Old Bay seasoning, and lemon juice. 2. Seal the foil packets, completely covering tails. Place into the air fryer basket. 3. Adjust the temperature to 375ºF (191ºC) and air fry for 12 minutes. 4. Once done, sprinkle with dried parsley and serve immediately

Lemon-Tarragon Fish en Papillote

Prep time: 10 minutes | Cook time: 15 minutes | Serves 2

- 2 tablespoons salted butter, melted
- 1 tablespoon fresh lemon juice
- ½ teaspoon dried tarragon, crushed, or 2 sprigs fresh tarragon
- 1 teaspoon kosher salt
- ½ cup julienned carrots
- ½ cup julienned fennel, or ¼ cup julienned celery
- ½ cup thinly sliced red bell pepper
- 2 (6 ounces / 170 g) cod fillets, thawed if frozen
- Vegetable oil spray
- ½ teaspoon black pepper

1. In a medium bowl, combine the butter, lemon juice, tarragon, and ½ teaspoon of the salt. Whisk well until you get a creamy sauce. Add the carrots, fennel, and bell pepper and toss to combine; set aside. 2. Cut two squares of parchment each large enough to hold one fillet and half the vegetables. Spray the fillets with vegetable oil spray. Season both sides with the remaining ½ teaspoon salt and the black pepper. 3. Lay one fillet down on each parchment square. Top each with half the vegetables. Pour any remaining sauce over the vegetables. 4. Fold over the parchment paper and crimp the sides in small, tight folds to hold the fish, vegetables, and sauce securely inside the packet. Place the packets in the air fryer basket. Set the air fryer to 350ºF (177ºC) for 15 minutes. 5. Transfer each packet to a plate. Cut open with scissors just before serving (be careful, as the steam inside will be hot).

Creamy Haddock

Prep time: 10 minutes | Cook time: 8 minutes | Serves 4

- 1 pound (454 g) haddock fillet
- 1 teaspoon cayenne pepper
- 1 teaspoon salt
- 1 teaspoon coconut oil
- ½ cup heavy cream

1. Grease a baking pan with coconut oil. 2. Then put haddock fillet inside and sprinkle it with cayenne pepper, salt, and heavy cream. Put the baking pan in the air fryer basket and cook at 375ºF (191ºC) for 8 minutes.

Italian Tuna Roast

Prep time: 15 minutes | Cook time: 21 to 24 minutes | Serves 8

- Cooking spray
- 1 tablespoon Italian seasoning
- ⅛ teaspoon ground black pepper
- 1 tablespoon extra-light
- olive oil
- 1 teaspoon lemon juice
- 1 tuna loin (approximately 2 pounds / 907 g, 3 to 4 inches thick)

1. Spray baking dish with cooking spray and place in air fryer basket. Preheat the air fryer to 390ºF (199ºC). 2. Mix together the Italian seasoning, pepper, oil, and lemon juice. 3. Using a dull table knife or butter knife, pierce top of tuna about every half inch: Insert knife into top of tuna roast and pierce almost all the way to the bottom. 4. Spoon oil mixture into each of the holes and use the knife to push seasonings into the tuna as deeply as possible. 5. Spread any remaining oil mixture on all outer surfaces of tuna. 6. Place tuna roast in baking dish and roast at 390ºF (199ºC) for 20 minutes. Check temperature with a meat thermometer. Cook for an additional 1 to 4 minutes or until temperature reaches 145ºF (63ºC). 7. Remove basket from the air fryer and let tuna sit in the basket for 10 minutes.

Chapter 7 Vegetables and Sides

Crispy Chickpeas

Prep time: 5 minutes | Cook time: 15 minutes | Serves 4

- 1 (15 ounces / 425 g) can chickpeas, drained but not rinsed
- 2 tablespoons olive oil
- 1 teaspoon salt
- 2 tablespoons lemon juice

1. Preheat the air fryer to 400°F (204°C). 2. Add all the ingredients together in a bowl and mix. Transfer this mixture to the air fryer basket. 3. Air fry for 15 minutes, ensuring the chickpeas become nice and crispy. 4. Serve immediately.

Spiced Honey-Walnut Carrots

Prep time: 5 minutes | Cook time: 12 minutes | Serves 6

- 1 pound (454 g) baby carrots
- 2 tablespoons olive oil
- ¼ cup raw honey
- ¼ teaspoon ground
- cinnamon
- ¼ cup black walnuts, chopped

1. Preheat the air fryer to 360°F(182°C). 2. In a large bowl, toss the baby carrots with olive oil, honey, and cinnamon until well coated. 3. Pour into the air fryer and roast for 6 minutes. Shake the basket, sprinkle the walnuts on top, and roast for 6 minutes more. 4. Remove the carrots from the air fryer and serve.

Roasted Sweet Potatoes

Prep time: 10 minutes | Cook time: 25 minutes | Serves 4

- Cooking oil spray
- 2 sweet potatoes, peeled and cut into 1-inch cubes
- 1 tablespoon extra-virgin olive oil
- Pinch salt
- Freshly ground black pepper, to taste
- ½ teaspoon dried thyme
- ½ teaspoon dried marjoram
- ¼ cup grated Parmesan cheese

1. Insert the crisper plate into the basket and the basket into the unit. Preheat the unit by selecting AIR ROAST, setting the temperature to 330°F (166°C), and setting the time to 3 minutes. Select START/STOP to begin. 2. Once the unit is preheated, spray the crisper plate with cooking oil. Put the sweet potato cubes into the basket and drizzle with olive oil. Toss gently to coat. Sprinkle with the salt, pepper, thyme, and marjoram and toss again. 3. Select AIR ROAST, set the temperature to 330°F (166°C), and set the time to 25 minutes. Select START/STOP to begin. 4. After 10 minutes, remove the basket and shake the potatoes. Reinsert the basket to resume cooking. After another 10 minutes, remove the basket and shake the potatoes one more time. Sprinkle evenly with the Parmesan cheese. Reinsert the basket to resume cooking. 5. When the cooking is complete, the potatoes should be tender. Serve immediately.

Roasted Eggplant

Prep time: 15 minutes | Cook time: 15 minutes | Serves 4

- 1 large eggplant
- 2 tablespoons olive oil
- ¼ teaspoon salt
- ½ teaspoon garlic powder

1. Remove top and bottom from eggplant. Slice eggplant into ¼-inch-thick round slices. 2. Brush slices with olive oil. Sprinkle with salt and garlic powder. Place eggplant slices into the air fryer basket. 3. Adjust the temperature to 390°F (199°C) and set the timer for 15 minutes. 4. Serve immediately.

Parmesan Herb Focaccia Bread

Prep time: 10 minutes | Cook time: 10 minutes | Serves 6

- 1 cup shredded Mozzarella cheese
- 1 ounce (28 g) full-fat cream cheese
- 1 cup blanched finely ground almond flour
- ¼ cup ground golden flaxseed
- ¼ cup grated Parmesan
- cheese
- ½ teaspoon baking soda
- 2 large eggs
- ½ teaspoon garlic powder
- ¼ teaspoon dried basil
- ¼ teaspoon dried rosemary
- 2 tablespoons salted butter, melted and divided

1. Place Mozzarella, cream cheese, and almond flour into a large microwave-safe bowl and microwave for 1 minute. Add the flaxseed, Parmesan, and baking soda and stir until smooth ball forms. If the mixture cools too much, it will be hard to mix. Return to microwave for 10 to 15 seconds to rewarm if necessary. 2. Stir in eggs. You may need to use your hands to get them fully incorporated. Just keep stirring and they will absorb into the dough. 3. Sprinkle dough with garlic powder, basil, and rosemary and knead into dough. Grease a baking pan with 1 tablespoon melted butter. Press the dough evenly into the pan. Place pan into the air fryer basket. 4. Adjust the temperature to 400°F (204°C) and bake for 10 minutes. 5. At 7 minutes, cover with foil if bread begins to get too dark. 6. Remove and let cool at least 30 minutes. Drizzle with remaining butter and serve.

Cauliflower Rice Balls

Prep time: 10 minutes | Cook time: 8 minutes | Serves 4

- 1 (10 ounces / 283 g) steamer bag cauliflower rice, cooked according to package instructions
- ½ cup shredded Mozzarella cheese
- 1 large egg
- 2 ounces (57 g) plain pork rinds, finely crushed
- ¼ teaspoon salt
- ½ teaspoon Italian seasoning

1. Place cauliflower into a large bowl and mix with Mozzarella. 2. Whisk egg in a separate medium bowl. Place pork rinds into another large bowl with salt and Italian seasoning. 3. Separate cauliflower mixture into four equal sections and form each into a ball. Carefully dip a ball into whisked egg, then roll in pork rinds. Repeat with remaining balls. 4. Place cauliflower balls into ungreased air fryer basket. Adjust the temperature to 400ºF (204ºC) and air fry for 8 minutes. Rice balls will be golden when done. 5. Use a spatula to carefully move cauliflower balls to a large dish for serving. Serve warm.

Tofu Bites

Prep time: 15 minutes | Cook time: 30 minutes | Serves 4

- 1 packaged firm tofu, cubed and pressed to remove excess water
- 1 tablespoon soy sauce
- 1 tablespoon ketchup
- 1 tablespoon maple syrup
- ½ teaspoon vinegar
- 1 teaspoon liquid smoke
- 1 teaspoon hot sauce
- 2 tablespoons sesame seeds
- 1 teaspoon garlic powder
- Salt and ground black pepper, to taste
- Cooking spray

1. Preheat the air fryer to 375ºF (191ºC). 2. Spritz a baking dish with cooking spray. 3. Combine all the ingredients to coat the tofu completely and allow the marinade to absorb for half an hour. 4. Transfer the tofu to the baking dish, then air fry for 15 minutes. Flip the tofu over and air fry for another 15 minutes on the other side. 5. Serve immediately.

Burger Bun for One

Prep time: 2 minutes | Cook time: 5 minutes | Serves 1

- 2 tablespoons salted butter, melted
- ¼ cup blanched finely ground almond flour
- ¼ teaspoon baking powder
- ⅛ teaspoon apple cider vinegar
- 1 large egg, whisked

1. Pour butter into an ungreased ramekin. Add flour, baking powder, and vinegar to ramekin and stir until combined. Add egg and stir until batter is mostly smooth. 2. Place ramekin into air fryer basket. Adjust the temperature to 350ºF (177ºC) and bake for 5 minutes. When done, the center will be firm and the top slightly browned.

Let cool, about 5 minutes, then remove from ramekin and slice in half. Serve.

Spicy Roasted Bok Choy

Prep time: 10 minutes | Cook time: 7 to 10 minutes | Serves 4

- 2 tablespoons olive oil
- 2 tablespoons reduced-sodium coconut aminos
- 2 teaspoons sesame oil
- 2 teaspoons chili garlic sauce
- 2 cloves garlic, minced
- 1 head (about 1 pound / 454 g) bok choy, sliced lengthwise into quarters
- 2 teaspoons black sesame seeds

1. Preheat the air fryer to 400ºF (204ºC). 2. In a large bowl, combine the olive oil, coconut aminos, sesame oil, chili garlic sauce, and garlic. Add the bok choy and toss, massaging the leaves with your hands if necessary, until thoroughly coated. 3. Arrange the bok choy in the basket of the air fryer. Pausing about halfway through the cooking time to shake the basket, air fry for 7 to 10 minutes until the bok choy is tender and the tips of the leaves begin to crisp. 4.Remove from the basket and let cool for a few minutes before coarsely chopping. Serve sprinkled with the sesame seeds.

Hasselback Potatoes with Chive Pesto

Prep time: 10 minutes | Cook time: 40 minutes | Serves 2

- 2 medium russet potatoes
- 5 tablespoons olive oil
- Kosher salt and freshly ground black pepper, to taste
- ¼ cup roughly chopped fresh chives
- 2 tablespoons packed fresh flat-leaf parsley leaves
- 1 tablespoon chopped walnuts
- 1 tablespoon grated Parmesan cheese
- 1 teaspoon fresh lemon juice
- 1 small garlic clove, peeled
- ¼ cup sour cream

1. Place the potatoes on a cutting board and lay a chopstick or thin-handled wooden spoon to the side of each potato. Thinly slice the potatoes crosswise, letting the chopstick or spoon handle stop the blade of your knife, and stop ½ inch short of each end of the potato. Rub the potatoes with 1 tablespoon of the olive oil and season with salt and pepper. 2. Place the potatoes, cut-side up, in the air fryer and air fry at 375ºF (191ºC) until golden brown and crisp on the outside and tender inside, about 40 minutes, drizzling the insides with 1 tablespoon more olive oil and seasoning with more salt and pepper halfway through. 3. Meanwhile, in a small blender or food processor, combine the remaining 3 tablespoons olive oil, the chives, parsley, walnuts, Parmesan, lemon juice, and garlic and purée until smooth. Season the chive pesto with salt and pepper. 4. Remove the potatoes from the air fryer and transfer to plates. Drizzle the potatoes with the pesto, letting it drip down into the grooves, then dollop each with sour cream and serve hot.

Sweet and Crispy Roasted Pearl Onions

Prep time: 5 minutes | Cook time: 18 minutes | Serves 3

- 1 (14½ ounces / 411 g) package frozen pearl onions (do not thaw)
- 2 tablespoons extra-virgin olive oil
- 2 tablespoons balsamic
- vinegar
- 2 teaspoons finely chopped fresh rosemary
- ½ teaspoon kosher salt
- ¼ teaspoon black pepper

1. In a medium bowl, combine the onions, olive oil, vinegar, rosemary, salt, and pepper until well coated. 2. Transfer the onions to the air fryer basket. Set the air fryer to 400°F (204°C) for 18 minutes, or until the onions are tender and lightly charred, stirring once or twice during the cooking time.

Indian Eggplant Bharta

Prep time: 15 minutes | Cook time: 20 minutes | Serves 4

- 1 medium eggplant
- 2 tablespoons vegetable oil
- ½ cup finely minced onion
- ½ cup finely chopped fresh tomato
- 2 tablespoons fresh lemon
- juice
- 2 tablespoons chopped fresh cilantro
- ½ teaspoon kosher salt
- ⅛ teaspoon cayenne pepper

1. Rub the eggplant all over with the vegetable oil. Place the eggplant in the air fryer basket. Set the air fryer to 400°F (204°C) for 20 minutes, or until the eggplant skin is blistered and charred. 2. Transfer the eggplant to a resealable plastic bag, seal, and set aside for 15 to 20 minutes (the eggplant will finish cooking in the residual heat trapped in the bag). 3. Transfer the eggplant to a large bowl. Peel off and discard the charred skin. Roughly mash the eggplant flesh. Add the onion, tomato, lemon juice, cilantro, salt, and cayenne. Stir to combine.

Lemony Broccoli

Prep time: 10 minutes | Cook time: 9 to 14 minutes per batch | Serves 4

- 1 large head broccoli, rinsed and patted dry
- 2 teaspoons extra-virgin olive oil
- 1 tablespoon freshly squeezed lemon juice
- Olive oil spray

1. Cut off the broccoli florets and separate them. You can use the stems, too; peel the stems and cut them into 1-inch chunks. 2. Insert the crisper plate into the basket and the basket into the unit. Preheat the unit by selecting AIR ROAST, setting the temperature to 390°F (199°C), and setting the time to 3 minutes. Select START/STOP to begin. 3. In a large bowl, toss together the broccoli, olive oil,

and lemon juice until coated. 4. Once the unit is preheated, spray the crisper plate with olive oil. Working in batches, place half the broccoli into the basket. 5. Select AIR ROAST, set the temperature to 390°F (199°C), and set the time to 14 minutes. Select START/STOP to begin. 6. After 5 minutes, remove the basket and shake the broccoli. Reinsert the basket to resume cooking. Check the broccoli after 5 minutes. If it is crisp-tender and slightly brown around the edges, it is done. If not, resume cooking. 7. When the cooking is complete, transfer the broccoli to a serving bowl. Repeat steps 5 and 6 with the remaining broccoli. Serve immediately.

Parmesan-Thyme Butternut Squash

Prep time: 15 minutes | Cook time: 20 minutes | Serves 4

- 2½ cups butternut squash, cubed into 1-inch pieces (approximately 1 medium)
- 2 tablespoons olive oil
- ¼ teaspoon salt
- ¼ teaspoon garlic powder
- ¼ teaspoon black pepper
- 1 tablespoon fresh thyme
- ¼ cup grated Parmesan

1. Preheat the air fryer to 360°F (182°C). 2. In a large bowl, combine the cubed squash with the olive oil, salt, garlic powder, pepper, and thyme until the squash is well coated. 3. Pour this mixture into the air fryer basket, and roast for 10 minutes. Stir and roast another 8 to 10 minutes more. 4. Remove the squash from the air fryer and toss with freshly grated Parmesan before serving.

Garlic-Parmesan Crispy Baby Potatoes

Prep time: 10 minutes | Cook time: 15 minutes | Serves 4

- Oil, for spraying
- 1 pound (454 g) baby potatoes
- ½ cup grated Parmesan cheese, divided
- 3 tablespoons olive oil
- 2 teaspoons granulated garlic
- ½ teaspoon onion powder
- ½ teaspoon salt
- ¼ teaspoon freshly ground black pepper
- ¼ teaspoon paprika
- 2 tablespoons chopped fresh parsley, for garnish

1. Line the air fryer basket with parchment and spray lightly with oil. 2. Rinse the potatoes, pat dry with paper towels, and place in a large bowl. 3. In a small bowl, mix together ¼ cup of Parmesan cheese, the olive oil, garlic, onion powder, salt, black pepper, and paprika. Pour the mixture over the potatoes and toss to coat. 4. Transfer the potatoes to the prepared basket and spread them out in an even layer, taking care to keep them from touching. You may need to work in batches, depending on the size of your air fryer. 5. Air fry at 400°F (204°C) for 15 minutes, stirring after 7 to 8 minutes, or until easily pierced with a fork. Continue to cook for another 1 to 2 minutes, if needed. 6. Sprinkle with the parsley and the remaining Parmesan cheese and serve.

Easy Rosemary Green Beans

Prep time: 5 minutes | Cook time: 5 minutes | Serves 1

- 1 tablespoon butter, melted
- 2 tablespoons rosemary
- ½ teaspoon salt
- 3 cloves garlic, minced
- ¾ cup chopped green beans

1. Preheat the air fryer to 390°F (199°C). 2. Combine the melted butter with the rosemary, salt, and minced garlic. Toss in the green beans, coating them well. 3. Air fry for 5 minutes. 4. Serve immediately.

Baked Jalapeño and Cheese Cauliflower Mash

Prep time: 10 minutes | Cook time: 15 minutes | Serves 6

- 1 (12 ounces / 340 g) steamer bag cauliflower florets, cooked according to package instructions
- 2 tablespoons salted butter, softened
- 2 ounces (57 g) cream
- cheese, softened
- ½ cup shredded sharp Cheddar cheese
- ¼ cup pickled jalapeños
- ½ teaspoon salt
- ¼ teaspoon ground black pepper

1. Place cooked cauliflower into a food processor with remaining ingredients. Pulse twenty times until cauliflower is smooth and all ingredients are combined. 2. Spoon mash into an ungreased round nonstick baking dish. Place dish into air fryer basket. Adjust the temperature to 380°F (193°C) and bake for 15 minutes. The top will be golden brown when done. Serve warm.

Citrus Sweet Potatoes and Carrots

Prep time: 5 minutes | Cook time: 20 to 25 minutes | Serves 4

- 2 large carrots, cut into 1-inch chunks
- 1 medium sweet potato, peeled and cut into 1-inch cubes
- ½ cup chopped onion
- 2 garlic cloves, minced
- 2 tablespoons honey
- 1 tablespoon freshly squeezed orange juice
- 2 teaspoons butter, melted

1. Insert the crisper plate into the basket and the basket into the unit. Preheat the unit by selecting AIR ROAST, setting the temperature to 400°F (204°C), and setting the time to 3 minutes. Select START/STOP to begin. 2. In a 6-by-2-inch round pan, toss together the carrots, sweet potato, onion, garlic, honey, orange juice, and melted butter to coat. 3. Once the unit is preheated, place the pan into the basket. 4. Select AIR ROAST, set the temperature to 400°F (204°C), and set the time to 25 minutes. Select START/STOP to begin. 5. After 15 minutes, remove the basket and shake the vegetables.

Reinsert the basket to resume cooking. After 5 minutes, if the vegetables are tender and glazed, they are done. If not, resume cooking. 6. When the cooking is complete, serve immediately.

Herbed Shiitake Mushrooms

Prep time: 10 minutes | Cook time: 5 minutes | Serves 4

- 8 ounces (227 g) shiitake mushrooms, stems removed and caps roughly chopped
- 1 tablespoon olive oil
- ½ teaspoon salt
- Freshly ground black pepper, to taste
- 1 teaspoon chopped fresh thyme leaves
- 1 teaspoon chopped fresh oregano
- 1 tablespoon chopped fresh parsley

1. Preheat the air fryer to 400°F (204°C). 2. Toss the mushrooms with the olive oil, salt, pepper, thyme and oregano. Air fry for 5 minutes, shaking the basket once or twice during the cooking process. The mushrooms will still be somewhat chewy with a meaty texture. If you'd like them a little more tender, add a couple of minutes to this cooking time. 3. Once cooked, add the parsley to the mushrooms and toss. Season again to taste and serve.

Bacon-Wrapped Asparagus

Prep time: 10 minutes | Cook time: 10 minutes | Serves 4

- 8 slices reduced-sodium bacon, cut in half
- 16 thick (about 1 pound /
- 454 g) asparagus spears, trimmed of woody ends

1. Preheat the air fryer to 350°F (177°C). 2. Wrap a half piece of bacon around the center of each stalk of asparagus. 3. Working in batches, if necessary, arrange seam-side down in a single layer in the air fryer basket. Air fry for 10 minutes until the bacon is crisp and the stalks are tender.

Parmesan and Herb Sweet Potatoes

Prep time: 10 minutes | Cook time: 18 minutes | Serves 4

- 2 large sweet potatoes, peeled and cubed
- ¼ cup olive oil
- 1 teaspoon dried rosemary
- ½ teaspoon salt
- 2 tablespoons shredded Parmesan

1. Preheat the air fryer to 360°F(182°C). 2. In a large bowl, toss the sweet potatoes with the olive oil, rosemary, and salt. 3. Pour the potatoes into the air fryer basket and roast for 10 minutes, then stir the potatoes and sprinkle the Parmesan over the top. Continue roasting for 8 minutes more. 4. Serve hot and enjoy.

Easy Potato Croquettes

Prep time: 15 minutes | Cook time: 15 minutes | Serves 10

- ¼ cup nutritional yeast
- 2 cups boiled potatoes, mashed
- 1 flax egg
- 1 tablespoon flour
- 2 tablespoons chopped chives
- Salt and ground black pepper, to taste
- 2 tablespoons vegetable oil
- ¼ cup bread crumbs

1. Preheat the air fryer to 400°F (204°C). 2. In a bowl, combine the nutritional yeast, potatoes, flax egg, flour, and chives. Sprinkle with salt and pepper as desired. 3. In a separate bowl, mix the vegetable oil and bread crumbs to achieve a crumbly consistency. 4. Shape the potato mixture into small balls and dip each one into the bread crumb mixture. 5. Put the croquettes inside the air fryer and air fry for 15 minutes, ensuring the croquettes turn golden brown. 6. Serve immediately.

Asparagus Fries

Prep time: 15 minutes | Cook time: 5 to 7 minutes per batch | Serves 4

- 12 ounces (340 g) fresh asparagus spears with tough ends trimmed off
- 2 egg whites
- ¼ cup water
- ¾ cup panko bread crumbs
- ¼ cup grated Parmesan cheese, plus 2 tablespoons
- ¼ teaspoon salt
- Oil for misting or cooking spray

1. Preheat the air fryer to 390°F (199°C). 2. In a shallow dish, beat egg whites and water until slightly foamy. 3. In another shallow dish, combine panko, Parmesan, and salt. 4. Dip asparagus spears in egg, then roll in crumbs. Spray with oil or cooking spray. 5. Place a layer of asparagus in air fryer basket, leaving just a little space in between each spear. Stack another layer on top, crosswise. Air fry at 390°F (199°C) for 5 to 7 minutes, until crispy and golden brown. 6. Repeat to cook remaining asparagus.

Marinara Pepperoni Mushroom Pizza

Prep time: 5 minutes | Cook time: 18 minutes | Serves 4

- 4 large portobello mushrooms, stems removed
- 4 teaspoons olive oil
- 1 cup marinara sauce
- 1 cup shredded Mozzarella cheese
- 10 slices sugar-free pepperoni

1. Preheat the air fryer to 375°F (191°C). 2. Brush each mushroom cap with the olive oil, one teaspoon for each cap. 3. Put on a baking sheet and bake, stem-side down, for 8 minutes. 4. Take out of the air fryer and divide the marinara sauce, Mozzarella cheese and pepperoni evenly among the caps. 5. Air fry for another 10 minutes until browned. 6. Serve hot.

Mole-Braised Cauliflower

Prep time: 10 minutes | Cook time: 15 minutes | Serves 2

- 8 ounces (227 g) medium cauliflower florets
- 1 tablespoon vegetable oil
- Kosher salt and freshly ground black pepper, to taste
- 1½ cups vegetable broth
- 2 tablespoons New Mexico chile powder (or regular chili powder)
- 2 tablespoons salted roasted peanuts
- 1 tablespoon toasted sesame seeds, plus more for garnish
- 1 tablespoon finely chopped golden raisins
- 1 teaspoon kosher salt
- 1 teaspoon dark brown sugar
- ½ teaspoon dried oregano
- ¼ teaspoon cayenne pepper
- ⅛ teaspoon ground cinnamon

1. In a large bowl, toss the cauliflower with the oil and season with salt and black pepper. Transfer to a cake pan. Place the pan in the air fryer and roast at 375°F (191°C) until the cauliflower is tender and lightly browned at the edges, about 10 minutes, stirring halfway through. 2. Meanwhile, in a small blender, combine the broth, chile powder, peanuts, sesame seeds, raisins, salt, brown sugar, oregano, cayenne, and cinnamon and purée until smooth. Pour into a small saucepan or skillet and bring to a simmer over medium heat, then cook until reduced by half, 3 to 5 minutes. 3. Pour the hot mole sauce over the cauliflower in the pan, stir to coat, then cook until the sauce is thickened and lightly charred on the cauliflower, about 5 minutes more. Sprinkle with more sesame seeds and serve warm.

Sausage-Stuffed Mushroom Caps

Prep time: 10 minutes | Cook time: 8 minutes | Serves 2

- 6 large portobello mushroom caps
- ½ pound (227 g) Italian sausage
- ¼ cup chopped onion
- 2 tablespoons blanched finely ground almond flour
- ¼ cup grated Parmesan cheese
- 1 teaspoon minced fresh garlic

1. Use a spoon to hollow out each mushroom cap, reserving scrapings. 2. In a medium skillet over medium heat, brown the sausage about 10 minutes or until fully cooked and no pink remains. Drain and then add reserved mushroom scrapings, onion, almond flour, Parmesan, and garlic. Gently fold ingredients together and continue cooking an additional minute, then remove from heat. 3. Evenly spoon the mixture into mushroom caps and place the caps into a 6-inch round pan. Place pan into the air fryer basket. 4. Adjust the temperature to 375°F (191°C) and set the timer for 8 minutes. 5. When finished cooking, the tops will be browned and bubbling. Serve warm.

Garlic Parmesan-Roasted Cauliflower

Prep time: 5 minutes | Cook time: 15 minutes | Serves 6

◀ 1 medium head cauliflower, leaves and core removed, cut into florets
◀ 2 tablespoons salted butter, melted
◀ ½ tablespoon salt
◀ 2 cloves garlic, peeled and finely minced
◀ ½ cup grated Parmesan cheese, divided

1. Toss cauliflower in a large bowl with butter. Sprinkle with salt, garlic, and ¼ cup Parmesan. 2. Place florets into ungreased air fryer basket. Adjust the temperature to 350ºF (177ºC) and roast for 15 minutes, shaking basket halfway through cooking. Cauliflower will be browned at the edges and tender when done. 3. Transfer florets to a large serving dish and sprinkle with remaining Parmesan. Serve warm.

Lemon-Thyme Asparagus

Prep time: 5 minutes | Cook time: 4 to 8 minutes | Serves 4

◀ 1 pound (454 g) asparagus, woody ends trimmed off
◀ 1 tablespoon avocado oil
◀ ½ teaspoon dried thyme or ½ tablespoon chopped fresh thyme
◀ Sea salt and freshly ground black pepper, to taste
◀ 2 ounces (57 g) goat cheese, crumbled
◀ Zest and juice of 1 lemon
◀ Flaky sea salt, for serving (optional)

1. In a medium bowl, toss together the asparagus, avocado oil, and thyme, and season with sea salt and pepper. 2. Place the asparagus in the air fryer basket in a single layer. Set the air fryer to 400ºF (204ºC) and air fry for 4 to 8 minutes, to your desired doneness. 3. Transfer to a serving platter. Top with the goat cheese, lemon zest, and lemon juice. If desired, season with a pinch of flaky salt.

Air-Fried Okra

Prep time: 10 minutes | Cook time: 10 minutes | Serves 4

◀ 1 egg
◀ ½ cup almond milk
◀ ½ cup crushed pork rinds
◀ ¼ cup grated Parmesan cheese
◀ ¼ cup almond flour
◀ 1 teaspoon garlic powder
◀ ¼ teaspoon freshly ground black pepper
◀ ½ pound (227 g) fresh okra, stems removed and chopped into 1-inch slices

1. Preheat the air fryer to 400ºF (204ºC). 2. In a shallow bowl, whisk together the egg and milk. 3. In a second shallow bowl, combine the pork rinds, Parmesan, almond flour, garlic powder, and black pepper. 4. Working with a few slices at a time, dip the okra into the egg mixture followed by the crumb mixture. Press lightly to ensure an even coating. 5. Working in batches if necessary, arrange the okra in a single layer in the air fryer basket and spray lightly with olive oil. Pausing halfway through the cooking time to turn the okra, air fry for 10 minutes until tender and golden brown. Serve warm.

Sesame ginger Broccoli

Prep time: 10 minutes | Cook time: 15 minutes | Serves 4

◀ 3 tablespoons toasted sesame oil
◀ 2 teaspoons sesame seeds
◀ 1 tablespoon chili garlic sauce
◀ 2 teaspoons minced fresh ginger
◀ ½ teaspoon kosher salt
◀ ½ teaspoon black pepper
◀ 1 (16 ounces / 454 g) package frozen broccoli florets (do not thaw)

1. In a large bowl, combine the sesame oil, sesame seeds, chili garlic sauce, ginger, salt, and pepper. Stir until well combined. Add the broccoli and toss until well coated. 2. Arrange the broccoli in the air fryer basket. Set the air fryer to 325ºF (163ºC) for 15 minutes, or until the broccoli is crisp, tender, and the edges are lightly browned, gently tossing halfway through the cooking time.

Zucchini Balls

Prep time: 5 minutes | Cook time: 10 minutes | Serves 4

◀ 4 zucchinis
◀ 1 egg
◀ ½ cup grated Parmesan
◀ cheese
◀ 1 tablespoon Italian herbs
◀ 1 cup grated coconut

1. Thinly grate the zucchinis and dry with a cheesecloth, ensuring to remove all the moisture. 2. In a bowl, combine the zucchinis with the egg, Parmesan, Italian herbs, and grated coconut, mixing well to incorporate everything. Using the hands, mold the mixture into balls. 3. Preheat the air fryer to 400ºF (204ºC). 4. Lay the zucchini balls in the air fryer basket and air fry for 10 minutes. 5. Serve hot.

Kohlrabi Fries

Prep time: 10 minutes | Cook time: 20 to 30 minutes | Serves 4

◀ 2 pounds (907 g) kohlrabi, peeled and cut into ¼ to ½-inch fries
◀ 2 tablespoons olive oil
◀ Salt and freshly ground black pepper, to taste

1. Preheat the air fryer to 400ºF (204ºC). 2. In a large bowl, combine the kohlrabi and olive oil. Season to taste with salt and black pepper. Toss gently until thoroughly coated. 3. Working in batches if necessary, spread the kohlrabi in a single layer in the air fryer basket. Pausing halfway through the cooking time to shake the basket, air fry for 20 to 30 minutes until the fries are lightly browned and crunchy.

Glazed Carrots

Prep time: 10 minutes | Cook time: 8 to 10 minutes | Serves 4

◀ 2 teaspoons honey
◀ 1 teaspoon orange juice
◀ ½ teaspoon grated orange rind
◀ ⅛ teaspoon ginger
◀ 1 pound (454 g) baby carrots
◀ 2 teaspoons olive oil
◀ ¼ teaspoon salt

1. Combine honey, orange juice, grated rind, and ginger in a small bowl and set aside. 2. Toss the carrots, oil, and salt together to coat well and pour them into the air fryer basket. 3. Roast at 390ºF (199ºC) for 5 minutes. Shake basket to stir a little and cook for 2 to 4 minutes more, until carrots are barely tender. 4. Pour carrots into a baking pan. 5. Stir the honey mixture to combine well, pour glaze over carrots, and stir to coat. 6. Roast at 360ºF (182ºC) for 1 minute or just until heated through.

Bacon Potatoes and Green Beans

Prep time: 10 minutes | Cook time: 25 minutes | Serves 4

◀ Oil, for spraying
◀ 2 pounds (907 g) medium russet potatoes, quartered
◀ ¾ cup bacon bits
◀ 10 ounces (283 g) fresh
green beans
◀ 1 teaspoon salt
◀ ½ teaspoon freshly ground black pepper

1. Line the air fryer basket with parchment and spray lightly with oil. 2. Place the potatoes in the prepared basket. Top with the bacon bits and green beans. Sprinkle with the salt and black pepper and spray liberally with oil. 3. Air fry at 355ºF (179ºC) for 25 minutes, stirring after 12 minutes and spraying with oil, until the potatoes are easily pierced with a fork.

Corn and Cilantro Salad

Prep time: 10 minutes | Cook time: 10 minutes | Serves 2

◀ 2 ears of corn, shucked (halved crosswise if too large to fit in your air fryer)
◀ 1 tablespoon unsalted butter, at room temperature
◀ 1 teaspoon chili powder
◀ ¼ teaspoon garlic powder
◀ Kosher salt and freshly ground black pepper, to taste
◀ 1 cup lightly packed fresh cilantro leaves
◀ 1 tablespoon sour cream
◀ 1 tablespoon mayonnaise
◀ 1 teaspoon adobo sauce (from a can of chipotle peppers in adobo sauce)
◀ 2 tablespoons crumbled queso fresco
◀ Lime wedges, for serving

1. Brush the corn all over with the butter, then sprinkle with the chili powder and garlic powder, and season with salt and pepper. Place the corn in the air fryer and air fry at 400ºF (204ºC), turning over halfway through, until the kernels are lightly charred and tender, about 10 minutes. 2. Transfer the ears to a cutting board, let stand 1 minute, then carefully cut the kernels off the cobs and move them to a bowl. Add the cilantro leaves and toss to combine (the cilantro leaves will wilt slightly). 3. In a small bowl, stir together the sour cream, mayonnaise, and adobo sauce. Divide the corn and cilantro among plates and spoon the adobo dressing over the top. Sprinkle with the queso fresco and serve with lime wedges on the side.

Lemon garlic Mushrooms

Prep time: 10 minutes | Cook time: 10 to 15 minutes | Serves 6

◀ 12 ounces (340 g) sliced mushrooms
◀ 1 tablespoon avocado oil
◀ Sea salt and freshly ground black pepper, to taste
◀ 3 tablespoons unsalted butter
◀ 1 teaspoon minced garlic
◀ 1 teaspoon freshly squeezed lemon juice
◀ ½ teaspoon red pepper flakes
◀ 2 tablespoons chopped fresh parsley

1. Place the mushrooms in a medium bowl and toss with the oil. Season to taste with salt and pepper. 2. Place the mushrooms in a single layer in the air fryer basket. Set your air fryer to 375ºF (191ºC) and roast for 10 to 15 minutes, until the mushrooms are tender. 3. While the mushrooms cook, melt the butter in a small pot or skillet over medium-low heat. Stir in the garlic and cook for 30 seconds. Remove the pot from the heat and stir in the lemon juice and red pepper flakes. 4. Toss the mushrooms with the lemon garlic butter and garnish with the parsley before serving.

Charred Okra with Peanut-Chile Sauce

Prep time: 10 minutes | Cook time: 16 minutes | Serves 2

◀ ¾ pound (340 g) okra pods
◀ 2 tablespoons vegetable oil
◀ Kosher salt and freshly ground black pepper, to taste
◀ 1 large shallot, minced
◀ 1 garlic clove, minced
◀ ½ Scotch bonnet chile,
minced (seeded if you want a milder sauce)
◀ 1 tablespoon tomato paste
◀ 1 cup vegetable stock or water
◀ 2 tablespoons natural peanut butter
◀ Juice of ½ lime

1. In a bowl, toss the okra with 1 tablespoon of the oil and season with salt and pepper. Transfer the okra to the air fryer and air fry at 400ºF (204ºC), shaking the basket halfway through, until the okra is tender and lightly charred at the edges, about 16 minutes. 2. Meanwhile, in a small skillet, heat the remaining 1 tablespoon oil over medium-high heat. Add the shallot, garlic, and chile and cook, stirring, until soft, about 2 minutes. Stir in the tomato paste and cook for 30 seconds, then stir in the vegetable stock and peanut butter. Reduce the heat to maintain a simmer and cook until the sauce is reduced slightly and thickened, 3 to 4 minutes. Remove the sauce from the heat, stir in the lime juice, and season with salt and pepper. 3. Place the peanut sauce on a plate, then pile the okra on top and serve hot.

Cheddar Broccoli with Bacon

Prep time: 10 minutes | Cook time: 10 minutes | Serves 2

- ◄ 3 cups fresh broccoli florets
- ◄ 1 tablespoon coconut oil
- ◄ ½ cup shredded sharp Cheddar cheese
- ◄ ¼ cup full-fat sour cream
- ◄ 4 slices sugar-free bacon, cooked and crumbled
- ◄ 1 scallion, sliced on the bias

1. Place broccoli into the air fryer basket and drizzle it with coconut oil. 2. Adjust the temperature to 350ºF (177ºC) and set the timer for 10 minutes. 3. Toss the basket two or three times during cooking to avoid burned spots. 4. When broccoli begins to crisp at ends, remove from fryer. Top with shredded cheese, sour cream, and crumbled bacon and garnish with scallion slices.

Crispy Green Beans

Prep time: 5 minutes | Cook time: 8 minutes | Serves 4

- ◄ 2 teaspoons olive oil
- ◄ ½ pound (227 g) fresh green beans, ends trimmed
- ◄ ¼ teaspoon salt
- ◄ ¼ teaspoon ground black pepper

1. In a large bowl, drizzle olive oil over green beans and sprinkle with salt and pepper. 2. Place green beans into ungreased air fryer basket. Adjust the temperature to 350ºF (177ºC) and set the timer for 8 minutes, shaking the basket two times during cooking. Green beans will be dark golden and crispy at the edges when done. Serve warm.

Parsnip Fries with Romesco Sauce

Prep time: 20 minutes | Cook time: 24 minutes | Serves 4

Romesco Sauce:
- ◄ 1 red bell pepper, halved and seeded
- ◄ 1 (1-inch) thick slice of Italian bread, torn into pieces (about 1 to 1½ cups)
- ◄ 1 cup almonds, toasted
- ◄ Olive oil
- ◄ ½ Jalapeño pepper, seeded
- ◄ 1 tablespoon fresh parsley leaves
- ◄ 1 clove garlic
- ◄ 2 Roma tomatoes, peeled
- and seeded (or ⅓ cup canned crushed tomatoes)
- ◄ 1 tablespoon red wine vinegar
- ◄ ¼ teaspoon smoked paprika
- ◄ ½ teaspoon salt
- ◄ ¾ cup olive oil
- ◄ 3 parsnips, peeled and cut into long strips
- ◄ 2 teaspoons olive oil
- ◄ Salt and freshly ground black pepper, to taste

1. Preheat the air fryer to 400ºF (204ºC). 2. Place the red pepper halves, cut side down, in the air fryer basket and air fry for 8 to 10 minutes, or until the skin turns black all over. Remove the pepper from the air fryer and let it cool. When it is cool enough to handle, peel the pepper. 3. Toss the torn bread and almonds with a little olive oil and air fry for 4 minutes, shaking the basket a couple times throughout the cooking time. When the bread and almonds are nicely toasted, remove them from the air fryer and let them cool for just a minute or two. 4. Combine the toasted bread, almonds, roasted red pepper, Jalapeño pepper, parsley, garlic, tomatoes, vinegar, smoked paprika and salt in a food processor or blender. Process until smooth. With the processor running, add the olive oil through the feed tube until the sauce comes together in a smooth paste that is barely pourable. 5. Toss the parsnip strips with the olive oil, salt and freshly ground black pepper and air fry at 400ºF (204ºC) for 10 minutes, shaking the basket a couple times during the cooking process so they brown and cook evenly. Serve the parsnip fries warm with the Romesco sauce to dip into.

Roasted Brussels Sprouts with Bacon

Prep time: 10 minutes | Cook time: 20 minutes | Serves 4

- ◄ 4 slices thick-cut bacon, chopped (about ¼ pound / 113 g)
- ◄ 1 pound (454 g) Brussels
- sprouts, halved (or quartered if large)
- ◄ Freshly ground black pepper, to taste

1. Preheat the air fryer to 380ºF (193ºC). 2. Air fry the bacon for 5 minutes, shaking the basket once or twice during the cooking time. 3. Add the Brussels sprouts to the basket and drizzle a little bacon fat from the bottom of the air fryer drawer into the basket. Toss the sprouts to coat with the bacon fat. Air fry for an additional 15 minutes, or until the Brussels sprouts are tender to a knifepoint. 4. Season with freshly ground black pepper.

Sesame Carrots and Sugar Snap Peas

Prep time: 10 minutes | Cook time: 16 minutes | Serves 4

- ◄ 1 pound (454 g) carrots, peeled sliced on the bias (½-inch slices)
- ◄ 1 teaspoon olive oil
- ◄ Salt and freshly ground black pepper, to taste
- ◄ ⅓ cup honey
- ◄ 1 tablespoon sesame oil
- ◄ 1 tablespoon soy sauce
- ◄ ½ teaspoon minced fresh ginger
- ◄ 4 ounces (113 g) sugar snap peas (about 1 cup)
- ◄ 1½ teaspoons sesame seeds

1. Preheat the air fryer to 360ºF (182ºC). 2. Toss the carrots with the olive oil, season with salt and pepper and air fry for 10 minutes, shaking the basket once or twice during the cooking process. 3. Combine the honey, sesame oil, soy sauce and minced ginger in a large bowl. Add the sugar snap peas and the air-fried carrots to the honey mixture, toss to coat and return everything to the air fryer basket. 4. Turn up the temperature to 400ºF (204ºC) and air fry for an additional 6 minutes, shaking the basket once during the cooking process. 5. Transfer the carrots and sugar snap peas to a serving bowl. Pour the sauce from the bottom of the cooker over the vegetables and sprinkle sesame seeds over top. Serve immediately.

Garlic Zucchini and Red Peppers

Prep time: 5 minutes | Cook time: 15 minutes | Serves 6

- ◄ 2 medium zucchini, cubed
- ◄ 1 red bell pepper, diced
- ◄ 2 garlic cloves, sliced
- ◄ 2 tablespoons olive oil
- ◄ ½ teaspoon salt

1. Preheat the air fryer to 380°F(193°C). 2. In a large bowl, mix together the zucchini, bell pepper, and garlic with the olive oil and salt. 3. Pour the mixture into the air fryer basket, and roast for 7 minutes. Shake or stir, then roast for 7 to 8 minutes more.

Fig, Chickpea, and Arugula Salad

Prep time: 15 minutes | Cook time: 20 minutes | Serves 4

- ◄ 8 fresh figs, halved
- ◄ 1½ cups cooked chickpeas
- ◄ 1 teaspoon crushed roasted cumin seeds
- ◄ 4 tablespoons balsamic vinegar
- ◄ 2 tablespoons extra-virgin
- olive oil, plus more for greasing
- ◄ Salt and ground black pepper, to taste
- ◄ 3 cups arugula rocket, washed and dried

1. Preheat the air fryer to 375°F (191°C). 2. Cover the air fryer basket with aluminum foil and grease lightly with oil. Put the figs in the air fryer basket and air fry for 10 minutes. 3. In a bowl, combine the chickpeas and cumin seeds. 4. Remove the air fried figs from the air fryer and replace with the chickpeas. Air fry for 10 minutes. Leave to cool. 5. In the meantime, prepare the dressing. Mix the balsamic vinegar, olive oil, salt and pepper. 6. In a salad bowl, combine the arugula rocket with the cooled figs and chickpeas. 7. Toss with the sauce and serve.

Broccoli-Cheddar Twice-Baked Potatoes

Prep time: 10 minutes | Cook time: 46 minutes | Serves 4

- ◄ Oil, for spraying
- ◄ 2 medium russet potatoes
- ◄ 1 tablespoon olive oil
- ◄ ¼ cup broccoli florets
- ◄ 1 tablespoon sour cream
- ◄ 1 teaspoon granulated garlic
- ◄ 1 teaspoon onion powder
- ◄ ½ cup shredded Cheddar cheese

1. Line the air fryer basket with parchment and spray lightly with oil. 2. Rinse the potatoes and pat dry with paper towels. Rub the outside of the potatoes with the olive oil and place them in the prepared basket. 3. Air fry at 400°F (204°C) for 40 minutes, or until easily pierced with a fork. Let cool just enough to handle, then cut the potatoes in half lengthwise. 4. Meanwhile, place the broccoli in a microwave-safe bowl, cover with water, and microwave on high for 5 to 8 minutes. Drain and set aside. 5. Scoop out most of the potato flesh and transfer to a medium bowl. 6. Add the sour cream, garlic, and onion powder and stir until the potatoes are mashed. 7. Spoon the potato mixture back into the hollowed potato skins, mounding it to fit, if necessary. Top with the broccoli and cheese. Return the potatoes to the basket. You may need to work in batches, depending on the size of your air fryer. 8. Air fry at 400°F (204°C) for 3 to 6 minutes, or until the cheese has melted. Serve immediately.

Chermoula-Roasted Beets

Prep time: 15 minutes | Cook time: 25 minutes | Serves 4

Chermoula:
- ◄ 1 cup packed fresh cilantro leaves
- ◄ ½ cup packed fresh parsley leaves
- ◄ 6 cloves garlic, peeled
- ◄ 2 teaspoons smoked paprika
- ◄ 2 teaspoons ground cumin

Beets:
- ◄ 3 medium beets, trimmed, peeled, and cut into 1-inch chunks
- ◄ 2 tablespoons chopped fresh

- ◄ 1 teaspoon ground coriander
- ◄ ½ to 1 teaspoon cayenne pepper
- ◄ Pinch crushed saffron (optional)
- ◄ ½ cup extra-virgin olive oil
- ◄ Kosher salt, to taste

- cilantro
- ◄ 2 tablespoons chopped fresh parsley

1. For the chermoula: In a food processor, combine the cilantro, parsley, garlic, paprika, cumin, coriander, and cayenne. Pulse until coarsely chopped. Add the saffron, if using, and process until combined. With the food processor running, slowly add the olive oil in a steady stream; process until the sauce is uniform. Season to taste with salt. 2. For the beets: In a large bowl, drizzle the beets with ½ cup of the chermoula, or enough to coat. Arrange the beets in the air fryer basket. Set the air fryer to 375°F (191°C) for 25 to minutes, or until the beets are tender. 3. Transfer the beets to a serving platter. Sprinkle with chopped cilantro and parsley and serve.

Rosemary New Potatoes

Prep time: 10 minutes | Cook time: 5 to 6 minutes | Serves 4

- ◄ 3 large red potatoes (enough to make 3 cups sliced)
- ◄ ¼ teaspoon ground rosemary
- ◄ ¼ teaspoon ground thyme
- ◄ ⅛ teaspoon salt
- ◄ ⅛ teaspoon ground black pepper
- ◄ 2 teaspoons extra-light olive oil

1. Preheat the air fryer to 330°F (166°C). 2. Place potatoes in large bowl and sprinkle with rosemary, thyme, salt, and pepper. 3. Stir with a spoon to distribute seasonings evenly. 4. Add oil to potatoes and stir again to coat well. 5. Air fry at 330°F (166°C) for 4 minutes. Stir and break apart any that have stuck together. 6. Cook an additional 1 to 2 minutes or until fork-tender.

Curry Roasted Cauliflower

Prep time: 10 minutes | Cook time: 20 minutes | Serves 4

◄ ¼ cup olive oil
◄ 2 teaspoons curry powder
◄ ½ teaspoon salt
◄ ¼ teaspoon freshly ground black pepper

◄ 1 head cauliflower, cut into bite-size florets
◄ ½ red onion, sliced
◄ 2 tablespoons freshly chopped parsley, for garnish (optional)

1. Preheat the air fryer to 400ºF (204ºC). 2. In a large bowl, combine the olive oil, curry powder, salt, and pepper. Add the cauliflower and onion. Toss gently until the vegetables are completely coated with the oil mixture. Transfer the vegetables to the basket of the air fryer. 3. Pausing about halfway through the cooking time to shake the basket, air fry for 20 minutes until the cauliflower is tender and beginning to brown. Top with the parsley, if desired, before serving.

Cabbage Wedges with Caraway Butter

Prep time: 30 minutes | Cook time: 35 to 40 minutes | Serves 6

◄ 1 tablespoon caraway seeds
◄ ½ cup (1 stick) unsalted butter, at room temperature
◄ ½ teaspoon grated lemon zest
◄ 1 small head green or red cabbage, cut into 6 wedges

◄ 1 tablespoon avocado oil
◄ ½ teaspoon sea salt
◄ ¼ teaspoon freshly ground black pepper

1. Place the caraway seeds in a small dry skillet over medium-high heat. Toast the seeds for 2 to 3 minutes, then remove them from the heat and let cool. Lightly crush the seeds using a mortar and pestle or with the back of a knife. 2. Place the butter in a small bowl and stir in the crushed caraway seeds and lemon zest. Form the butter into a log and wrap it in parchment paper or plastic wrap. Refrigerate for at least 1 hour or freeze for 20 minutes. 3. Brush or spray the cabbage wedges with the avocado oil, and sprinkle with the salt and pepper. 4. Set the air fryer to 375ºF (191ºC). Place the cabbage in a single layer in the air fryer basket and roast for 20 minutes. Flip and cook for 15 to 20 minutes more, until the cabbage is tender and lightly charred. Plate the cabbage and dot with caraway butter. Tent with foil for 5 minutes to melt the butter, and serve.

Saltine Wax Beans

Prep time: 10 minutes | Cook time: 7 minutes | Serves 4

◄ ½ cup flour
◄ 1 teaspoon smoky chipotle powder
◄ ½ teaspoon ground black pepper
◄ 1 teaspoon sea salt flakes

◄ 2 eggs, beaten
◄ ½ cup crushed saltines
◄ 10 ounces (283 g) wax beans
◄ Cooking spray

1. Preheat the air fryer to 360ºF (182ºC). 2. Combine the flour, chipotle powder, black pepper, and salt in a bowl. Put the eggs in a second bowl. Put the crushed saltines in a third bowl. 3. Wash the beans with cold water and discard any tough strings. 4. Coat the beans with the flour mixture, before dipping them into the beaten egg. Cover them with the crushed saltines. 5. Spritz the beans with cooking spray. 6. Air fry for 4 minutes. Give the air fryer basket a good shake and continue to air fry for 3 minutes. Serve hot.

Chapter 8 Vegetarian Mains

Black Bean and Tomato Chili

Prep time: 15 minutes | Cook time: 23 minutes | Serves 6

- 1 tablespoon olive oil
- 1 medium onion, diced
- 3 garlic cloves, minced
- 1 cup vegetable broth
- 3 cans black beans, drained and rinsed
- 2 cans diced tomatoes
- 2 chipotle peppers, chopped
- 2 teaspoons cumin
- 2 teaspoons chili powder
- 1 teaspoon dried oregano
- ½ teaspoon salt

1. Over a medium heat, fry the garlic and onions in the olive oil for 3 minutes. 2. Add the remaining ingredients, stirring constantly and scraping the bottom to prevent sticking. 3. Preheat the air fryer to 400ºF (204ºC). 4. Take a dish and place the mixture inside. Put a sheet of aluminum foil on top. 5. Transfer to the air fryer and bake for 20 minutes. 6. When ready, plate up and serve immediately.

Roasted Spaghetti Squash

Prep time: 10 minutes | Cook time: 45 minutes | Serves 6

- 1 (4 pounds / 1.8 kg) spaghetti squash, halved and seeded
- 2 tablespoons coconut oil
- 4 tablespoons salted butter, melted
- 1 teaspoon garlic powder
- 2 teaspoons dried parsley

1. Brush shell of spaghetti squash with coconut oil. Brush inside with butter. Sprinkle inside with garlic powder and parsley. 2. Place squash skin side down into ungreased air fryer basket, working in batches if needed. Adjust the temperature to 350ºF (177ºC) and set the timer for 30 minutes. When the timer beeps, flip squash and cook an additional 15 minutes until fork-tender. 3. Use a fork to remove spaghetti strands from shell and serve warm.

Vegetable Burgers

Prep time: 10 minutes | Cook time: 12 minutes | Serves 4

- 8 ounces (227 g) cremini mushrooms
- 2 large egg yolks
- ½ medium zucchini, trimmed and chopped
- ¼ cup peeled and chopped
- yellow onion
- 1 clove garlic, peeled and finely minced
- ½ teaspoon salt
- ¼ teaspoon ground black pepper

1. Place all ingredients into a food processor and pulse twenty times until finely chopped and combined. 2. Separate mixture into four equal sections and press each into a burger shape. Place burgers into ungreased air fryer basket. Adjust the temperature to 375ºF (191ºC) and air fry for 12 minutes, turning burgers halfway through cooking. Burgers will be browned and firm when done. 3. Place burgers on a large plate and let cool 5 minutes before serving.

Greek Stuffed Eggplant

Prep time: 15 minutes | Cook time: 20 minutes | Serves 2

- 1 large eggplant
- 2 tablespoons unsalted butter
- ¼ medium yellow onion, diced
- ¼ cup chopped artichoke
- hearts
- 1 cup fresh spinach
- 2 tablespoons diced red bell pepper
- ½ cup crumbled feta

1. Slice eggplant in half lengthwise and scoop out flesh, leaving enough inside for shell to remain intact. Take eggplant that was scooped out, chop it, and set aside. 2. In a medium skillet over medium heat, add butter and onion. Sauté until onions begin to soften, about 3 to 5 minutes. Add chopped eggplant, artichokes, spinach, and bell pepper. Continue cooking 5 minutes until peppers soften and spinach wilts. Remove from the heat and gently fold in the feta. 3. Place filling into each eggplant shell and place into the air fryer basket. 4. Adjust the temperature to 320ºF (160ºC) and air fry for 20 minutes. 5. Eggplant will be tender when done. Serve warm.

Italian Baked Egg and Veggies

Prep time: 10 minutes | Cook time: 10 minutes | Serves 2

- 2 tablespoons salted butter
- 1 small zucchini, sliced lengthwise and quartered
- ½ medium green bell pepper, seeded and diced
- 1 cup fresh spinach, chopped
- 1 medium Roma tomato,
- diced
- 2 large eggs
- ¼ teaspoon onion powder
- ¼ teaspoon garlic powder
- ½ teaspoon dried basil
- ¼ teaspoon dried oregano

1. Grease two ramekins with 1 tablespoon butter each. 2. In a large bowl, toss zucchini, bell pepper, spinach, and tomatoes. Divide the mixture in two and place half in each ramekin. 3. Crack an egg on top of each ramekin and sprinkle with onion powder, garlic powder, basil, and oregano. Place into the air fryer basket. 4. Adjust the temperature to 330ºF (166ºC) and bake for 10 minutes. 5. Serve immediately.

Spaghetti Squash Alfredo

Prep time: 10 minutes | Cook time: 15 minutes | Serves 2

- ½ large cooked spaghetti squash
- 2 tablespoons salted butter, melted
- ½ cup low-carb Alfredo sauce
- ¼ cup grated vegetarian
- Parmesan cheese
- ½ teaspoon garlic powder
- 1 teaspoon dried parsley
- ¼ teaspoon ground peppercorn
- ½ cup shredded Italian blend cheese

1. Using a fork, remove the strands of spaghetti squash from the shell. Place into a large bowl with butter and Alfredo sauce. Sprinkle with Parmesan, garlic powder, parsley, and peppercorn. 2. Pour into a 4-cup round baking dish and top with shredded cheese. Place dish into the air fryer basket. 3. Adjust the temperature to 320ºF (160ºC) and bake for 15 minutes. When finished, cheese will be golden and bubbling. Serve immediately.

Quiche-Stuffed Peppers

Prep time: 5 minutes | Cook time: 15 minutes | Serves 2

- 2 medium green bell peppers
- 3 large eggs
- ¼ cup full-fat ricotta cheese
- ¼ cup diced yellow onion
- ½ cup chopped broccoli
- ½ cup shredded medium Cheddar cheese

1. Cut the tops off of the peppers and remove the seeds and white membranes with a small knife. 2. In a medium bowl, whisk eggs and ricotta. 3. Add onion and broccoli. Pour the egg and vegetable mixture evenly into each pepper. Top with Cheddar. Place peppers into a 4-cup round baking dish and place into the air fryer basket. 4. Adjust the temperature to 350ºF (177ºC) and bake for 15 minutes. 5. Eggs will be mostly firm and peppers tender when fully cooked. Serve immediately.

Whole Roasted Lemon Cauliflower

Prep time: 5 minutes | Cook time: 15 minutes | Serves 4

- 1 medium head cauliflower
- 2 tablespoons salted butter, melted
- 1 medium lemon
- ½ teaspoon garlic powder
- 1 teaspoon dried parsley

1. Remove the leaves from the head of cauliflower and brush it with melted butter. Cut the lemon in half and zest one half onto the cauliflower. Squeeze the juice of the zested lemon half and pour it over the cauliflower. 2. Sprinkle with garlic powder and parsley. Place cauliflower head into the air fryer basket. 3. Adjust the temperature to 350ºF (177ºC) and air fry for 15 minutes. 4. Check cauliflower every 5 minutes to avoid overcooking. It should be fork tender. 5. To serve, squeeze juice from other lemon half over cauliflower. Serve immediately.

Stuffed Portobellos

Prep time: 10 minutes | Cook time: 8 minutes | Serves 4

- 3 ounces (85 g) cream cheese, softened
- ½ medium zucchini, trimmed and chopped
- ¼ cup seeded and chopped red bell pepper
- 1½ cups chopped fresh
- spinach leaves
- 4 large portobello mushrooms, stems removed
- 2 tablespoons coconut oil, melted
- ½ teaspoon salt

1. In a medium bowl, mix cream cheese, zucchini, pepper, and spinach. 2. Drizzle mushrooms with coconut oil and sprinkle with salt. Scoop ¼ zucchini mixture into each mushroom. 3. Place mushrooms into ungreased air fryer basket. Adjust the temperature to 400ºF (204ºC) and air fry for 8 minutes. Portobellos will be tender and tops will be browned when done. Serve warm.

Garlicky Sesame Carrots

Prep time: 5 minutes | Cook time: 16 minutes | Serves 4 to 6

- 1 pound (454 g) baby carrots
- 1 tablespoon sesame oil
- ½ teaspoon dried dill
- Pinch salt
- Freshly ground black pepper, to taste
- 6 cloves garlic, peeled
- 3 tablespoons sesame seeds

1. Preheat the air fryer to 380ºF (193ºC). 2. In a medium bowl, drizzle the baby carrots with the sesame oil. Sprinkle with the dill, salt, and pepper and toss to coat well. 3. Place the baby carrots in the air fryer basket and roast for 8 minutes. 4. Remove the basket and stir in the garlic. Return the basket to the air fryer and roast for another 8 minutes, or until the carrots are lightly browned. 5. Serve sprinkled with the sesame seeds.

Air Fryer Veggies with Halloumi

Prep time: 5 minutes | Cook time: 14 minutes | Serves 2

- 2 zucchinis, cut into even chunks
- 1 large eggplant, peeled, cut into chunks
- 1 large carrot, cut into chunks
- 6 ounces (170 g) halloumi
- cheese, cubed
- 2 teaspoons olive oil
- Salt and black pepper, to taste
- 1 teaspoon dried mixed herbs

1. Preheat the air fryer to 340ºF (171ºC). 2. Combine the zucchinis, eggplant, carrot, cheese, olive oil, salt, and pepper in a large bowl and toss to coat well. 3. Spread the mixture evenly in the air fryer basket and air fry for 14 minutes until crispy and golden, shaking the basket once during cooking. Serve topped with mixed herbs.

Basmati Risotto

Prep time: 10 minutes | Cook time: 30 minutes | Serves 2

◄ 1 onion, diced
◄ 1 small carrot, diced
◄ 2 cups vegetable broth, boiling
◄ ½ cup grated Cheddar cheese

◄ 1 clove garlic, minced
◄ ¾ cup long grain basmati rice
◄ 1 tablespoon olive oil
◄ 1 tablespoon unsalted butter

1. Preheat the air fryer to 390ºF (199ºC). 2. Grease a baking tin with oil and stir in the butter, garlic, carrot, and onion. 3. Put the tin in the air fryer and bake for 4 minutes. 4. Pour in the rice and bake for a further 4 minutes, stirring three times throughout the baking time. 5. Turn the temperature down to 320ºF (160ºC). 6. Add the vegetable broth and give the dish a gentle stir. Bake for 22 minutes, leaving the air fryer uncovered. 7. Pour in the cheese, stir once more and serve.

Cheese Stuffed Peppers

Prep time: 20 minutes | Cook time: 15 minutes | Serves 2

◄ 1 red bell pepper, top and seeds removed
◄ 1 yellow bell pepper, top and seeds removed

◄ Salt and pepper, to taste
◄ 1 cup Cottage cheese
◄ 4 tablespoons mayonnaise
◄ 2 pickles, chopped

1. Arrange the peppers in the lightly greased air fryer basket. Cook in the preheated air fryer at 400ºF (204ºC) for 15 minutes, turning them over halfway through the cooking time. 2. Season with salt and pepper. Then, in a mixing bowl, combine the cream cheese with the mayonnaise and chopped pickles. Stuff the pepper with the cream cheese mixture and serve. Enjoy!

Crispy Eggplant Rounds

Prep time: 15 minutes | Cook time: 10 minutes | Serves 4

◄ 1 large eggplant, ends trimmed, cut into ½-inch slices
◄ ½ teaspoon salt
◄ 2 ounces (57 g) Parmesan

100% cheese crisps, finely ground
◄ ½ teaspoon paprika
◄ ¼ teaspoon garlic powder
◄ 1 large egg

1. Sprinkle eggplant rounds with salt. Place rounds on a kitchen towel for 30 minutes to draw out excess water. Pat rounds dry. 2. In a medium bowl, mix cheese crisps, paprika, and garlic powder. In a separate medium bowl, whisk egg. Dip each eggplant round in egg, then gently press into cheese crisps to coat both sides. 3. Place eggplant rounds into ungreased air fryer basket. Adjust the temperature to 400ºF (204ºC) and air fry for 10 minutes, turning rounds halfway through cooking. Eggplant will be golden and crispy when done. Serve warm.

Tangy Asparagus and Broccoli

Prep time: 25 minutes | Cook time: 22 minutes | Serves 4

◄ ½ pound (227 g) asparagus, cut into 1½-inch pieces
◄ ½ pound (227 g) broccoli, cut into 1½-inch pieces
◄ 2 tablespoons olive oil

◄ Salt and white pepper, to taste
◄ ½ cup vegetable broth
◄ 2 tablespoons apple cider vinegar

1. Place the vegetables in a single layer in the lightly greased air fryer basket. Drizzle the olive oil over the vegetables. 2. Sprinkle with salt and white pepper. 3. Cook at 380ºF (193ºC) for 15 minutes, shaking the basket halfway through the cooking time. 4. Add ½ cup of vegetable broth to a saucepan; bring to a rapid boil and add the vinegar. Cook for 5 to 7 minutes or until the sauce has reduced by half. 5. Spoon the sauce over the warm vegetables and serve immediately. Bon appétit!

Broccoli with Garlic Sauce

Prep time: 19 minutes | Cook time: 15 minutes | Serves 4

◄ 2 tablespoons olive oil
◄ Kosher salt and freshly ground black pepper, to taste
◄ 1 pound (454 g) broccoli florets
◄ Dipping Sauce:

◄ 2 teaspoons dried rosemary, crushed
◄ 3 garlic cloves, minced
◄ ⅓ teaspoon dried marjoram, crushed
◄ ¼ cup sour cream
◄ ⅓ cup mayonnaise

1. Lightly grease your broccoli with a thin layer of olive oil. Season with salt and ground black pepper. 2. Arrange the seasoned broccoli in the air fryer basket. Bake at 395ºF (202ºC) for 15 minutes, shaking once or twice. In the meantime, prepare the dipping sauce by mixing all the sauce ingredients. Serve warm broccoli with the dipping sauce and enjoy!

Mediterranean Pan Pizza

Prep time: 5 minutes | Cook time: 8 minutes | Serves 2

◄ 1 cup shredded Mozzarella cheese
◄ ¼ medium red bell pepper, seeded and chopped
◄ ½ cup chopped fresh spinach

leaves
◄ 2 tablespoons chopped black olives
◄ 2 tablespoons crumbled feta cheese

1. Sprinkle Mozzarella into an ungreased round nonstick baking dish in an even layer. Add remaining ingredients on top. 2. Place dish into air fryer basket. Adjust the temperature to 350ºF (177ºC) and bake for 8 minutes, checking halfway through to avoid burning. Top of pizza will be golden brown and the cheese melted when done. 3. Remove dish from fryer and let cool 5 minutes before slicing and serving.

Broccoli-Cheese Fritters

Prep time: 5 minutes | Cook time: 20 to 25 minutes | Serves 4

◀ 1 cup broccoli florets
◀ 1 cup shredded Mozzarella cheese
◀ ¾ cup almond flour
◀ ½ cup flaxseed meal, divided
◀ 2 teaspoons baking powder

◀ 1 teaspoon garlic powder
◀ Salt and freshly ground black pepper, to taste
◀ 2 eggs, lightly beaten
◀ ½ cup ranch dressing

1. Preheat the air fryer to 400°F (204°C). 2. In a food processor fitted with a metal blade, pulse the broccoli until very finely chopped. 3. Transfer the broccoli to a large bowl and add the Mozzarella, almond flour, ¼ cup of the flaxseed meal, baking powder, and garlic powder. Stir until thoroughly combined. Season to taste with salt and black pepper. Add the eggs and stir again to form a sticky dough. Shape the dough into 1¼-inch fritters. 4. Place the remaining ¼ cup flaxseed meal in a shallow bowl and roll the fritters in the meal to form an even coating. 5. Working in batches if necessary, arrange the fritters in a single layer in the basket of the air fryer and spray generously with olive oil. Pausing halfway through the cooking time to shake the basket, air fry for 20 to 25 minutes until the fritters are golden brown and crispy. Serve with the ranch dressing for dipping.

Mediterranean Air Fried Veggies

Prep time: 10 minutes | Cook time: 6 minutes | Serves 4

◀ 1 large zucchini, sliced
◀ 1 cup cherry tomatoes, halved
◀ 1 parsnip, sliced
◀ 1 green pepper, sliced
◀ 1 carrot, sliced

◀ 1 teaspoon mixed herbs
◀ 1 teaspoon mustard
◀ 1 teaspoon garlic purée
◀ 6 tablespoons olive oil
◀ Salt and ground black pepper, to taste

1. Preheat the air fryer to 400°F (204°C). 2. Combine all the ingredients in a bowl, making sure to coat the vegetables well. 3. Transfer to the air fryer and air fry for 6 minutes, ensuring the vegetables are tender and browned. 4. Serve immediately.

Crispy Cabbage Steaks

Prep time: 5 minutes | Cook time: 10 minutes | Serves 4

◀ 1 small head green cabbage, cored and cut into ½-inch-thick slices
◀ ¼ teaspoon salt
◀ ¼ teaspoon ground black pepper

◀ 2 tablespoons olive oil
◀ 1 clove garlic, peeled and finely minced
◀ ½ teaspoon dried thyme
◀ ½ teaspoon dried parsley

1. Sprinkle each side of cabbage with salt and pepper, then place into ungreased air fryer basket, working in batches if needed. 2. Drizzle each side of cabbage with olive oil, then sprinkle with remaining ingredients on both sides. Adjust the temperature to 350°F (177°C) and air fry for 10 minutes, turning "steaks" halfway through cooking. 3.Cabbage will be browned at the edges and tender when done. Serve warm.

Chapter 9 Snacks and Appetizers

Cinnamon-Apple Chips

Prep time: 10 minutes | Cook time: 32 minutes | Serves 4

- Oil, for spraying
- 2 Red Delicious or Honeycrisp apples
- ¼ teaspoon ground cinnamon, divided

1. Line the air fryer basket with parchment and spray lightly with oil. 2. Trim the uneven ends off the apples. Using a mandoline on the thinnest setting or a sharp knife, cut the apples into very thin slices. Discard the cores. 3. Place half of the apple slices in a single layer in the prepared basket and sprinkle with half of the cinnamon. 4. Place a metal air fryer trivet on top of the apples to keep them from flying around while they are cooking. 5. Air fry at 300ºF (149ºC) for 16 minutes, flipping every 5 minutes to ensure even cooking. Repeat with the remaining apple slices and cinnamon. 6. Let cool to room temperature before serving. The chips will firm up as they cool.

Baked Spanakopita Dip

Prep time: 10 minutes | Cook time: 15 minutes | Serves 2

- Olive oil cooking spray
- 3 tablespoons olive oil, divided
- 2 tablespoons minced white onion
- 2 garlic cloves, minced
- 4 cups fresh spinach
- 4 ounces (113 g) cream cheese, softened
- 4 ounces (113 g) feta cheese, divided
- Zest of 1 lemon
- ¼ teaspoon ground nutmeg
- 1 teaspoon dried dill
- ½ teaspoon salt
- Pita chips, carrot sticks, or sliced bread for serving (optional)

1. Preheat the air fryer to 360°F(182ºC). Coat the inside of a 6-inch ramekin or baking dish with olive oil cooking spray. 2. In a large skillet over medium heat, heat 1 tablespoon of the olive oil. Add the onion, then cook for 1 minute. 3. Add in the garlic and cook, stirring for 1 minute more. 4. Reduce the heat to low and mix in the spinach and water. Let this cook for 2 to 3 minutes, or until the spinach has wilted. Remove the skillet from the heat. 5. In a medium bowl, combine the cream cheese, 2 ounces (57 g) of the feta, and the remaining 2 tablespoons of olive oil, along with the lemon zest, nutmeg, dill, and salt. Mix until just combined. 6. Add the vegetables to the cheese base and stir until combined. 7. Pour the dip mixture into the prepared ramekin and top with the remaining 2 ounces (57 g) of feta cheese. 8. Place the dip into the air fryer basket and cook for 10 minutes, or until heated through and bubbling. 9. Serve with pita chips, carrot sticks, or sliced bread.

Vegetable Pot Stickers

Prep time: 12 minutes | Cook time: 11 to 18 minutes | Makes 12 pot stickers

- 1 cup shredded red cabbage
- ¼ cup chopped button mushrooms
- ¼ cup grated carrot
- 2 tablespoons minced onion
- 2 garlic cloves, minced
- 2 teaspoons grated fresh ginger
- 12 gyoza/pot sticker wrappers
- 2½ teaspoons olive oil, divided

1. In a baking pan, combine the red cabbage, mushrooms, carrot, onion, garlic, and ginger. Add 1 tablespoon of water. Place in the air fryer and air fry at 370ºF (188ºC) for 3 to 6 minutes, until the vegetables are crisp-tender. Drain and set aside. 2. Working one at a time, place the pot sticker wrappers on a work surface. Top each wrapper with a scant 1 tablespoon of the filling. Fold half of the wrapper over the other half to form a half circle. Dab one edge with water and press both edges together. 3. To another pan, add 1¼ teaspoons of olive oil. Put half of the pot stickers, seam-side up, in the pan. Air fry for 5 minutes, or until the bottoms are light golden brown. Add 1 tablespoon of water and return the pan to the air fryer. 4. Air fry for 4 to 6 minutes more, or until hot. Repeat with the remaining pot stickers, remaining 1¼ teaspoons of oil, and another tablespoon of water. Serve immediately.

Roasted Pearl Onion Dip

Prep time: 5 minutes | Cook time: 12 minutes | Serves 4

- 2 cups peeled pearl onions
- 3 garlic cloves
- 3 tablespoons olive oil, divided
- ½ teaspoon salt
- 1 cup nonfat plain Greek yogurt
- 1 tablespoon lemon juice
- ¼ teaspoon black pepper
- ⅛ teaspoon red pepper flakes
- Pita chips, vegetables, or toasted bread for serving (optional)

1. Preheat the air fryer to 360°F(182ºC). 2. In a large bowl, combine the pearl onions and garlic with 2 tablespoons of the olive oil until the onions are well coated. 3. Pour the garlic-and-onion mixture into the air fryer basket and roast for 12 minutes. 4. Transfer the garlic and onions to a food processor. Pulse the vegetables several times, until the onions are minced but still have some chunks. 5. In a large bowl, combine the garlic and onions and the remaining 1 tablespoon of olive oil, along with the salt, yogurt, lemon juice, black pepper, and red pepper flakes. 6. Cover and chill for 1 hour before serving with pita chips, vegetables, or toasted bread.

Spiralized Potato Nest with Tomato Ketchup

Prep time: 10 minutes | Cook time: 15 minutes | Serves 2

- 1 large russet potato (about 12 ounces / 340 g)
- 2 tablespoons vegetable oil
- 1 tablespoon hot smoked paprika
- ½ teaspoon garlic powder
- Kosher salt and freshly ground black pepper, to taste
- ½ cup canned crushed tomatoes
- 2 tablespoons apple cider vinegar
- 1 tablespoon dark brown sugar
- 1 tablespoon Worcestershire sauce
- 1 teaspoon mild hot sauce

1. Using a spiralizer, spiralize the potato, then place in a large colander. (If you don't have a spiralizer, cut the potato into thin ⅛-inch-thick matchsticks.) Rinse the potatoes under cold running water until the water runs clear. Spread the potatoes out on a double-thick layer of paper towels and pat completely dry. 2. In a large bowl, combine the potatoes, oil, paprika, and garlic powder. Season with salt and pepper and toss to combine. Transfer the potatoes to the air fryer and air fry at 400ºF (204ºC) until the potatoes are browned and crisp, 15 minutes, shaking the basket halfway through. 3. Meanwhile, in a small blender, purée the tomatoes, vinegar, brown sugar, Worcestershire, and hot sauce until smooth. Pour into a small saucepan or skillet and simmer over medium heat until reduced by half, 3 to 5 minutes. Pour the homemade ketchup into a bowl and let cool. 4. Remove the spiralized potato nest from the air fryer and serve hot with the ketchup.

Crispy Green Tomatoes with Horseradish

Prep time: 18 minutes | Cook time: 10 to 15 minutes | Serves 4

- 2 eggs
- ¼ cup buttermilk
- ½ cup bread crumbs
- ½ cup cornmeal
- ¼ teaspoon salt
- Horseradish Sauce:
- ¼ cup sour cream
- ¼ cup mayonnaise
- 2 teaspoons prepared horseradish
- 1½ pounds (680 g) firm green tomatoes, cut into ¼-inch slices
- Cooking spray
- ½ teaspoon lemon juice
- ½ teaspoon Worcestershire sauce
- ⅛ teaspoon black pepper

1. Preheat air fryer to 390ºF (199ºC). Spritz the air fryer basket with cooking spray. 2. In a small bowl, whisk together all the ingredients for the horseradish sauce until smooth. Set aside. 3. In a shallow dish, beat the eggs and buttermilk. 4. In a separate shallow dish, thoroughly combine the bread crumbs, cornmeal, and salt. 5. Dredge the tomato slices, one at a time, in the egg mixture, then roll in the bread crumb mixture until evenly coated. 6. Working in batches, place the tomato slices in the air fryer basket in a single layer. Spray them with cooking spray. 7. Air fry for 10 to 15 minutes, flipping the slices halfway through, or until the tomato slices are nicely browned and crisp. 8. Remove from the basket to a platter and repeat with the remaining tomato slices. 9. Serve drizzled with the prepared horseradish sauce.

Shrimp Toasts with Sesame Seeds

Prep time: 15 minutes | Cook time: 6 to 8 minutes | Serves 4 to 6

- ½ pound (227 g) raw shrimp, peeled and deveined
- 1 egg, beaten
- 2 scallions, chopped, plus more for garnish
- 2 tablespoons chopped fresh cilantro
- 2 teaspoons grated fresh ginger
- 1 to 2 teaspoons sriracha
- sauce
- 1 teaspoon soy sauce
- ½ teaspoon toasted sesame oil
- 6 slices thinly sliced white sandwich bread
- ½ cup sesame seeds
- Cooking spray
- Thai chili sauce, for serving

1. Preheat the air fryer to 400ºF (204ºC). Spritz the air fryer basket with cooking spray. 2. In a food processor, add the shrimp, egg, scallions, cilantro, ginger, sriracha sauce, soy sauce and sesame oil, and pulse until chopped finely. You'll need to stop the food processor occasionally to scrape down the sides. Transfer the shrimp mixture to a bowl. 3. On a clean work surface, cut the crusts off the sandwich bread. Using a brush, generously brush one side of each slice of bread with shrimp mixture. 4. Place the sesame seeds on a plate. Press bread slices, shrimp-side down, into sesame seeds to coat evenly. Cut each slice diagonally into quarters. 5. Spread the coated slices in a single layer in the air fryer basket. 6. Air fry in batches for 6 to 8 minutes, or until golden and crispy. Flip the bread slices halfway through. Repeat with the remaining bread slices. 7. Transfer to a plate and let cool for 5 minutes. Top with the chopped scallions and serve warm with Thai chili sauce.

Roasted Grape Dip

Prep time: 10 minutes | Cook time: 8 to 12 minutes | Serves 6

- 2 cups seedless red grapes, rinsed and patted dry
- 1 tablespoon apple cider vinegar
- 1 tablespoon honey
- 1 cup low-fat Greek yogurt
- 2 tablespoons 2% milk
- 2 tablespoons minced fresh basil

1. In the air fryer basket, sprinkle the grapes with the cider vinegar and drizzle with the honey. Toss to coat. Roast the grapes at 380ºF (193ºC) for 8 to 12 minutes, or until shriveled but still soft. Remove from the air fryer. 2. In a medium bowl, stir together the yogurt and milk. 3. Gently blend in the grapes and basil. Serve immediately, or cover and chill for 1 to 2 hours.

Crispy Cajun Dill Pickle Chips

Prep time: 5 minutes | Cook time: 10 minutes | Makes 16 slices

- ¼ cup all-purpose flour
- ½ cup panko bread crumbs
- 1 large egg, beaten
- 2 teaspoons Cajun seasoning
- 2 large dill pickles, sliced into 8 rounds each
- Cooking spray

1. Preheat the air fryer to 390ºF (199ºC). 2. Place the all-purpose flour, panko bread crumbs, and egg into 3 separate shallow bowls, then stir the Cajun seasoning into the flour. 3. Dredge each pickle chip in the flour mixture, then the egg, and finally the bread crumbs. Shake off any excess, then place each coated pickle chip on a plate. 4. Spritz the air fryer basket with cooking spray, then place 8 pickle chips in the basket and air fry for 5 minutes, or until crispy and golden brown. Repeat this process with the remaining pickle chips. 5. Remove the chips and allow to slightly cool on a wire rack before serving.

Cheesy Hash Brown Bruschetta

Prep time: 5 minutes | Cook time: 6 to 8 minutes | Serves 4

- 4 frozen hash brown patties
- 1 tablespoon olive oil
- ⅓ cup chopped cherry tomatoes
- 3 tablespoons diced fresh Mozzarella
- 2 tablespoons grated Parmesan cheese
- 1 tablespoon balsamic vinegar
- 1 tablespoon minced fresh basil

1. Preheat the air fryer to 400ºF (204ºC). 2. Place the hash brown patties in the air fryer in a single layer. Air fry for 6 to 8 minutes, or until the potatoes are crisp, hot, and golden brown. 3. Meanwhile, combine the olive oil, tomatoes, Mozzarella, Parmesan, vinegar, and basil in a small bowl. 4. When the potatoes are done, carefully remove from the basket and arrange on a serving plate. Top with the tomato mixture and serve.

Honey-Mustard Chicken Wings

Prep time: 10 minutes | Cook time: 24 minutes | Serves 2

- 2 pounds (907 g) chicken wings
- Salt and freshly ground black pepper, to taste
- 2 tablespoons butter
- ¼ cup honey
- ¼ cup spicy brown mustard
- Pinch ground cayenne pepper
- 2 teaspoons Worcestershire sauce

1. Prepare the chicken wings by cutting off the wing tips and discarding (or freezing for chicken stock). Divide the drumettes from the wingettes by cutting through the joint. Place the chicken wing pieces in a large bowl. 2. Preheat the air fryer to 400ºF (204ºC).

3. Season the wings with salt and freshly ground black pepper and air fry the wings in two batches for 10 minutes per batch, shaking the basket half way through the cooking process. 4. While the wings are air frying, combine the remaining ingredients in a small saucepan over low heat. 5. When both batches are done, toss all the wings with the honey-mustard sauce and toss them all back into the basket for another 4 minutes to heat through and finish cooking. Give the basket a good shake part way through the cooking process to redistribute the wings. Remove the wings from the air fryer and serve.

Golden Onion Rings

Prep time: 15 minutes | Cook time: 14 minutes per batch | Serves 4

- 1 large white onion, peeled and cut into ½ to ¾-inch-thick slices (about 2 cups)
- ½ cup 2% milk
- 1 cup whole-wheat pastry flour, or all-purpose flour
- 2 tablespoons cornstarch
- ¾ teaspoon sea salt, divided
- ½ teaspoon freshly ground black pepper, divided
- ¾ teaspoon granulated garlic, divided
- 1½ cups whole grain bread crumbs, or gluten-free bread crumbs
- Cooking oil spray (coconut, sunflower, or safflower)
- Ketchup, for serving (optional)

1. Carefully separate the onion slices into rings—a gentle touch is important here. 2. Place the milk in a shallow bowl and set aside. 3. Make the first breading: In a medium bowl, stir together the flour, cornstarch, ¼ teaspoon of salt, ¼ teaspoon of pepper, and ¼ teaspoon of granulated garlic. Set aside. 4. Make the second breading: In a separate medium bowl, stir together the bread crumbs with the remaining ½ teaspoon of salt, the remaining ½ teaspoon of garlic, and the remaining ½ teaspoon of pepper. Set aside. 5. Insert the crisper plate into the basket and the basket into the unit. Preheat the unit by selecting AIR FRY, setting the temperature to 390ºF (199ºC), and setting the time to 3 minutes. Select START/ STOP to begin. 6. Once the unit is preheated, spray the crisper plate and the basket with cooking oil. 7. To make the onion rings, dip one ring into the milk and into the first breading mixture. Dip the ring into the milk again and back into the first breading mixture, coating thoroughly. Dip the ring into the milk one last time and then into the second breading mixture, coating thoroughly. Gently lay the onion ring in the basket. Repeat with additional rings and, as you place them into the basket, do not overlap them too much. Once all the onion rings are in the basket, generously spray the tops with cooking oil. 8. Select AIR FRY, set the temperature to 390ºF (199ºC), and set the time to 14 minutes. Insert the basket into the unit. Select START/STOP to begin. 9. After 4 minutes, open the unit and spray the rings generously with cooking oil. Close the unit to resume cooking. After 3 minutes, remove the basket and spray the onion rings again. Remove the rings, turn them over, and place them back into the basket. Generously spray them again with oil. Reinsert the basket to resume cooking. After 4 minutes, generously spray the rings with oil one last time. Resume cooking for the remaining 3 minutes, or until the onion rings are very crunchy and brown. 10. When the cooking is complete, serve the hot rings with ketchup, or other sauce of choice.

Cream Cheese Wontons

Prep time: 15 minutes | Cook time: 6 minutes | Makes 20 wontons

◄ Oil, for spraying
◄ 20 wonton wrappers
◄ 4 ounces (113 g) cream cheese

1. Line the air fryer basket with parchment and spray lightly with oil. 2. Pour some water in a small bowl. 3. Lay out a wonton wrapper and place 1 teaspoon of cream cheese in the center. 4. Dip your finger in the water and moisten the edge of the wonton wrapper. Fold over the opposite corners to make a triangle and press the edges together. 5. Pinch the corners of the triangle together to form a classic wonton shape. Place the wonton in the prepared basket. Repeat with the remaining wrappers and cream cheese. You may need to work in batches, depending on the size of your air fryer. 6. Air fry at 400ºF (204ºC) for 6 minutes, or until golden brown around the edges.

Air Fried Pot Stickers

Prep time: 10 minutes | Cook time: 18 to 20 minutes | Makes 30 pot stickers

◄ ½ cup finely chopped cabbage
◄ ¼ cup finely chopped red bell pepper
◄ 2 green onions, finely chopped
◄ 1 egg, beaten
◄ 2 tablespoons cocktail sauce
◄ 2 teaspoons low-sodium soy sauce
◄ 30 wonton wrappers
◄ 1 tablespoon water, for brushing the wrappers

1. Preheat the air fryer to 360ºF (182ºC). 2. In a small bowl, combine the cabbage, pepper, green onions, egg, cocktail sauce, and soy sauce, and mix well. 3. Put about 1 teaspoon of the mixture in the center of each wonton wrapper. Fold the wrapper in half, covering the filling; dampen the edges with water, and seal. You can crimp the edges of the wrapper with your fingers so they look like the pot stickers you get in restaurants. Brush them with water. 4. Place the pot stickers in the air fryer basket and air fry in 2 batches for 9 to 10 minutes, or until the pot stickers are hot and the bottoms are lightly browned. 5. Serve hot.

Lemony Endive in Curried Yogurt

Prep time: 5 minutes | Cook time: 10 minutes | Serves 6

◄ 6 heads endive
◄ ½ cup plain and fat-free yogurt
◄ 3 tablespoons lemon juice
◄ 1 teaspoon garlic powder
◄ ½ teaspoon curry powder
◄ Salt and ground black pepper, to taste

1. Wash the endives, and slice them in half lengthwise. 2. In a bowl, mix together the yogurt, lemon juice, garlic powder, curry powder, salt and pepper. 3. Brush the endive halves with the marinade, coating them completely. Allow to sit for at least 30 minutes or up to 24 hours. 4. Preheat the air fryer to 320ºF (160ºC). 5. Put the endives in the air fryer basket and air fry for 10 minutes. 6. Serve hot.

Egg Roll Pizza Sticks

Prep time: 10 minutes | Cook time: 5 minutes | Serves 4

◄ Olive oil
◄ 8 pieces reduced-fat string cheese
◄ 8 egg roll wrappers
◄ 24 slices turkey pepperoni
◄ Marinara sauce, for dipping (optional)

1. Spray the air fryer basket lightly with olive oil. Fill a small bowl with water. 2. Place each egg roll wrapper diagonally on a work surface. It should look like a diamond. 3. Place 3 slices of turkey pepperoni in a vertical line down the center of the wrapper. 4. Place 1 Mozzarella cheese stick on top of the turkey pepperoni. 5. Fold the top and bottom corners of the egg roll wrapper over the cheese stick. 6. Fold the left corner over the cheese stick and roll the cheese stick up to resemble a spring roll. Dip a finger in the water and seal the edge of the roll 7. Repeat with the rest of the pizza sticks. 8. Place them in the air fryer basket in a single layer, making sure to leave a little space between each one. Lightly spray the pizza sticks with oil. You may need to cook these in batches. 9. Air fry at 375ºF (191ºC) until the pizza sticks are lightly browned and crispy, about 5 minutes. 10. These are best served hot while the cheese is melted. Accompany with a small bowl of marinara sauce, if desired.

Eggplant Fries

Prep time: 10 minutes | Cook time: 7 to 8 minutes per batch | Serves 4

◄ 1 medium eggplant
◄ 1 teaspoon ground coriander
◄ 1 teaspoon cumin
◄ 1 teaspoon garlic powder
◄ ½ teaspoon salt
◄ 1 cup crushed panko bread
crumbs
◄ 1 large egg
◄ 2 tablespoons water
◄ Oil for misting or cooking spray

1. Peel and cut the eggplant into fat fries, ⅜- to ½-inch thick. 2. Preheat the air fryer to 390ºF (199ºC). 3. In a small cup, mix together the coriander, cumin, garlic, and salt. 4. Combine 1 teaspoon of the seasoning mix and panko crumbs in a shallow dish. 5. Place eggplant fries in a large bowl, sprinkle with remaining seasoning, and stir well to combine. 6. Beat eggs and water together and pour over eggplant fries. Stir to coat. 7. Remove eggplant from egg wash, shaking off excess, and roll in panko crumbs. 8. Spray with oil. 9. Place half of the fries in air fryer basket. You should have only a single layer, but it's fine if they overlap a little. 10. Cook for 5 minutes. Shake basket, mist lightly with oil, and cook 2 to 3 minutes longer, until browned and crispy. 11. Repeat step 10 to cook remaining eggplant.

Crunchy Tex-Mex Tortilla Chips

Prep time: 5 minutes | Cook time: 5 minutes | Serves 4

- Olive oil
- ½ teaspoon salt
- ½ teaspoon ground cumin
- ½ teaspoon chili powder
- ½ teaspoon paprika
- Pinch cayenne pepper
- 8 (6-inch) corn tortillas, each cut into 6 wedges

1. Spray fryer basket lightly with olive oil. 2. In a small bowl, combine the salt, cumin, chili powder, paprika, and cayenne pepper. 3. Place the tortilla wedges in the air fryer basket in a single layer. Spray the tortillas lightly with oil and sprinkle with some of the seasoning mixture. You will need to cook the tortillas in batches. 4. Air fry at 375ºF (191ºC) for 2 to 3 minutes. Shake the basket and cook until the chips are light brown and crispy, an additional 2 to 3 minutes. Watch the chips closely so they do not burn.

Bacon-Wrapped Pickle Spears

Prep time: 10 minutes | Cook time: 8 minutes | Serves 4

- 8 to 12 slices bacon
- ¼ cup (2 ounces / 57 g) cream cheese, softened
- ¼ cup shredded Mozzarella
- cheese
- 8 dill pickle spears
- ½ cup ranch dressing

1. Lay the bacon slices on a flat surface. In a medium bowl, combine the cream cheese and Mozzarella. Stir until well blended. Spread the cheese mixture over the bacon slices. 2. Place a pickle spear on a bacon slice and roll the bacon around the pickle in a spiral, ensuring the pickle is fully covered. (You may need to use more than one slice of bacon per pickle to fully cover the spear.) Tuck in the ends to ensure the bacon stays put. Repeat to wrap all the pickles. 3. Place the wrapped pickles in the air fryer basket in a single layer. Set the air fryer to 400ºF (204ºC) for 8 minutes, or until the bacon is cooked through and crisp on the edges. 4. Serve the pickle spears with ranch dressing on the side.

Asian Rice Logs

Prep time: 30 minutes | Cook time: 5 minutes | Makes 8 rice logs

- 1½ cups cooked jasmine or sushi rice
- ¼ teaspoon salt
- 2 teaspoons five-spice powder
- 2 teaspoons diced shallots
- 1 tablespoon tamari sauce
- 1 egg, beaten
- 1 teaspoon sesame oil
- 2 teaspoons water
- ⅓ cup plain bread crumbs
- ¾ cup panko bread crumbs
- 2 tablespoons sesame seeds
- Orange Marmalade Dipping Sauce:
- ½ cup all-natural orange marmalade
- 1 tablespoon soy sauce

1. Make the rice according to package instructions. While the rice is cooking, make the dipping sauce by combining the marmalade

and soy sauce and set aside. 2. Stir together the cooked rice, salt, five-spice powder, shallots, and tamari sauce. 3. Divide rice into 8 equal pieces. With slightly damp hands, mold each piece into a log shape. Chill in freezer for 10 to 15 minutes. 4. Mix the egg, sesame oil, and water together in a shallow bowl. 5. Place the plain bread crumbs on a sheet of wax paper. 6. Mix the panko bread crumbs with the sesame seeds and place on another sheet of wax paper. 7. Roll the rice logs in plain bread crumbs, then dip in egg wash, and then dip in the panko and sesame seeds. 8. Cook the logs at 390ºF (199ºC) for approximately 5 minutes, until golden brown. 9. Cool slightly before serving with Orange Marmalade Dipping Sauce.

Pickle Chips

Prep time: 30 minutes | Cook time: 12 minutes | Serves 4

- Oil, for spraying
- 2 cups sliced dill or sweet pickles, drained
- 1 cup buttermilk
- 2 cups all-purpose flour
- 2 large eggs, beaten
- 2 cups panko bread crumbs
- ¼ teaspoon salt

1. Line the air fryer basket with parchment and spray lightly with oil. 2. In a shallow bowl, combine the pickles and buttermilk and let soak for at least 1 hour, then drain. 3. Place the flour, beaten eggs, and bread crumbs in separate bowls. 4. Coat each pickle chip lightly in the flour, dip in the eggs, and dredge in the bread crumbs. Be sure each one is evenly coated. 5. Place the pickle chips in the prepared basket, sprinkle with the salt, and spray lightly with oil. You may need to work in batches, depending on the size of your air fryer. 6. Air fry at 390ºF (199ºC) for 5 minutes, flip, and cook for another 5 to 7 minutes, or until crispy. Serve hot.

Feta and Quinoa Stuffed Mushrooms

Prep time: 5 minutes | Cook time: 8 minutes | Serves 6

- 2 tablespoons finely diced red bell pepper
- 1 garlic clove, minced
- ¼ cup cooked quinoa
- ⅛ teaspoon salt
- ¼ teaspoon dried oregano
- 24 button mushrooms,
- stemmed
- 2 ounces (57 g) crumbled feta
- 3 tablespoons whole wheat bread crumbs
- Olive oil cooking spray

1. Preheat the air fryer to 360°F(182°C). 2. In a small bowl, combine the bell pepper, garlic, quinoa, salt, and oregano. 3. Spoon the quinoa stuffing into the mushroom caps until just filled. 4. Add a small piece of feta to the top of each mushroom. 5. Sprinkle a pinch bread crumbs over the feta on each mushroom. 6. Spray the basket of the air fryer with olive oil cooking spray, then gently place the mushrooms into the basket, making sure that they don't touch each other. (Depending on the size of the air fryer, you may have to cook them in two batches.) 7. Place the basket into the air fryer and bake for 8 minutes. 8. Remove from the air fryer and serve.

Dark Chocolate and Cranberry Granola Bars

Prep time: 5 minutes | Cook time: 15 minutes | Serves 6

- ◄ 2 cups certified gluten-free quick oats
- ◄ 2 tablespoons sugar-free dark chocolate chunks
- ◄ 2 tablespoons unsweetened dried cranberries
- ◄ 3 tablespoons unsweetened shredded coconut
- ◄ ½ cup raw honey
- ◄ 1 teaspoon ground cinnamon
- ◄ ⅛ teaspoon salt
- ◄ 2 tablespoons olive oil

1. Preheat the air fryer to 360°F(182°C). Line an 8-by-8-inch baking dish with parchment paper that comes up the side so you can lift it out after cooking. 2. In a large bowl, mix together all of the ingredients until well combined. 3. Press the oat mixture into the pan in an even layer. 4. Place the pan into the air fryer basket and bake for 15 minutes. 5. Remove the pan from the air fryer, and lift the granola cake out of the pan using the edges of the parchment paper. 6. Allow to cool for 5 minutes before slicing into 6 equal bars. 7. Serve immediately, or wrap in plastic wrap and store at room temperature for up to 1 week.

Kale Chips with Sesame

Prep time: 15 minutes | Cook time: 8 minutes | Serves 5

- ◄ 8 cups deribbed kale leaves, torn into 2-inch pieces
- ◄ 1½ tablespoons olive oil
- ◄ ¾ teaspoon chili powder
- ◄ ¼ teaspoon garlic powder
- ◄ ½ teaspoon paprika
- ◄ 2 teaspoons sesame seeds

1. Preheat air fryer to 350°F (177°C). 2. In a large bowl, toss the kale with the olive oil, chili powder, garlic powder, paprika, and sesame seeds until well coated. 3. Put the kale in the air fryer basket and air fry for 8 minutes, flipping the kale twice during cooking, or until the kale is crispy. 4. Serve warm.

Skinny Fries

Prep time: 10 minutes | Cook time: 15 minutes per batch | Serves 2

- ◄ 2 to 3 russet potatoes, peeled and cut into ¼-inch sticks
- ◄ 2 to 3 teaspoons olive or
- vegetable oil
- ◄ Salt, to taste

1. Cut the potatoes into ¼-inch strips. (A mandolin with a julienne blade is really helpful here.) Rinse the potatoes with cold water several times and let them soak in cold water for at least 10 minutes or as long as overnight. 2. Preheat the air fryer to 380°F (193°C). 3. Drain and dry the potato sticks really well, using a clean kitchen towel. Toss the fries with the oil in a bowl and then air fry the fries in two batches at 380°F (193°C) for 15 minutes, shaking the basket a couple of times while they cook. 4. Add the first batch of French

fries back into the air fryer basket with the finishing batch and let everything warm through for a few minutes. As soon as the fries are done, season them with salt and transfer to a plate or basket. Serve them warm with ketchup or your favorite dip.

Browned Ricotta with Capers and Lemon

Prep time: 10 minutes | Cook time: 8 to 10 minutes | Serves 4 to 6

- ◄ 1½ cups whole milk ricotta cheese
- ◄ 2 tablespoons extra-virgin olive oil
- ◄ 2 tablespoons capers, rinsed
- ◄ Zest of 1 lemon, plus more for garnish
- ◄ 1 teaspoon finely chopped
- fresh rosemary
- ◄ Pinch crushed red pepper flakes
- ◄ Salt and freshly ground black pepper, to taste
- ◄ 1 tablespoon grated Parmesan cheese

1. Preheat the air fryer to 380°F (193°C). 2. In a mixing bowl, stir together the ricotta cheese, olive oil, capers, lemon zest, rosemary, red pepper flakes, salt, and pepper until well combined. 3. Spread the mixture evenly in a baking dish and place it in the air fryer basket. 4. Air fry for 8 to 10 minutes until the top is nicely browned. 5. Remove from the basket and top with a sprinkle of grated Parmesan cheese. 6. Garnish with the lemon zest and serve warm.

Sweet Potato Fries with Mayonnaise

Prep time: 5 minutes | Cook time: 20 minutes | Serves 2 to 3

- ◄ 1 large sweet potato (about 1 pound / 454 g), scrubbed
- ◄ 1 teaspoon vegetable or canola oil
- ◄ Salt, to taste
- ◄ Dipping Sauce:
- ◄ ¼ cup light mayonnaise
- ◄ ½ teaspoon sriracha sauce
- ◄ 1 tablespoon spicy brown mustard
- ◄ 1 tablespoon sweet Thai chili sauce

1. Preheat the air fryer to 200°F (93°C). 2. On a flat work surface, cut the sweet potato into fry-shaped strips about ¼ inch wide and ¼ inch thick. You can use a mandoline to slice the sweet potato quickly and uniformly. 3. In a medium bowl, drizzle the sweet potato strips with the oil and toss well. 4. Transfer to the air fryer basket and air fry for 10 minutes, shaking the basket twice during cooking. 5. Remove the air fryer basket and sprinkle with the salt and toss to coat. 6. Increase the air fryer temperature to 400°F (204°C) and air fry for an additional 10 minutes, or until the fries are crispy and tender. Shake the basket a few times during cooking. 7. Meanwhile, whisk together all the ingredients for the sauce in a small bowl. 8. Remove the sweet potato fries from the basket to a plate and serve warm alongside the dipping sauce.

Tangy Fried Pickle Spears

Prep time: 5 minutes | Cook time: 15 minutes | Serves 6

◄ 2 jars sweet and sour pickle spears, patted dry
◄ 2 medium-sized eggs
◄ ⅓ cup milk
◄ 1 teaspoon garlic powder
◄ 1 teaspoon sea salt
◄ ½ teaspoon shallot powder
◄ ⅓ teaspoon chili powder
◄ ⅓ cup all-purpose flour
◄ Cooking spray

1. Preheat the air fryer to 385ºF (196ºC). Spritz the air fryer basket with cooking spray. 2. In a bowl, beat together the eggs with milk. In another bowl, combine garlic powder, sea salt, shallot powder, chili powder and all-purpose flour until well blended. 3. One by one, roll the pickle spears in the powder mixture, then dredge them in the egg mixture. Dip them in the powder mixture a second time for additional coating. 4. Arrange the coated pickles in the prepared basket. Air fry for 15 minutes until golden and crispy, shaking the basket halfway through to ensure even cooking. 5. Transfer to a plate and let cool for 5 minutes before serving.

Asiago Shishito Peppers

Prep time: 5 minutes | Cook time: 10 minutes | Serves 4

◄ Oil, for spraying
◄ 6 ounces (170 g) shishito peppers
◄ 1 tablespoon olive oil
◄ ½ teaspoon salt
◄ ½ teaspoon lemon pepper
◄ ⅓ cup grated Asiago cheese, divided

1. Line the air fryer basket with parchment and spray lightly with oil. 2. Rinse the shishitos and pat dry with paper towels. 3. In a large bowl, mix together the shishitos, olive oil, salt, and lemon pepper. Place the shishitos in the prepared basket. 4. Roast at 350ºF (177ºC) for 10 minutes, or until blistered but not burned. 5. Sprinkle with half of the cheese and cook for 1 more minute. 6. Transfer to a serving plate. Immediately sprinkle with the remaining cheese and serve.

Onion Pakoras

Prep time: 30 minutes | Cook time: 10 minutes per batch | Serves 2

◄ 2 medium yellow or white onions, sliced (2 cups)
◄ ½ cup chopped fresh cilantro
◄ 2 tablespoons vegetable oil
◄ 1 tablespoon chickpea flour
◄ 1 tablespoon rice flour, or 2
tablespoons chickpea flour
◄ 1 teaspoon ground turmeric
◄ 1 teaspoon cumin seeds
◄ 1 teaspoon kosher salt
◄ ½ teaspoon cayenne pepper
◄ Vegetable oil spray

1. In a large bowl, combine the onions, cilantro, oil, chickpea flour, rice flour, turmeric, cumin seeds, salt, and cayenne. Stir to combine. Cover and let stand for 30 minutes or up to overnight. (This allows the onions to release moisture, creating a batter.) Mix well before using. 2. Spray the air fryer basket generously with vegetable oil spray. Drop half of the batter in 6 heaping tablespoons into the basket. Set the air fryer to 350ºF (177ºC) for 8 minutes. Carefully turn the pakoras over and spray with oil spray. Set the air fryer for 2 minutes, or until the batter is cooked through and crisp. 3. Repeat with remaining batter to make 6 more pakoras, checking at 6 minutes for doneness. Serve hot.

Authentic Scotch Eggs

Prep time: 15 minutes | Cook time: 11 to 13 minutes | Serves 6

◄ 1½ pounds (680 g) bulk lean chicken or turkey sausage
◄ 3 raw eggs, divided
◄ 1½ cups dried bread crumbs,
divided
◄ ½ cup all-purpose flour
◄ 6 hardboiled eggs, peeled
◄ Cooking oil spray

1. In a large bowl, combine the chicken sausage, 1 raw egg, and ½ cup of bread crumbs and mix well. Divide the mixture into 6 pieces and flatten each into a long oval. 2. In a shallow bowl, beat the remaining 2 raw eggs. 3. Place the flour in a small bowl. 4. Place the remaining 1 cup of bread crumbs in a second small bowl. 5. Roll each hardboiled egg in the flour and wrap one of the chicken sausage pieces around each egg to encircle it completely. 6. One at a time, roll the encased eggs in the flour, dip in the beaten eggs, and finally dip in the bread crumbs to coat. 7. Insert the crisper plate into the basket and the basket into the unit. Preheat the unit by selecting AIR FRY, setting the temperature to 375ºF (191ºC), and setting the time to 3 minutes. Select START/STOP to begin. 8. Once the unit is preheated, spray the crisper plate with cooking oil. Place the eggs in a single layer into the basket and spray them with oil. 9. Select AIR FRY, set the temperature to 375ºF (191ºC), and set the time to 13 minutes. Select START/STOP to begin. 10. After about 6 minutes, use tongs to turn the eggs and spray them with more oil. Resume cooking for 5 to 7 minutes more, or until the chicken is thoroughly cooked and the Scotch eggs are browned. 11. When the cooking is complete, serve warm.

Garlic-Parmesan Croutons

Prep time: 3 minutes | Cook time: 12 minutes | Serves 4

◄ Oil, for spraying
◄ 4 cups cubed French bread
◄ 1 tablespoon grated Parmesan cheese
◄ 3 tablespoons olive oil
◄ 1 tablespoon granulated garlic
◄ ½ teaspoon unsalted salt

1. Line the air fryer basket with parchment and spray lightly with oil. 2. In a large bowl, mix together the bread, Parmesan cheese, olive oil, garlic, and salt, tossing with your hands to evenly distribute the seasonings. Transfer the coated bread cubes to the prepared basket. 3. Air fry at 350ºF (177ºC) for 10 to 12 minutes, stirring once after 5 minutes, or until crisp and golden brown.

Spicy Chicken Bites

Prep time: 10 minutes | Cook time: 10 to 12 minutes | Makes 30 bites

◄ 8 ounces boneless and skinless chicken thighs, cut into 30 pieces
◄ ¼ teaspoon kosher salt
◄ 2 tablespoons hot sauce
◄ Cooking spray

1. Preheat the air fryer to 390ºF (199ºC). 2. Spray the air fryer basket with cooking spray and season the chicken bites with the kosher salt, then place in the basket and air fry for 10 to 12 minutes or until crispy. 3. While the chicken bites cook, pour the hot sauce into a large bowl. 4. Remove the bites and add to the sauce bowl, tossing to coat. Serve warm.

Asian Five-Spice Wings

Prep time: 30 minutes | Cook time: 13 to 15 minutes | Serves 4

◄ 2 pounds (907 g) chicken wings
◄ ½ cup Asian-style salad dressing
◄ 2 tablespoons Chinese five-spice powder

1. Cut off wing tips and discard or freeze for stock. Cut remaining wing pieces in two at the joint. 2. Place wing pieces in a large sealable plastic bag. Pour in the Asian dressing, seal bag, and massage the marinade into the wings until well coated. Refrigerate for at least an hour. 3. Remove wings from bag, drain off excess marinade, and place wings in air fryer basket. 4. Air fry at 360ºF (182ºC) for 13 to 15 minutes or until juices run clear. About halfway through cooking time, shake the basket or stir wings for more even cooking. 5. Transfer cooked wings to plate in a single layer. Sprinkle half of the Chinese five-spice powder on the wings, turn, and sprinkle other side with remaining seasoning.

Chile-Brined Fried Calamari

Prep time: 20 minutes | Cook time: 8 minutes | Serves 2

◄ 1 (8 ounces / 227 g) jar sweet or hot pickled cherry peppers
◄ ½ pound (227 g) calamari bodies and tentacles, bodies cut into ½-inch-wide rings
◄ 1 lemon
◄ 2 cups all-purpose flour
◄ Kosher salt and freshly

ground black pepper, to taste
◄ 3 large eggs, lightly beaten
◄ Cooking spray
◄ ½ cup mayonnaise
◄ 1 teaspoon finely chopped rosemary
◄ 1 garlic clove, minced

1. Drain the pickled pepper brine into a large bowl and tear the peppers into bite-size strips. Add the pepper strips and calamari to the brine and let stand in the refrigerator for 20 minutes or up to 2 hours. 2. Grate the lemon zest into a large bowl then whisk in the flour and season with salt and pepper. Dip the calamari and pepper strips in the egg, then toss them in the flour mixture until fully coated. Spray the calamari and peppers liberally with cooking spray, then transfer half to the air fryer. Air fry at 400ºF (204ºC), shaking the basket halfway into cooking, until the calamari is cooked through and golden brown, about 8 minutes. Transfer to a plate and repeat with the remaining pieces. 3. In a small bowl, whisk together the mayonnaise, rosemary, and garlic. Squeeze half the zested lemon to get 1 tablespoon of juice and stir it into the sauce. Season with salt and pepper. Cut the remaining zested lemon half into 4 small wedges and serve alongside the calamari, peppers, and sauce.

Root Veggie Chips with Herb Salt

Prep time: 10 minutes | Cook time: 8 minutes | Serves 2

◄ 1 parsnip, washed
◄ 1 small beet, washed
◄ 1 small turnip, washed
◄ ½ small sweet potato, washed
◄ 1 teaspoon olive oil
◄ Cooking spray
◄ Herb Salt:
◄ ¼ teaspoon kosher salt
◄ 2 teaspoons finely chopped fresh parsley

1. Preheat the air fryer to 360ºF (182ºC). 2. Peel and thinly slice the parsnip, beet, turnip, and sweet potato, then place the vegetables in a large bowl, add the olive oil, and toss. 3. Spray the air fryer basket with cooking spray, then place the vegetables in the basket and air fry for 8 minutes, gently shaking the basket halfway through. 4. While the chips cook, make the herb salt in a small bowl by combining the kosher salt and parsley. 5. Remove the chips and place on a serving plate, then sprinkle the herb salt on top and allow to cool for 2 to 3 minutes before serving.

Spinach and Crab Meat Cups

Prep time: 10 minutes | Cook time: 10 minutes | Makes 30 cups

◄ 1 (6 ounces / 170 g) can crab meat, drained to yield ⅓ cup meat
◄ ¼ cup frozen spinach, thawed, drained, and chopped
◄ 1 clove garlic, minced
◄ ½ cup grated Parmesan

cheese
◄ 3 tablespoons plain yogurt
◄ ¼ teaspoon lemon juice
◄ ½ teaspoon Worcestershire sauce
◄ 30 mini frozen phyllo shells, thawed
◄ Cooking spray

1. Preheat the air fryer to 390ºF (199ºC). 2. Remove any bits of shell that might remain in the crab meat. 3. Mix the crab meat, spinach, garlic, and cheese together. 4. Stir in the yogurt, lemon juice, and Worcestershire sauce and mix well. 5. Spoon a teaspoon of filling into each phyllo shell. 6. Spray the air fryer basket with cooking spray and arrange half the shells in the basket. Air fry for 5 minutes. Repeat with the remaining shells. 7. Serve immediately.

Crunchy Basil White Beans

Prep time: 2 minutes | Cook time: 19 minutes | Serves 2

- 1 (15 ounces / 425 g) can cooked white beans
- 2 tablespoons olive oil
- 1 teaspoon fresh sage, chopped
- ¼ teaspoon garlic powder
- ¼ teaspoon salt, divided
- 1 teaspoon chopped fresh basil

1. Preheat the air fryer to 380°F(193°C). 2. In a medium bowl, mix together the beans, olive oil, sage, garlic, ⅛ teaspoon salt, and basil. 3. Pour the white beans into the air fryer and spread them out in a single layer. 4. Bake for 10 minutes. Stir and continue cooking for an additional 5 to 9 minutes, or until they reach your preferred level of crispiness. 5. Toss with the remaining ⅛ teaspoon salt before serving.

Red Pepper Tapenade

Prep time: 5 minutes | Cook time: 5 minutes | Serves 4

- 1 large red bell pepper
- 2 tablespoons plus 1 teaspoon olive oil, divided
- ½ cup Kalamata olives,
- pitted and roughly chopped
- 1 garlic clove, minced
- ½ teaspoon dried oregano
- 1 tablespoon lemon juice

1. Preheat the air fryer to 380°F(193°C). 2. Brush the outside of a whole red pepper with 1 teaspoon olive oil and place it inside the air fryer basket. Roast for 5 minutes. 3. Meanwhile, in a medium bowl combine the remaining 2 tablespoons of olive oil with the olives, garlic, oregano, and lemon juice. 4. Remove the red pepper from the air fryer, then gently slice off the stem and remove the seeds. Roughly chop the roasted pepper into small pieces. 5. Add the red pepper to the olive mixture and stir all together until combined. 6. Serve with pita chips, crackers, or crusty bread.

Zucchini Fries with Roasted Garlic Aïoli

Prep time: 20 minutes | Cook time: 12 minutes | Serves 4

- 1 tablespoon vegetable oil
- ½ head green or savoy cabbage, finely shredded
- Roasted Garlic Aïoli:
- 1 teaspoon roasted garlic
Zucchini Fries:
- ½ cup flour
- 2 eggs, beaten
- 1 cup seasoned bread crumbs
- Salt and pepper, to taste
- ½ cup mayonnaise
- 2 tablespoons olive oil
- Juice of ½ lemon
- Salt and pepper, to taste

- 1 large zucchini, cut into ½-inch sticks
- Olive oil

1. Make the aïoli: Combine the roasted garlic, mayonnaise, olive oil and lemon juice in a bowl and whisk well. Season the aïoli with salt and pepper to taste. 2. Prepare the zucchini fries. Create a dredging station with three shallow dishes. Place the flour in the first shallow dish and season well with salt and freshly ground black pepper. Put the beaten eggs in the second shallow dish. In the third shallow dish, combine the bread crumbs, salt and pepper. Dredge the zucchini sticks, coating with flour first, then dipping them into the eggs to coat, and finally tossing in bread crumbs. Shake the dish with the bread crumbs and pat the crumbs onto the zucchini sticks gently with your hands so they stick evenly. 3. Place the zucchini fries on a flat surface and let them sit at least 10 minutes before air frying to let them dry out a little. Preheat the air fryer to 400°F (204°C). 4. Spray the zucchini sticks with olive oil, and place them into the air fryer basket. You can air fry the zucchini in two layers, placing the second layer in the opposite direction to the first. Air fry for 12 minutes turning and rotating the fries halfway through the cooking time. Spray with additional oil when you turn them over. 5. Serve zucchini fries warm with the roasted garlic aïoli.

Zucchini Feta Roulades

Prep time: 10 minutes | Cook time: 10 minutes | Serves 6

- ½ cup feta
- 1 garlic clove, minced
- 2 tablespoons fresh basil, minced
- 1 tablespoon capers, minced
- ⅛ teaspoon salt
- ⅛ teaspoon red pepper flakes
- 1 tablespoon lemon juice
- 2 medium zucchini
- 12 toothpicks

1. Preheat the air fryer to 360°F (182°C).(If using a grill attachment, make sure it is inside the air fryer during preheating.) 2. In a small bowl, combine the feta, garlic, basil, capers, salt, red pepper flakes, and lemon juice. 3. Slice the zucchini into ⅛-inch strips lengthwise. (Each zucchini should yield around 6 strips.) 4. Spread 1 tablespoon of the cheese filling onto each slice of zucchini, then roll it up and secure it with a toothpick through the middle. 5. Place the zucchini roulades into the air fryer basket in a single layer, making sure that they don't touch each other. 6. Bake or grill in the air fryer for 10 minutes. 7. Remove the zucchini roulades from the air fryer and gently remove the toothpicks before serving.

Crispy Breaded Beef Cubes

Prep time: 10 minutes | Cook time: 12 to 16 minutes | Serves 4

- 1 pound (454 g) sirloin tip, cut into 1-inch cubes
- 1 cup cheese pasta sauce
- 1½ cups soft bread crumbs
- 2 tablespoons olive oil
- ½ teaspoon dried marjoram

1. Preheat the air fryer to 360°F (182°C). 2. In a medium bowl, toss the beef with the pasta sauce to coat. 3. In a shallow bowl, combine the bread crumbs, oil, and marjoram, and mix well. Drop the beef cubes, one at a time, into the bread crumb mixture to coat thoroughly. 4. Air fry the beef in two batches for 6 to 8 minutes, shaking the basket once during cooking time, until the beef is at least 145°F (63°C) and the outside is crisp and brown. 5. Serve hot.

Cheese-Stuffed Blooming Onion

Prep time: 10 minutes | Cook time: 15 minutes | Serves 2

- 1 large yellow onion (14 ounces / 397 g)
- 1 tablespoon olive oil
- Kosher salt and freshly ground black pepper, to taste
- ¼ cup plus 2 tablespoons panko bread crumbs
- ¼ cup grated Parmesan
- cheese
- 3 tablespoons mayonnaise
- 1 tablespoon fresh lemon juice
- 1 tablespoon chopped fresh flat-leaf parsley
- 2 teaspoons whole grain Dijon mustard
- 1 garlic clove, minced

1. Place the onion on a cutting board and trim the top off and peel off the outer skin. Turn the onion upside down and use a paring knife, cut vertical slits halfway through the onion at ½-inch intervals around the onion, keeping the root intact. When you turn the onion right side up, it should open up like the petals of a flower. Drizzle the cut sides of the onion with the olive oil and season with salt and pepper. Place petal-side up in the air fryer and air fry at 350°F (177°C) for 10 minutes. 2. Meanwhile, in a bowl, stir together the panko, Parmesan, mayonnaise, lemon juice, parsley, mustard, and garlic until incorporated into a smooth paste. 3. Remove the onion from the fryer and stuff the paste all over and in between the onion "petals." Return the onion to the air fryer and air fry at 375°F (191°C) until the onion is tender in the center and the bread crumb mixture is golden brown, about 5 minutes. Remove the onion from the air fryer, transfer to a plate, and serve hot.

Shrimp Pirogues

Prep time: 15 minutes | Cook time: 4 to 5 minutes | Serves 8

- 12 ounces (340 g) small, peeled, and deveined raw shrimp
- 3 ounces (85 g) cream cheese, room temperature
- 2 tablespoons plain yogurt
- 1 teaspoon lemon juice
- 1 teaspoon dried dill weed, crushed
- Salt, to taste
- 4 small hothouse cucumbers, each approximately 6 inches long

1. Pour 4 tablespoons water in bottom of air fryer drawer. 2. Place shrimp in air fryer basket in single layer and air fry at 390°F (199°C) for 4 to 5 minutes, just until done. Watch carefully because shrimp cooks quickly, and overcooking makes it tough. 3. Chop shrimp into small pieces, no larger than ½ inch. Refrigerate while mixing the remaining ingredients. 4. With a fork, mash and whip the cream cheese until smooth. 5. Stir in the yogurt and beat until smooth. Stir in lemon juice, dill weed, and chopped shrimp. 6. Taste for seasoning. If needed, add ¼ to ½ teaspoon salt to suit your taste. 7. Store in refrigerator until serving time. 8. When ready to serve, wash and dry cucumbers and split them lengthwise. Scoop out the seeds and turn cucumbers upside down on paper towels to drain for 10 minutes. 9. Just before filling, wipe centers of cucumbers dry. Spoon the shrimp mixture into the pirogues and cut in half crosswise. Serve immediately.

Italian Rice Balls

Prep time: 20 minutes | Cook time: 10 minutes | Makes 8 rice balls

- 1½ cups cooked sticky rice
- ½ teaspoon Italian seasoning blend
- ¾ teaspoon salt, divided
- 8 black olives, pitted
- 1 ounce (28 g) Mozzarella cheese, cut into tiny pieces
- (small enough to stuff into olives)
- 2 eggs
- ⅓ cup Italian bread crumbs
- ¾ cup panko bread crumbs
- Cooking spray

1. Preheat air fryer to 390°F (199°C). 2. Stuff each black olive with a piece of Mozzarella cheese. Set aside. 3. In a bowl, combine the cooked sticky rice, Italian seasoning blend, and ½ teaspoon of salt and stir to mix well. Form the rice mixture into a log with your hands and divide it into 8 equal portions. Mold each portion around a black olive and roll into a ball. 4. Transfer to the freezer to chill for 10 to 15 minutes until firm. 5. In a shallow dish, place the Italian bread crumbs. In a separate shallow dish, whisk the eggs. In a third shallow dish, combine the panko bread crumbs and remaining salt. 6. One by one, roll the rice balls in the Italian bread crumbs, then dip in the whisked eggs, finally coat them with the panko bread crumbs. 7. Arrange the rice balls in the air fryer basket and spritz both sides with cooking spray. 8. Air fry for 10 minutes until the rice balls are golden brown. Flip the balls halfway through the cooking time. 9. Serve warm.

Lemon Shrimp with Garlic Olive Oil

Prep time: 5 minutes | Cook time: 6 minutes | Serves 4

- 1 pound (454 g) medium shrimp, cleaned and deveined
- ¼ cup plus 2 tablespoons olive oil, divided
- Juice of ½ lemon
- 3 garlic cloves, minced and
- divided
- ½ teaspoon salt
- ¼ teaspoon red pepper flakes
- Lemon wedges, for serving (optional)
- Marinara sauce, for dipping (optional)

1. Preheat the air fryer to 380°F(193°C). 2. In a large bowl, combine the shrimp with 2 tablespoons of the olive oil, as well as the lemon juice, ⅓ of the minced garlic, salt, and red pepper flakes. Toss to coat the shrimp well. 3. In a small ramekin, combine the remaining ¼ cup of olive oil and the remaining minced garlic. 4. Tear off a 12-by-12-inch sheet of aluminum foil. Pour the shrimp into the center of the foil, then fold the sides up and crimp the edges so that it forms an aluminum foil bowl that is open on top. Place this packet into the air fryer basket. 5. Roast the shrimp for 4 minutes, then open the air fryer and place the ramekin with oil and garlic in the basket beside the shrimp packet. Cook for 2 more minutes. 6. Transfer the shrimp on a serving plate or platter with the ramekin of garlic olive oil on the side for dipping. You may also serve with lemon wedges and marinara sauce, if desired.

Beef and Mango Skewers

Prep time: 10 minutes | Cook time: 4 to 7 minutes | Serves 4

- ◄ ¾ pound (340 g) beef sirloin tip, cut into 1-inch cubes
- ◄ 2 tablespoons balsamic vinegar
- ◄ 1 tablespoon olive oil
- ◄ 1 tablespoon honey
- ◄ ½ teaspoon dried marjoram
- ◄ Pinch of salt
- ◄ Freshly ground black pepper, to taste
- ◄ 1 mango

1. Preheat the air fryer to 390°F (199°C). 2. Put the beef cubes in a medium bowl and add the balsamic vinegar, olive oil, honey, marjoram, salt, and pepper. Mix well, then massage the marinade into the beef with your hands. Set aside. 3. To prepare the mango, stand it on end and cut the skin off, using a sharp knife. Then carefully cut around the oval pit to remove the flesh. Cut the mango into 1-inch cubes. 4. Thread metal skewers alternating with three beef cubes and two mango cubes. 5. Roast the skewers in the air fryer basket for 4 to 7 minutes, or until the beef is browned and at least 145°F (63°C). 6. Serve hot.

Mozzarella Arancini

Prep time: 5 minutes | Cook time: 8 to 11 minutes | Makes 16 arancini

- ◄ 2 cups cooked rice, cooled
- ◄ 2 eggs, beaten
- ◄ 1½ cups panko bread crumbs, divided
- ◄ ½ cup grated Parmesan cheese
- ◄ 2 tablespoons minced fresh basil
- ◄ 16 ¾-inch cubes Mozzarella cheese
- ◄ 2 tablespoons olive oil

1. Preheat the air fryer to 400°F (204°C). 2. In a medium bowl, combine the rice, eggs, ½ cup of the bread crumbs, Parmesan cheese, and basil. Form this mixture into 16 1½-inch balls. 3. Poke a hole in each of the balls with your finger and insert a Mozzarella cube. Form the rice mixture firmly around the cheese. 4. On a shallow plate, combine the remaining 1 cup of the bread crumbs with the olive oil and mix well. Roll the rice balls in the bread crumbs to coat. 5. Air fry the arancini in batches for 8 to 11 minutes or until golden brown. 6. Serve hot.

Baked Ricotta

Prep time: 10 minutes | Cook time: 15 minutes | Makes 2 cups

- ◄ 1 (15 ounces / 425 g) container whole milk Ricotta cheese
- ◄ 3 tablespoons grated Parmesan cheese, divided
- ◄ 2 tablespoons extra-virgin olive oil
- ◄ 1 teaspoon chopped fresh
- thyme leaves
- ◄ 1 teaspoon grated lemon zest
- ◄ 1 clove garlic, crushed with press
- ◄ ¼ teaspoon salt
- ◄ ¼ teaspoon pepper
- ◄ Toasted baguette slices or crackers, for serving

1. Preheat the air fryer to 380°F (193°C). 2. To get the baking dish in and out of the air fryer, create a sling using a 24-inch length of foil, folded lengthwise into thirds. 3. Whisk together the Ricotta, 2 tablespoons of the Parmesan, oil, thyme, lemon zest, garlic, salt, and pepper. Pour into a baking dish. Cover the dish tightly with foil. 4. Place the sling under dish and lift by the ends into the air fryer, tucking the ends of the sling around the dish. Bake for 10 minutes. Remove the foil cover and sprinkle with the remaining 1 tablespoon of the Parmesan. Air fry for 5 more minutes, or until bubbly at edges and the top is browned. 5. Serve warm with toasted baguette slices or crackers.

Cinnamon Apple Chips

Prep time: 5 minutes | Cook time: 7 to 8 hours | Serves 4

- ◄ 4 medium apples, any type, cored and cut into ⅓-inch-thick slices (thin slices yield crunchy chips)
- ◄ ¼ teaspoon ground cinnamon
- ◄ ¼ teaspoon ground nutmeg

1. Place the apple slices in a large bowl. Sprinkle the cinnamon and nutmeg onto the apple slices and toss to coat. 2. Insert the crisper plate into the basket and the basket into the unit. Preheat the unit by selecting DEHYDRATE, setting the temperature to 135°F (57°C), and setting the time to 3 minutes. Select START/STOP to begin. 3. Once the unit is preheated, place the apple chips into the basket. It is okay to stack them. 4. Select DEHYDRATE, set the temperature to 135°F (57°C), and set the time to 7 or 8 hours. Select START/STOP to begin. 5. When the cooking is complete, cool the apple chips. Serve or store at room temperature in an airtight container for up to 1 week.

Chapter 10 Desserts

Bourbon and Spice Monkey Bread

Prep time: 5 minutes | Cook time: 25 minutes | Serves 6 to 8

- 1 (16.3 ounces / 462 g) can store-bought refrigerated biscuit dough
- ¼ cup packed light brown sugar
- 1 teaspoon ground cinnamon
- ½ teaspoon freshly grated nutmeg
- ½ teaspoon ground ginger
- ½ teaspoon kosher salt
- ¼ teaspoon ground allspice
- ⅛ teaspoon ground cloves
- 4 tablespoons (½ stick) unsalted butter, melted
- ½ cup powdered sugar
- 2 teaspoons bourbon
- 2 tablespoons chopped candied cherries
- 2 tablespoons chopped pecans

1. Open the can and separate the biscuits, then cut each into quarters. Toss the biscuit quarters in a large bowl with the brown sugar, cinnamon, nutmeg, ginger, salt, allspice, and cloves until evenly coated. Transfer the dough pieces and any sugar left in the bowl to a cake pan and drizzle evenly with the melted butter. Place the pan in the air fryer and bake at 310ºF (154ºC) until the monkey bread is golden brown and cooked through in the middle, about 25 minutes. Transfer the pan to a wire rack and let cool completely. Unmold from the pan. 2. In a small bowl, whisk the powdered sugar and the bourbon into a smooth glaze. Drizzle the glaze over the cooled monkey bread and, while the glaze is still wet, sprinkle with the cherries and pecans to serve.

Nutty Pear Crumble

Prep time: 10 minutes | Cook time: 30 minutes | Serves 2 to 4

- 2 ripe d'Anjou pears (1 pound / 454 g), peeled, cored, and roughly chopped
- ¼ cup packed light brown sugar
- 2 tablespoons cornstarch
- 1 teaspoon kosher salt
- ¼ cup granulated sugar
- 3 tablespoons unsalted
- butter, at room temperature
- ⅓ cup all-purpose flour
- 2½ tablespoons Dutch-process cocoa powder
- ¼ cup chopped blanched hazelnuts
- Vanilla ice cream or whipped cream, for serving (optional)

1. In a cake pan, combine the pears, brown sugar, cornstarch, and ½ teaspoon salt and toss until the pears are evenly coated in the sugar. 2. In a bowl, combine the remaining ½ teaspoon salt with the granulated sugar, butter, flour, and cocoa powder and pinch and press the butter into the other ingredients with your fingers until a sandy, shaggy crumble dough forms. Stir in the hazelnuts. Sprinkle the crumble topping evenly over the pears. 3. Place the pan in the air fryer and bake at 320ºF (160ºC) until the crumble is crisp and the pears are bubbling in the center, about 30 minutes. 4. Carefully remove the pan from the air fryer and serve the hot crumble in bowls, topped with ice cream or whipped cream, if you like.

Brownies for Two

Prep time: 5 minutes | Cook time: 15 minutes | Serves 2

- ½ cup blanched finely ground almond flour
- 3 tablespoons granular erythritol
- 3 tablespoons unsweetened cocoa powder
- ½ teaspoon baking powder
- 1 teaspoon vanilla extract
- 2 large eggs, whisked
- 2 tablespoons salted butter, melted

1. In a medium bowl, combine flour, erythritol, cocoa powder, and baking powder. 2. Add in vanilla, eggs, and butter, and stir until a thick batter forms. 3. Pour batter into two ramekins greased with cooking spray and place ramekins into air fryer basket. Adjust the temperature to 325ºF (163ºC) and bake for 15 minutes. Centers will be firm when done. Let ramekins cool 5 minutes before serving.

Gluten-Free Spice Cookies

Prep time: 10 minutes | Cook time: 12 minutes | Serves 4

- 4 tablespoons (½ stick) unsalted butter, at room temperature
- 2 tablespoons agave nectar
- 1 large egg
- 2 tablespoons water
- 2½ cups almond flour
- ½ cup sugar
- 2 teaspoons ground ginger
- 1 teaspoon ground cinnamon
- ½ teaspoon freshly grated nutmeg
- 1 teaspoon baking soda
- ¼ teaspoon kosher salt

1. Line the bottom of the air fryer basket with parchment paper cut to fit. 2. In a large bowl using a hand mixer, beat together the butter, agave, egg, and water on medium speed until light and fluffy. 3. Add the almond flour, sugar, ginger, cinnamon, nutmeg, baking soda, and salt. Beat on low speed until well combined. 4. Roll the dough into 2-tablespoon balls and arrange them on the parchment paper in the basket. (They don't really spread too much, but try to leave a little room between them.) Set the air fryer to 325ºF (163ºC) for 12 minutes, or until the tops of cookies are lightly browned. 5. Transfer to a wire rack and let cool completely. Store in an airtight container for up to a week.

Pumpkin-Spice Bread Pudding

Prep time: 15 minutes | Cook time: 35 minutes | Serves 6

Bread Pudding:
- ¾ cup heavy whipping cream
- ½ cup canned pumpkin
- ⅓ cup whole milk
- ⅓ cup sugar
- 1 large egg plus 1 yolk
- ½ teaspoon pumpkin pie
- spice
- ⅛ teaspoon kosher salt
- 4 cups 1-inch cubed day-old baguette or crusty country bread
- 4 tablespoons (½ stick) unsalted butter, melted

Sauce:
- ⅓ cup pure maple syrup
- 1 tablespoon unsalted butter
- ½ cup heavy whipping
- cream
- ½ teaspoon pure vanilla extract

1. For the bread pudding: In a medium bowl, combine the cream, pumpkin, milk, sugar, egg and yolk, pumpkin pie spice, and salt. Whisk until well combined. 2. In a large bowl, toss the bread cubes with the melted butter. Add the pumpkin mixture and gently toss until the ingredients are well combined. 3. Transfer the mixture to a baking pan. Place the pan in the air fryer basket. Set the fryer to 350ºF (177ºC) for 35 minutes, or until custard is set in the middle. 4. Meanwhile, for the sauce: In a small saucepan, combine the syrup and butter. Heat over medium heat, stirring, until the butter melts. Stir in the cream and simmer, stirring often, until the sauce has thickened, about 15 minutes. Stir in the vanilla. Remove the pudding from the air fryer. 5. Let the pudding stand for 10 minutes before serving with the warm sauce.

Carrot Cake with Cream Cheese Icing

Prep time: 10 minutes | Cook time: 55 minutes | Serves 6 to 8

- 1¼ cups all-purpose flour
- 1 teaspoon baking powder
- ½ teaspoon baking soda
- 1 teaspoon ground cinnamon
- ¼ teaspoon ground nutmeg
- ¼ teaspoon salt
- 2 cups grated carrot (about

Icing:
- 8 ounces (227 g) cream cheese, softened at room temperature
- 8 tablespoons butter (1 stick), softened at room
- 3 to 4 medium carrots or 2 large)
- ¾ cup granulated sugar
- ¼ cup brown sugar
- 2 eggs
- ¾ cup canola or vegetable oil
- temperature
- 1 cup powdered sugar
- 1 teaspoon pure vanilla extract

1. Grease a cake pan. 2. Combine the flour, baking powder, baking soda, cinnamon, nutmeg and salt in a bowl. Add the grated carrots and toss well. In a separate bowl, beat the sugars and eggs together until light and frothy. Drizzle in the oil, beating constantly. Fold the egg mixture into the dry ingredients until everything is just combined and you no longer see any traces of flour. Pour the batter into the cake pan and wrap the pan completely in greased aluminum foil. 3. Preheat the air fryer to 350ºF (177ºC). 4. Lower the cake pan into the air fryer basket using a sling made of aluminum foil (fold a piece of aluminum foil into a strip about 2-inches wide by 24-inches long). Fold the ends of the aluminum foil into the air fryer, letting them rest on top of the cake. Air fry for 40 minutes. Remove the aluminum foil cover and air fry for an additional 15 minutes or until a skewer inserted into the center of the cake comes out clean and the top is nicely browned. 5. While the cake is cooking, beat the cream cheese, butter, powdered sugar and vanilla extract together using a hand mixer, stand mixer or food processor (or a lot of elbow grease!). 6. Remove the cake pan from the air fryer and let the cake cool in the cake pan for 10 minutes or so. Then remove the cake from the pan and let it continue to cool completely. Frost the cake with the cream cheese icing and serve.

Pears with Honey-Lemon Ricotta

Prep time: 10 minutes | Cook time: 8 minutes | Serves 4

- 2 large Bartlett pears
- 3 tablespoons butter, melted
- 3 tablespoons brown sugar
- ½ teaspoon ground ginger
- ¼ teaspoon ground cardamom
- ½ cup whole-milk ricotta
- cheese
- 1 tablespoon honey, plus additional for drizzling
- 1 teaspoon pure almond extract
- 1 teaspoon pure lemon extract

1. Peel each pear and cut in half lengthwise. Use a melon baller to scoop out the core. Place the pear halves in a medium bowl, add the melted butter, and toss. Add the brown sugar, ginger, and cardamom; toss to coat. 2. Place the pear halves, cut side down, in the air fryer basket. Set the air fryer to 375ºF (191ºC) for 8 to 10 minutes, or until the pears are lightly browned and tender, but not mushy. 3. Meanwhile, in a medium bowl, combine the ricotta, honey, and almond and lemon extracts. Beat with an electric mixer on medium speed until the mixture is light and fluffy, about 1 minute. 4. To serve, divide the ricotta mixture among four small shallow bowls. Place a pear half, cut side up, on top of the cheese. Drizzle with additional honey and serve.

Pecan Brownies

Prep time: 10 minutes | Cook time: 20 minutes | Serves 6

- ½ cup blanched finely ground almond flour
- ½ cup powdered erythritol
- 2 tablespoons unsweetened cocoa powder
- ½ teaspoon baking powder
- ¼ cup unsalted butter, softened
- 1 large egg
- ¼ cup chopped pecans
- ¼ cup low-carb, sugar-free chocolate chips

1. In a large bowl, mix almond flour, erythritol, cocoa powder, and baking powder. Stir in butter and egg. 2. Fold in pecans and chocolate chips. Scoop mixture into a round baking pan. Place pan into the air fryer basket. 3. Adjust the temperature to 300ºF (149ºC) and bake for 20 minutes. 4. When fully cooked a toothpick inserted in center will come out clean. Allow 20 minutes to fully cool and firm up.

Almond-Roasted Pears

Prep time: 10 minutes | Cook time: 15 to 20 minutes | Serves 4

Yogurt Topping:
- ◀ 1 container vanilla Greek yogurt (5 to 6 ounces / 142 to 170 g)
- ◀ ¼ teaspoon almond flavoring
- ◀ 2 whole pears
- ◀ ¼ cup crushed Biscoff cookies (approx. 4 cookies)
- ◀ 1 tablespoon sliced almonds
- ◀ 1 tablespoon butter

1. Stir almond flavoring into yogurt and set aside while preparing pears. 2. Halve each pear and spoon out the core. 3. Place pear halves in air fryer basket. 4. Stir together the cookie crumbs and almonds. Place a quarter of this mixture into the hollow of each pear half. 5. Cut butter into 4 pieces and place one piece on top of crumb mixture in each pear. 6. Roast at 360ºF (182ºC) for 15 to 20 minutes or until pears have cooked through but are still slightly firm. 7. Serve pears warm with a dollop of yogurt topping.

Pecan Bars

Prep time: 5 minutes | Cook time: 40 minutes | Serves 12

- ◀ 2 cups coconut flour
- ◀ 5 tablespoons erythritol
- ◀ 4 tablespoons coconut oil, softened
- ◀ ½ cup heavy cream
- ◀ 1 egg, beaten
- ◀ 4 pecans, chopped

1. Mix coconut flour, erythritol, coconut oil, heavy cream, and egg. 2. Pour the batter in the air fryer basket and flatten well. 3. Top the mixture with pecans and cook the meal at 350ºF (177ºC) for 40 minutes. 4. Cut the cooked meal into the bars.

Protein Powder Doughnut Holes

Prep time: 25 minutes | Cook time: 6 minutes | Makes 12 holes

- ◀ ½ cup blanched finely ground almond flour
- ◀ ½ cup low-carb vanilla protein powder
- ◀ ½ cup granular erythritol
- ◀ ½ teaspoon baking powder
- ◀ 1 large egg
- ◀ 5 tablespoons unsalted butter, melted
- ◀ ½ teaspoon vanilla extract

1. Mix all ingredients in a large bowl. Place into the freezer for 20 minutes. 2. Wet your hands with water and roll the dough into twelve balls. 3. Cut a piece of parchment to fit your air fryer basket. Working in batches as necessary, place doughnut holes into the air fryer basket on top of parchment. 4. Adjust the temperature to 380ºF (193ºC) and air fry for 6 minutes. 5. Flip doughnut holes halfway through the cooking time. 6. Let cool completely before serving.

Glazed Cherry Turnovers

Prep time: 10 minutes | Cook time: 14 minutes per batch | Serves 8

- ◀ 2 sheets frozen puff pastry, thawed
- ◀ 1 (21 ounces / 595 g) can premium cherry pie filling
- ◀ 2 teaspoons ground
- ◀ cinnamon
- ◀ 1 egg, beaten
- ◀ 1 cup sliced almonds
- ◀ 1 cup powdered sugar
- ◀ 2 tablespoons milk

1. Roll a sheet of puff pastry out into a square that is approximately 10-inches by 10-inches. Cut this large square into quarters. 2. Mix the cherry pie filling and cinnamon together in a bowl. Spoon ¼ cup of the cherry filling into the center of each puff pastry square. Brush the perimeter of the pastry square with the egg wash. Fold one corner of the puff pastry over the cherry pie filling towards the opposite corner, forming a triangle. Seal the two edges of the pastry together with the tip of a fork, making a design with the tines. Brush the top of the turnovers with the egg wash and sprinkle sliced almonds over each one. Repeat these steps with the second sheet of puff pastry. You should have eight turnovers at the end. 3. Preheat the air fryer to 370ºF (188ºC). 4. Air fry two turnovers at a time for 14 minutes, carefully turning them over halfway through the cooking time. 5. While the turnovers are cooking, make the glaze by whisking the powdered sugar and milk together in a small bowl until smooth. Let the glaze sit for a minute so the sugar can absorb the milk. If the consistency is still too thick to drizzle, add a little more milk, a drop at a time, and stir until smooth. 6. Let the cooked cherry turnovers sit for at least 10 minutes. Then drizzle the glaze over each turnover in a zigzag motion. Serve warm or at room temperature.

Zucchini Nut Muffins

Prep time: 15 minutes | Cook time: 15 minutes | Serves 4

- ◀ ¼ cup vegetable oil, plus more for greasing
- ◀ ¾ cup all-purpose flour
- ◀ ¾ teaspoon ground cinnamon
- ◀ ¼ teaspoon kosher salt
- ◀ ¼ teaspoon baking soda
- ◀ ¼ teaspoon baking powder
- ◀ 2 large eggs
- ◀ ½ cup sugar
- ◀ ½ cup grated zucchini
- ◀ ¼ cup chopped walnuts

1. Generously grease four 4 ounces (113 g) ramekins or a baking pan with vegetable oil. 2. In a medium bowl, sift together the flour, cinnamon, salt, baking soda, and baking powder. 3. In a separate medium bowl, beat together the eggs, sugar, and vegetable oil. Add the dry ingredients to the wet ingredients. Add the zucchini and nuts and stir gently until well combined. Transfer the batter to the prepared ramekins or baking pan. 4. Place the ramekins or pan in the air fryer basket. Set the air fryer to 325ºF (163ºC) for 15 minutes, or until a cake tester or toothpick inserted into the center comes out clean. If it doesn't, cook for 3 to 5 minutes more and test again. 5. Let cool in the ramekins or pan on a wire rack for 10 minutes. Carefully remove from the ramekins or pan and let cool completely on the rack before serving.

Cinnamon-Sugar Almonds

Prep time: 5 minutes | Cook time: 8 minutes | Serves 4

- ◁ 1 cup whole almonds
- ◁ 2 tablespoons salted butter, melted
- ◁ 1 tablespoon sugar
- ◁ ½ teaspoon ground cinnamon

1. In a medium bowl, combine the almonds, butter, sugar, and cinnamon. Mix well to ensure all the almonds are coated with the spiced butter. 2. Transfer the almonds to the air fryer basket and shake so they are in a single layer. Set the air fryer to 300ºF (149ºC) for 8 minutes, stirring the almonds halfway through the cooking time. 3. Let cool completely before serving.

Simple Pineapple Sticks

Prep time: 5 minutes | Cook time: 10 minutes | Serves 4

- ◁ ½ fresh pineapple, cut into sticks
- ◁ ¼ cup desiccated coconut

1. Preheat the air fryer to 400ºF (204ºC). 2. Coat the pineapple sticks in the desiccated coconut and put each one in the air fryer basket. 3. Air fry for 10 minutes. 4. Serve immediately

Homemade Mint Pie

Prep time: 15 minutes | Cook time: 25 minutes | Serves 2

- ◁ 1 tablespoon instant coffee
- ◁ 2 tablespoons almond butter, softened
- ◁ 2 tablespoons erythritol
- ◁ 1 teaspoon dried mint
- ◁ 3 eggs, beaten
- ◁ 1 teaspoon spearmint, dried
- ◁ 4 teaspoons coconut flour
- ◁ Cooking spray

1. Spray the air fryer basket with cooking spray. 2. Then mix all ingredients in the mixer bowl. 3. When you get a smooth mixture, transfer it in the air fryer basket. Flatten it gently. 4. Cook the pie at 365ºF (185ºC) for 25 minutes.

Funnel Cake

Prep time: 10 minutes | Cook time: 5 minutes | Serves 4

- ◁ Oil, for spraying
- ◁ 1 cup self-rising flour, plus more for dusting
- ◁ 1 cup fat-free vanilla Greek
- yogurt
- ◁ ½ teaspoon ground cinnamon
- ◁ ¼ cup confectioners' sugar

1. Preheat the air fryer to 375ºF (191ºC). Line the air fryer basket with parchment and spray lightly with oil. 2. In a large bowl, mix together the flour, yogurt, and cinnamon until the mixture forms a ball. 3. Place the dough on a lightly floured work surface and knead

for about 2 minutes. 4. Cut the dough into 4 equal pieces, then cut each of those into 6 pieces. You should have 24 total pieces. 5. Roll the pieces into 8- to 10-inch-long ropes. Loosely mound the ropes into 4 piles of 6 ropes. 6. Place the dough piles in the prepared basket and spray liberally with oil. You may need to work in batches, depending on the size of your air fryer. 7. Cook for 5 minutes, or until lightly browned. 8. Dust with the confectioners' sugar before serving.

Air Fryer Apple Fritters

Prep time: 30 minutes | Cook time: 7 to 8 minutes | Serves 6

- ◁ 1 cup chopped, peeled Granny Smith apple
- ◁ ½ cup granulated sugar
- ◁ 1 teaspoon ground cinnamon
- ◁ 1 cup all-purpose flour
- ◁ 1 teaspoon baking powder
- ◁ 1 teaspoon salt
- ◁ 2 tablespoons milk
- ◁ 2 tablespoons butter, melted
- ◁ 1 large egg, beaten
- ◁ Cooking spray
- ◁ ¼ cup confectioners' sugar (optional)

1. Mix together the apple, granulated sugar, and cinnamon in a small bowl. Allow to sit for 30 minutes. 2. Combine the flour, baking powder, and salt in a medium bowl. Add the milk, butter, and egg and stir to incorporate. 3. Pour the apple mixture into the bowl of flour mixture and stir with a spatula until a dough forms. 4. Make the fritters: On a clean work surface, divide the dough into 12 equal portions and shape into 1-inch balls. Flatten them into patties with your hands. 5. Preheat the air fryer to 350ºF (177ºC). Line the air fryer basket with parchment paper and spray it with cooking spray. 6. Transfer the apple fritters onto the parchment paper, evenly spaced but not too close together. Spray the fritters with cooking spray. 7. Bake for 7 to 8 minutes until lightly browned. Flip the fritters halfway through the cooking time. 8. Remove from the basket to a plate and serve with the confectioners' sugar sprinkled on top, if desired.

Fried Oreos

Prep time: 7 minutes | Cook time: 6 minutes per batch | Makes 12 cookies

- ◁ Oil for misting or nonstick spray
- ◁ 1 cup complete pancake and waffle mix
- ◁ 1 teaspoon vanilla extract
- ◁ ½ cup water, plus 2
- tablespoons
- ◁ 12 Oreos or other chocolate sandwich cookies
- ◁ 1 tablespoon confectioners' sugar

1. Spray baking pan with oil or nonstick spray and place in basket. 2. Preheat the air fryer to 390ºF (199ºC). 3. In a medium bowl, mix together the pancake mix, vanilla, and water. 4. Dip 4 cookies in batter and place in baking pan. 5. Cook for 6 minutes, until browned. 6. Repeat steps 4 and 5 for the remaining cookies. 7. Sift sugar over warm cookies.

Baked Peaches with Yogurt and Blueberries

Prep time: 10 minutes | Cook time: 7 to 11 minutes | Serves 6

- 3 peaches, peeled, halved, and pitted
- 2 tablespoons packed brown sugar
- 1 cup plain Greek yogurt
- ¼ teaspoon ground cinnamon
- 1 teaspoon pure vanilla extract
- 1 cup fresh blueberries

1. Preheat the air fryer to 380ºF (193ºC). 2. Arrange the peaches in the air fryer basket, cut-side up. Top with a generous sprinkle of brown sugar. 3. Bake in the preheated air fryer for 7 to 11 minutes, or until the peaches are lightly browned and caramelized. 4. Meanwhile, whisk together the yogurt, cinnamon, and vanilla in a small bowl until smooth. 5. Remove the peaches from the basket to a plate. Serve topped with the yogurt mixture and fresh blueberries.

Olive Oil Cake

Prep time: 10 minutes | Cook time: 30 minutes | Serves 8

- 2 cups blanched finely ground almond flour
- 5 large eggs, whisked
- ¾ cup extra-virgin olive oil
- ⅓ cup granular erythritol
- 1 teaspoon vanilla extract
- 1 teaspoon baking powder

1. In a large bowl, mix all ingredients. Pour batter into an ungreased round nonstick baking dish. 2. Place dish into air fryer basket. Adjust the temperature to 300ºF (149ºC) and bake for 30 minutes. The cake will be golden on top and firm in the center when done. 3. Let cake cool in dish 30 minutes before slicing and serving.

Molten Chocolate Almond Cakes

Prep time: 5 minutes | Cook time: 13 minutes | Serves 3

- Butter and flour for the ramekins
- 4 ounces (113 g) bittersweet chocolate, chopped
- ½ cup (1 stick) unsalted butter
- 2 eggs
- 2 egg yolks
- ¼ cup sugar
- ½ teaspoon pure vanilla extract, or almond extract
- 1 tablespoon all-purpose flour
- 3 tablespoons ground almonds
- 8 to 12 semisweet chocolate discs (or 4 chunks of chocolate)
- Cocoa powder or powdered sugar, for dusting
- Toasted almonds, coarsely chopped

1. Butter and flour three (6 ounces / 170 g) ramekins. (Butter the ramekins and then coat the butter with flour by shaking it around in the ramekin and dumping out any excess.) 2. Melt the chocolate and butter together, either in the microwave or in a double boiler.

In a separate bowl, beat the eggs, egg yolks and sugar together until light and smooth. Add the vanilla extract. Whisk the chocolate mixture into the egg mixture. Stir in the flour and ground almonds. 3. Preheat the air fryer to 330ºF (166ºC). 4. Transfer the batter carefully to the buttered ramekins, filling halfway. Place two or three chocolate discs in the center of the batter and then fill the ramekins to ½-inch below the top with the remaining batter. Place the ramekins into the air fryer basket and air fry at 330ºF (166ºC) for 13 minutes. The sides of the cake should be set, but the centers should be slightly soft. Remove the ramekins from the air fryer and let the cakes sit for 5 minutes. (If you'd like the cake a little less molten, air fry for 14 minutes and let the cakes sit for 4 minutes.) 5. Run a butter knife around the edge of the ramekins and invert the cakes onto a plate. Lift the ramekin off the plate slowly and carefully so that the cake doesn't break. Dust with cocoa powder or powdered sugar and serve with a scoop of ice cream and some coarsely chopped toasted almonds.

Mini Peanut Butter Tarts

Prep time: 25 minutes | Cook time: 12 to 15 minutes | Serves 8

- 1 cup pecans
- 1 cup finely ground blanched almond flour
- 2 tablespoons unsalted butter, at room temperature
- ½ cup plus 2 tablespoons Swerve, divided
- ½ cup heavy (whipping) cream
- 2 tablespoons mascarpone cheese
- 4 ounces (113 g) cream
- cheese
- ½ cup sugar-free peanut butter
- 1 teaspoon pure vanilla extract
- ⅛ teaspoon sea salt
- ½ cup stevia-sweetened chocolate chips
- 1 tablespoon coconut oil
- ¼ cup chopped peanuts or pecans

1. Place the pecans in the bowl of a food processor; process until they are finely ground. 2. Transfer the ground pecans to a medium bowl and stir in the almond flour. Add the butter and 2 tablespoons of Swerve, and stir until the mixture becomes wet and crumbly. 3. Divide the mixture among 8 silicone muffin cups, pressing the crust firmly with your fingers into the bottom and part way up the sides of each cup. 4. Arrange the muffin cups in the air fryer basket, working in batches if necessary. Set the air fryer to 300ºF (149ºC) and bake for 12 to 15 minutes, until the crusts begin to brown. Remove the cups from the air fryer and set them aside to cool. 5. In the bowl of a stand mixer, combine the heavy cream and mascarpone cheese. Beat until peaks form. Transfer to a large bowl. 6. In the same stand mixer bowl, combine the cream cheese, peanut butter, remaining ½ cup of Swerve, vanilla, and salt. Beat at medium-high speed until smooth. 7. Reduce the speed to low and add the heavy cream mixture back a spoonful at a time, beating after each addition. 8. Spoon the peanut butter mixture over the crusts, and freeze the tarts for 30 minutes. 9. Place the chocolate chips and coconut oil in the top of a double boiler over high heat. Stir until melted, then remove from the heat. 10. Drizzle the melted chocolate over the peanut butter tarts. Top with the chopped nuts and freeze the tarts for another 15 minutes, until set. 11. Store the peanut butter tarts in an airtight container in the refrigerator for up to 1 week or in the freezer for up to 1 month.

Cream Cheese Danish

Prep time: 20 minutes | Cook time: 15 minutes | Serves 6

- ¾ cup blanched finely ground almond flour
- 1 cup shredded Mozzarella cheese
- 5 ounces (142 g) full-fat cream cheese, divided
- 2 large egg yolks
- ¾ cup powdered erythritol, divided
- 2 teaspoons vanilla extract, divided

1. In a large microwave-safe bowl, add almond flour, Mozzarella, and 1 ounce (28 g) cream cheese. Mix and then microwave for 1 minute. 2. Stir and add egg yolks to the bowl. Continue stirring until soft dough forms. Add ½ cup erythritol to dough and 1 teaspoon vanilla. 3. Cut a piece of parchment to fit your air fryer basket. Wet your hands with warm water and press out the dough into a ¼-inch-thick rectangle. 4. In a medium bowl, mix remaining cream cheese, erythritol, and vanilla. Place this cream cheese mixture on the right half of the dough rectangle. Fold over the left side of the dough and press to seal. Place into the air fryer basket. 5. Adjust the temperature to 330ºF (166ºC) and bake for 15 minutes. 6. After 7 minutes, flip over the Danish. 7. When done, remove the Danish from parchment and allow to completely cool before cutting.

Cardamom Custard

Prep time: 10 minutes | Cook time: 25 minutes | Serves 2

- 1 cup whole milk
- 1 large egg
- 2 tablespoons plus 1 teaspoon sugar
- ¼ teaspoon vanilla bean
- paste or pure vanilla extract
- ¼ teaspoon ground cardamom, plus more for sprinkling

1. In a medium bowl, beat together the milk, egg, sugar, vanilla, and cardamom. 2. Place two 8 ounces (227 g) ramekins in the air fryer basket. Divide the mixture between the ramekins. Sprinkle lightly with cardamom. Cover each ramekin tightly with aluminum foil. Set the air fryer to 350ºF (177ºC) for 25 minutes, or until a toothpick inserted in the center comes out clean. 3. Let the custards cool on a wire rack for 5 to 10 minutes. 4. Serve warm, or refrigerate until cold and serve chilled.

Fried Golden Bananas

Prep time: 5 minutes | Cook time: 7 minutes | Serves 6

- 1 large egg
- ¼ cup cornstarch
- ¼ cup plain bread crumbs
- 3 bananas, halved crosswise
- Cooking oil
- Chocolate sauce, for drizzling

1. Preheat the air fryer to 375ºF (191ºC) 2. Separate the biscuit dough into 8 biscuits and place them on a flat work surface. Use a small circle cookie cutter or a biscuit cutter to cut a hole in the center of each biscuit. You can also cut the holes using a knife. 3. Spray the air fryer basket with cooking oil. 4. Put 4 donuts in the air fryer. Do not stack. Spray with cooking oil. Air fry for 4 minutes. 5. Open the air fryer and flip the donuts. Air fry for an additional 4 minutes. 6. Remove the cooked donuts from the air fryer, then repeat steps 3 and 4 for the remaining 4 donuts. 7. Drizzle chocolate sauce over the donuts and enjoy while warm.

Lime Bars

Prep time: 10 minutes | Cook time: 33 minutes | Makes 12 bars

- 1½ cups blanched finely ground almond flour, divided
- ¾ cup confectioners' erythritol, divided
- 4 tablespoons salted butter, melted
- ½ cup fresh lime juice
- 2 large eggs, whisked

1. In a medium bowl, mix together 1 cup flour, ¼ cup erythritol, and butter. Press mixture into bottom of an ungreased round nonstick cake pan. 2. Place pan into air fryer basket. Adjust the temperature to 300ºF (149ºC) and bake for 13 minutes. Crust will be brown and set in the middle when done. 3. Allow to cool in pan 10 minutes. 4. In a medium bowl, combine remaining flour, remaining erythritol, lime juice, and eggs. Pour mixture over cooled crust and return to air fryer for 20 minutes at 300ºF (149ºC). Top will be browned and firm when done. 5. Let cool completely in pan, about 30 minutes, then chill covered in the refrigerator 1 hour. Serve chilled.

Ricotta Lemon Poppy Seed Cake

Prep time: 10 minutes | Cook time: 55 minutes | Serves 4

- Unsalted butter, at room temperature
- 1 cup almond flour
- ½ cup sugar
- 3 large eggs
- ¼ cup heavy cream
- ¼ cup full-fat ricotta cheese
- ¼ cup coconut oil, melted
- 2 tablespoons poppy seeds
- 1 teaspoon baking powder
- 1 teaspoon pure lemon extract
- Grated zest and juice of 1 lemon, plus more zest for garnish

1. Generously butter a baking pan. Line the bottom of the pan with parchment paper cut to fit. 2. In a large bowl, combine the almond flour, sugar, eggs, cream, ricotta, coconut oil, poppy seeds, baking powder, lemon extract, lemon zest, and lemon juice. Beat with a hand mixer on medium speed until well blended and fluffy. 3. Pour the batter into the prepared pan. Cover the pan tightly with aluminum foil. Set the pan in the air fryer basket. Set the air fryer to 325ºF (163ºC) for 45 minutes. Remove the foil and cook for 10 to 15 minutes more, until a knife (do not use a toothpick) inserted into the center of the cake comes out clean. 4. Let the cake cool in the pan on a wire rack for 10 minutes. Remove the cake from pan and let it cool on the rack for 15 minutes before slicing. 5. Top with additional lemon zest, slice and serve.

Butter Flax Cookies

Prep time: 25 minutes | Cook time: 20 minutes | Serves 4

- 8 ounces (227 g) almond meal
- 2 tablespoons flaxseed meal
- 1 ounce (28 g) monk fruit
- 1 teaspoon baking powder
- A pinch of grated nutmeg
- A pinch of coarse salt
- 1 large egg, room temperature.
- 1 stick butter, room temperature
- 1 teaspoon vanilla extract

1. Mix the almond meal, flaxseed meal, monk fruit, baking powder, grated nutmeg, and salt in a bowl. 2. In a separate bowl, whisk the egg, butter, and vanilla extract. 3. Stir the egg mixture into dry mixture; mix to combine well or until it forms a nice, soft dough. 4. Roll your dough out and cut out with a cookie cutter of your choice. Bake in the preheated air fryer at 350°F (177°C) for 10 minutes. Decrease the temperature to 330°F (166°C) and cook for 10 minutes longer. Bon appétit!

Eggless Farina Cake

Prep time: 30 minutes | Cook time: 25 minutes | Serves 6

- Vegetable oil
- 2 cups hot water
- 1 cup chopped dried fruit, such as apricots, golden raisins, figs, and/or dates
- 1 cup farina (or very fine semolina)
- 1 cup milk
- 1 cup sugar
- ¼ cup ghee, butter, or coconut oil, melted
- 2 tablespoons plain Greek yogurt or sour cream
- 1 teaspoon ground cardamom
- 1 teaspoon baking powder
- ½ teaspoon baking soda
- Whipped cream, for serving

1. Grease a baking pan with vegetable oil. 2. In a small bowl, combine the hot water and dried fruit; set aside for 20 minutes to plump the fruit. 3. Meanwhile, in a large bowl, whisk together the farina, milk, sugar, ghee, yogurt, and cardamom. Let stand for 20 minutes to allow the farina to soften and absorb some of the liquid. 4. Drain the dried fruit and gently stir it into the batter. Add the baking powder and baking soda and stir until thoroughly combined. 5. Pour the batter into the prepared pan. Set the pan in the air fryer basket. Set the air fryer to 325°F (163°C) for 25 minutes, or until a toothpick inserted into the center of the cake comes out clean. 6. Let the cake cool in the pan on a wire rack for 10 minutes. Remove the cake from the pan and let cool on the rack for 20 minutes before slicing. 7. Slice and serve topped with whipped cream.

Appendix Air Fryer Cooking Chart

Air Fryer Cooking Chart

Beef

Item	Temp (°F)	Time (mins)	Item	Temp (°F)	Time (mins)
Beef Eye Round Roast (4 lbs.)	400 °F	45 to 55	Meatballs (1-inch)	370 °F	7
Burger Patty (4 oz.)	370 °F	16 to 20	Meatballs (3-inch)	380 °F	10
Filet Mignon (8 oz.)	400 °F	18	Ribeye, bone-in (1-inch, 8 oz)	400 °F	10 to 15
Flank Steak (1.5 lbs.)	400 °F	12	Sirloin steaks (1-inch, 12 oz)	400 °F	9 to 14
Flank Steak (2 lbs.)	400 °F	20 to 28			

Chicken

Item	Temp (°F)	Time (mins)	Item	Temp (°F)	Time (mins)
Breasts, bone in (1 ¼ lb.)	370 °F	25	Legs, bone-in (1 ¾ lb.)	380 °F	30
Breasts, boneless (4 oz)	380 °F	12	Thighs, boneless (1 ½ lb.)	380 °F	18 to 20
Drumsticks (2 ½ lb.)	370 °F	20	Wings (2 lb.)	400 °F	12
Game Hen (halved 2 lb.)	390 °F	20	Whole Chicken	360 °F	75
Thighs, bone-in (2 lb.)	380 °F	22	Tenders	360 °F	8 to 10

Pork & Lamb

Item	Temp (°F)	Time (mins)	Item	Temp (°F)	Time (mins)
Bacon (regular)	400 °F	5 to 7	Pork Tenderloin	370 °F	15
Bacon (thick cut)	400 °F	6 to 10	Sausages	380 °F	15
Pork Loin (2 lb.)	360 °F	55	Lamb Loin Chops (1-inch thick)	400 °F	8 to 12
Pork Chops, bone in (1-inch, 6.5 oz)	400 °F	12	Rack of Lamb (1.5 – 2 lb.)	380 °F	22

Fish & Seafood

Item	Temp (°F)	Time (mins)	Item	Temp (°F)	Time (mins)
Calamari (8 oz)	400 °F	4	Tuna Steak	400 °F	7 to 10
Fish Fillet (1-inch, 8 oz)	400 °F	10	Scallops	400 °F	5 to 7
Salmon, fillet (6 oz)	380 °F	12	Shrimp	400 °F	5
Swordfish steak	400 °F	10			

Air Fryer Cooking Chart

	Vegetables				
INGREDIENT	AMOUNT	PREPARATION	OIL	TEMP	COOK TIME
Asparagus	2 bunches	Cut in half, trim stems	2 Tbsp	420°F	12-15 mins
Beets	1½ lbs	Peel, cut in ½-inch cubes	1Tbsp	390°F	28-30 mins
Bell peppers (for roasting)	4 peppers	Cut in quarters, remove seeds	1Tbsp	400°F	15-20 mins
Broccoli	1 large head	Cut in 1-2-inch florets	1Tbsp	400°F	15-20 mins
Brussels sprouts	1lb	Cut in half, remove stems	1Tbsp	425°F	15-20 mins
Carrots	1lb	Peel, cut in ¼-inch rounds	1 Tbsp	425°F	10-15 mins
Cauliflower	1 head	Cut in 1-2-inch florets	2 Tbsp	400°F	20-22 mins
Corn on the cob	7 ears	Whole ears, remove husks	1 Tbps	400°F	14-17 mins
Green beans	1 bag (12 oz)	Trim	1 Tbps	420°F	18-20 mins
Kale (for chips)	4 oz	Tear into pieces,remove stems	None	325°F	5-8 mins
Mushrooms	16 oz	Rinse, slice thinly	1 Tbps	390°F	25-30 mins
Potatoes, russet	1½ lbs	Cut in 1-inch wedges	1 Tbps	390°F	25-30 mins
Potatoes, russet	1lb	Hand-cut fries, soak 30 mins in cold water, then pat dry	½ -3 Tbps	400°F	25-28 mins
Potatoes, sweet	1lb	Hand-cut fries, soak 30 mins in cold water, then pat dry	1 Tbps	400°F	25-28 mins
Zucchini	1lb	Cut in eighths lengthwise, then cut in half	1 Tbps	400°F	15-20 mins

Made in the USA
Las Vegas, NV
03 May 2024

89471517R00057